SL Fallon 08

# FLYING
# THROUGH
# TIME

A Journey into History in a World War II Biplane

JAMES M. DOYLE

*Illustrated by the Author*

Potomac Books, Inc.
Washington, D.C.

Library of Congress Cataloging-in-Publication Data

Doyle, James M.
   Flying through time : a journey into history in a World War II biplane
/ James M. Doyle.
      p.   cm.
Includes index.
   ISBN 1-57488-447-6 (hard : alk. paper)
   1. World War, 1939–1945—Personal narratives, American.   2. World War,
1939–1945—Aerial operations, American.   3. Air pilots, Military—United
States—Biography.   4. Stearman airplanes.   5. Doyle, James M.   I. Title.
   D811.A2 D67   2002
   940.54′4973′092—dc21

                                                          2002008437


ISBN 1-57488-701-7 (paperback)


Printed in Canada



Potomac Books, Inc.
22841 Quicksilver Drive
Dulles, Virginia 20166

First Edition

10   9   8   7   6   5   4   3   2   1

Stearman cover photo courtesy of Robert M. Brown.
B-24 crew cover photo courtesy of Bill Blair.

*This book is dedicated*
*to all the young American fliers*
*who made such a profound difference*
*in our world, almost sixty years ago.*

The friends I left, that parting day,
How changed as time has sped!
Young childhood grown, strong man had gray,
And half of all are dead.

Abraham Lincoln, *My Childhood Home I See Again*

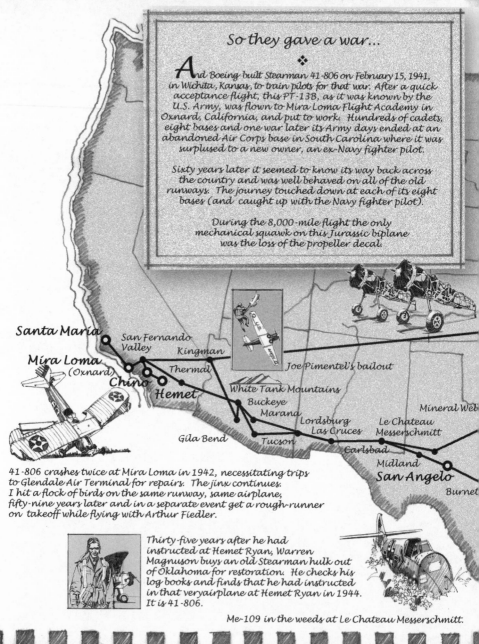

## So they gave a war...

❖

**A**nd Boeing built Stearman 41-806 on February 15, 1941, in Wichita, Kansas, to train pilots for that war. After a quick acceptance flight, this PT-13B, as it was known by the U.S. Army, was flown to Mira Loma Flight Academy in Oxnard, California, and put to work. Hundreds of cadets, eight bases and one war later its Army days ended at an abandoned Air Corps base in South Carolina where it was surplused to a new owner, an ex-Navy fighter pilot.

Sixty years later it seemed to know its way back across the country and was well behaved on all of the old runways. The journey touched down at each of its eight bases (and caught up with the Navy fighter pilot).

During the 8,000-mile flight the only mechanical squawk on this Jurassic biplane was the loss of the propeller decal.

Santa Maria

Mira Loma
(Oxnard)

San Fernando Valley

Chino

Kingman

Hemet

Thermal

Joe Pimentel's bailout

White Tank Mountains

Buckeye

Marana

Mineral Wel

Gila Bend

Lordsburg
Las Cruces

Le Chateau
Messerschmitt

Tucson

Carlsbad

Midland

San Angelo

Burnet

41-806 crashes twice at Mira Loma in 1942, necessitating trips to Glendale Air Terminal for repairs. The jinx continues. I hit a flock of birds on the same runway, same airplane, fifty-nine years later and in a separate event get a rough-runner on takeoff while flying with Arthur Fiedler.

Thirty-five years after he had instructed at Hemet Ryan, Warren Magnuson buys an old Stearman hulk out of Oklahoma for restoration. He checks his log books and finds that he had instructed in that very airplane at Hemet Ryan in 1944. It is 41-806.

Me-109 in the weeds at Le Chateau Messerschmitt.

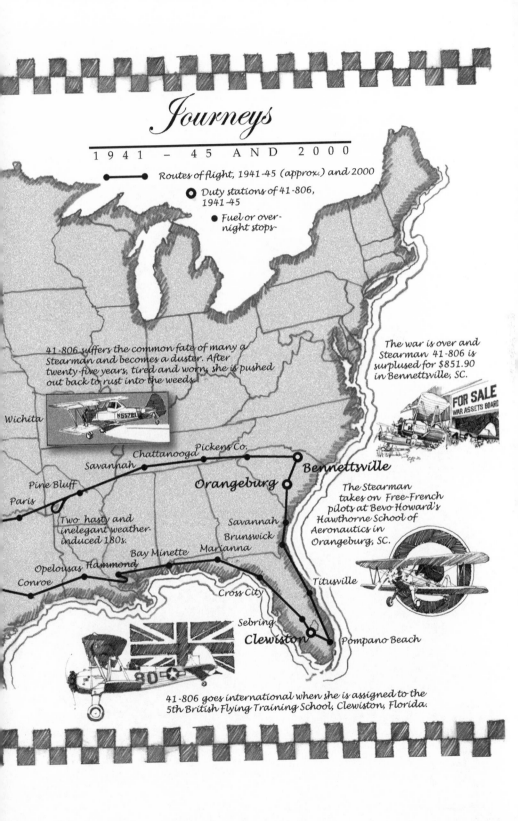

# Journeys

## 1941 — 45 AND 2000

● — Routes of flight, 1941-45 (approx.) and 2000

◎ Duty stations of 41-806, 1941-45

● Fuel or over-
night stops

41-806 suffers the common fate of many a
Stearman and becomes a duster. After
twenty-five years, tired and worn, she is pushed
out back to rust into the weeds.

The war is over and
Stearman 41-806 is
surplused for $851.90
in Bennettsville, SC.

Wichita

FOR SALE
WAR ASSETS BOARD

Chattanooga    Pickens Co.
Savannah                        Bennettsville

Pine Bluff                Orangeburg

Paris

The Stearman
takes on Free-French
pilots at Bevo Howard's
Hawthorne School of
Aeronautics in
Orangeburg, SC.

Two hasty and         Savannah
inelegant weather-    Brunswick
induced 180s.
                Marianna
Bay Minette
Opelousas Hammond
Conroe                        Titusville
              Cross City

              Sebring
              Clewiston        Pompano Beach

41-806 goes international when she is assigned to the
5th British Flying Training School, Clewiston, Florida.

# CONTENTS

# Contents

# PREFACE

The stories in this book are true and were gathered in three ways. During an eight-thousand-mile circuit of the country in a World War II Stearman biplane, I revisited a string of old Army Air Corps bases. At some of these bases and at reunions and air shows, I met and flew with World War II pilots as I could find them and as they were attracted to the old airplane. The stories of that trip itself and those flights make up about a third of this book and are subject to only the normal slight exaggerations, which are the birthright of pilots everywhere and to which I confess I am not immune.

Most of those pilots were interviewed about their wartime experiences and provided the stories that make up the second third of this book. They have lived with these tales for almost sixty years, sharing them only with family and friends. Some were recalled reluctantly and some with obvious relish, but always they were recalled long after the event. With these men I was able to work back and forth to smooth out the bumps between the spoken word and the written word to our mutual satisfaction.

The final third are transcripts of oral histories that I discovered during the trip in a stop at the American Airpower Heritage Museum in Midland, Texas. This little gold mine of stories gathered by interviewers of the Confederate Air Force (now called the Commemorative Air Force) had been laying quietly untouched for the last twelve years. With their kind permission I touched them. But there is a tradition among authors of historical literature of leaving interview transcripts exactly as spoken, and I must confess to violating that tradition. Sometimes the spoken word does not translate well. Sometimes there is an inflection, a pause, an erroneous recollection, or a backtracking of chronology in an interview that can make it difficult to follow. And sometimes there are just plain errors in typing the written transcript. To the best of my ability, without changing content I tried to make these transcriptions of the interviews a bit more readable.

For various reasons it was impossible to contact any of these men to clarify their narratives, thus the only alternative would have been to not use the particular story, and that would have been a disservice.

So with those ground rules, strap in, punch the starter, and bring the throttle up. Let's go flying.

# CHAPTER I

LT. ALBERT (Bill) BARLOW, over the Hürtgen Forest, September 1944
*"It exploded right underneath the aircraft . . . almost a direct hit."*

The Hürtgen Forest, Germany

The Luftwaffe gun crew slid the long eighty-eight-millimeter shell into the breech of the *flugabwehrkanone* (flak gun) with their customary Teutonic competency and locked it into place. Spinning the azimuth and elevation wheels on the side of the weapon, the crew quickly matched their indicators to those of the gun director that was engaged in tracking the flight of P-47 Thunderbolt fighters. As the "88" pointed its muzzle like an accusing finger at the offending American aircraft, the other weapons in the battery did the same and the powerful guns exploded into a lethal crackle of ripple fire. For the crews, it was an everyday impersonal thing. They were not even able to see their target, cruising serenely three miles above the overcast gray skies over Aachen, Germany. But for Bill

Barlow, in Republic Thunderbolt 42–22759, it was very personal. Today they were trying to kill him.

> We were at about sixteen thousand feet and flying maybe fifty or a hundred feet apart in a finger-four formation, which we always used, when all of a sudden there was a burst of flak over to my right. It was closer to my flight leader than to me, so I decided to move over. I moved to the left to give them a harder target and make the spacing a little wider, and I'll be darned if I didn't move over right on top of the next burst. It exploded right underneath the aircraft, maybe ten feet below, something like that, almost a direct hit. It tore up the cockpit somewhat and set the wings on fire, and I could hear the bullets exploding as the ammunition burned. I called another pilot in the flight and asked him if it looked like I could make it back, because I couldn't see any of the outside damage. I could hear it, but I couldn't see it.
>
> He said, "Just get out! That plane's not going very far, and you don't want to be in it."
>
> I pulled the nose up, rolled over, released my seat belt, and just dropped out.

This was not a new experience for Bill Barlow. His luck in the P-47 had never been good. But then this was not his first choice of airplanes.

> I flew [P-51] Mustangs in England to start with, but not in combat, just in an operational training unit. There were nine of us who were assigned to the 339th Fighter Group, which was a Mustang unit that had just come over, and they didn't want us. They hadn't had any casualties and they didn't need us. They sent us back down to wing headquarters, who reassigned us to a P-47 ["Jug"] outfit. And we called ourselves "The Bitter Nine," because we resented going from Mustangs to Jugs.
>
> And then, as we started watching—they had Teletype messages that were posted on the bulletin board showing various outfits and their casualties—we could see that our friends who were in the '51s weren't faring so well. Our nine stuck together for quite awhile, and I think seven of us came home. And of all things, three of us lost legs, which is unusual for fighter pilots.
>
> I was in the Eighth Air Force, 353rd Fighter Group, and our aircraft had yellow-and-black-checkerboard noses. I flew a razorback Thunderbolt [the early models of the Thunderbolt had a faired-in canopy with

sharp "spine" down the top of the rear fuselage], but most everybody else had the bubble canopy model. My aircraft was named *Flak Bait,* because if only one aircraft got hit on a mission, that one was me. Never bad, just a hole here or a hole there.

Early on I dumped one in the North Sea. I don't know exactly what happened. There had been some flak, and all of a sudden the engine just quit. I bailed out off of the Dutch coast and got picked up by the British in a Supermarine Walrus. That was the prettiest plane I ever saw. It looked like a poor man's PBY [a far more advanced American amphibian] with a fixed-pitch carved wooden prop on it. After they picked me up they'd start across the water, across the tops of the waves, and it wouldn't quite take off. Then we'd go back again and take off in another direction. In the meantime the Germans on the shore saw us out there, and they were sending a few shells in our direction, but they didn't get anywhere near us.

I lost a couple of aircraft down the runway while landing and wiped them out. Flak damage! Three airplanes down so far and I was on my way to becoming a German ace, but it was all due to flak.

On my third mission, the C.O. called over the radio and said that he had three or four Germans surrounded but was running out of ammunition and needed somebody to come and help him. Two of us took out in his direction, and pretty soon he called up and said there was one less German. I think he shot down two or three of them. When we arrived, there were still a couple left and I headed in their direction. We had been told, "Keep your nose pointed at the Germans at all times. Don't ever let them out of your sight." So I did.

But the German was a squadron leader or something and obviously an old hand at this sort of thing. He had chevrons on the side of his plane and really knew his business. So all he did—as I was heading up for him—was go into a circle. As I tried to follow him around, he just tightened the circle. I was concentrating on keeping my nose pointed at him and not getting in any trouble when first thing that I knew, I had spun out. When I came out of the spin he was on my tail, shooting, and he put a bunch of holes in the plane. I put the water injection on, and fortunately at that time I was heading toward England, and I don't think that I varied one degree from that course.

I had everything going, water injection, the whole works, but he finally pulled up beside me—for some reason I wasn't very fast yet—and waggled his wings. He fired his guns, waved, and then off he went, letting me go. He had control of the situation and he wanted me to know it.

That happened to other people, too, so it wasn't unique. He was a squadron leader or something and probably knew that I was a newcomer who didn't know what I was doing and was going to get shot down anyway—and he didn't want to murder me.

My final shoot-down was in September, a week before we were to switch to P-51s. That was the one plane I wanted to get back to, except that I know for a fact that if I had been in a P-51 during this shoot-down, I wouldn't have survived. The '51 was too fragile. It wasn't the rugged plane that the P-47 was.

We were dive-bombing and strafing near Aachen, Germany. My outfit, even though we were Eighth Air Force, would usually escort the bombers in and then we'd hit the deck on the way out. My C.O.'s firm conviction was that escorting bombers was an important part of the job, but only a part. Killing Germans was our main job, and we could get more when we were on the deck.

We were through strafing and had gained altitude coming back, because there were the front lines to come over and it was just a good idea to have fifteen or sixteen thousand feet underneath us. That was when I got hit and bailed out.

Since we were high and there was a bit of flak, mostly eighty-eight-millimeter, I decided that I wasn't going to pull the ripcord until I got out of the flak area. I felt safer. I knew that the cloud deck was at about three thousand feet, because that's where it had been when we went in. I decided to pull the ripcord at just above the cloud deck and hope that somebody would see me and know that I had made it out of the plane safely, because it's pretty hard to see somebody falling in an unopened chute.

The chute opened just above the cloud deck, and in the meantime I could hear the plane sputtering and then a big explosion. I found out later that the plane had tumbled, end over end. Nobody had ever seen the Jug do that before, but it just made four or five tumbles and then blew up.

I came down through the clouds, which had bases at maybe two thousand feet, and they started opening up on me with twenty-millimeters from the ground, but there was nothing I could do about that. A couple of Me-109s came along, saw what was going on, circled around me, and that kept the ground fire down. Apparently they weren't interested in seeing other pilots shot in their chute.

I landed in a firebreak in the Hürtgen Forest in Germany.

When I came down I knew that I was behind the German lines. I hit the ground, took my chute off, hid it in the brush, and started running. I had a little compass that they had issued us, so I used that and headed in a westerly direction. Go west, young man—that was the plan. I wanted to get out of the area, because I knew the Germans had seen me coming down and they would be looking for me. I ran across a road and into the woods and came across a creek. There was a bank above the creek, maybe twelve to fifteen feet high, with a path on it that eventually turned down to the creek and crossed it.

I heard dogs and thought, "Uh-oh, they're after me."

I didn't think they were tracking dogs. I thought they were probably guard dogs, so I got into the creek and doubled back parallel to the path and hid in the underbrush. I stayed down until I heard the searchers go past, then climbed back up onto the path and followed it back down to where it joined the creek. Most of the searchers had gone either up or down the creek, so I just crossed it, headed off into the woods, and started walking west.

I went on that way for a couple of days. If I heard people I thought were Germans, I would head in the other direction. I probably circled around quite a bit. My main problem was that I didn't know which side of the Rhine River I was on. The Rhine moves down through there, and I was concerned that if I were on the German side, I would have very little chance of getting out. If I were on the American side, I would have every chance.

I walked for three or four days and had nothing to eat and no water. We had escape kits with Halizone tablets in them, which were chemicals that you were supposed to be able to put into water to make it potable. So what I would do is find a mud puddle, put a pill in it, and drink a little of the water. In the escape kit they had a big chunk of chocolate and that was the only sustenance. Of course being twenty years old, I ate it almost before I hit the ground, so I didn't have anything left.

I kept on going, and once or twice I ran across Germans. One time they saw me and opened fire, but I was close enough to the edge of the clearing to run into the woods. They didn't follow very far or very long.

I was getting weaker and my feet started swelling and giving me problems, so I took my shoes off, which was a mistake. I had a GI sweater, and in the escape kit that we had there was a razor blade and a needle and thread, of all things. I sewed the ends of the sleeves up from the sweater and made little booties out of them, because my feet were cold and wet from the creek.

I kept going, and finally after about seven days my feet were hurting so bad I was kind of losing track of what was going on, so I decided that I'd better give up.

The morning of the eighth day some Germans appeared near where I was hiding. The Hürtgen Forest had fir trees whose thick branches hung down to the ground and made a kind of a tent shelter. I could see the Germans but they couldn't see me, and I was under one of the trees when a German patrol came by. I didn't realize it at the time, but they were planting mines. I could hear the shovels and hear them talking, and one of them came near my hiding place and threw down a cigarette that was still lit. He kept on going, so I picked up the cigarette and finished it. We were smoking all the time in those days.

After they had left, I started out and came to a clearing just as a German convoy came along a road on the far side. I had decided by then that I was going to have to give up, but I didn't want to give up to a whole bunch of troops. I figured that I'd better kind of pick and choose and let the German convoy go by. Pretty soon a vehicle with four wheels in back and two in the front, a kind of a staff car, came by with troops sitting in it, just like the newsreels. They looked like Germans on parade with their big cars and guns, so I staggered up to it, used the only German I knew, "*kamerad*," and surrendered.

But as I got to the car, I just couldn't go on and passed out. I woke up in the back of the car as it was driving along and heard one of the troops say, "You want a cigarette, buddy?"

I asked, "Who are you. What's going on?"

"We're taking you into the field hospital—the Forty-Fifth Evac."

I found out later as we were going back that we were still behind the German lines and these GIs were following the German convoy and evidently radioing information on it. They were in American uniforms, but if you go eight days without food and very little, if any, water, you don't see things too well. It just wasn't that clear to me. I had not been aware of who they were or what kind of unit they were with. It was just a group that had fewer people in it and seemed less likely to shoot me.

I had dry gangrene in both feet. Trench foot. In the Canadian army, and probably the American Army, it was a court-martial offense to get it, but they never gave us any training in the Air Corps, and we didn't know anything about it.

And so, I spent the next three and a half years in various Army hospitals.

# Tulare, California

Fifty-seven years later under a hot sun at a Tulare/Sequoia pilots' reunion, Bill Barlow walks out to U.S. Army Air Corps Stearman 41-806, determined to renew his acquaintance with a military aircraft. He hasn't been in one since he left his Thunderbolt high over Aachen in September of 1944. He has a slight limp on this day, and as we chat he cautions me that he might not be able to get up into the aircraft. I'm a bit surprised, because although it can be a difficult airplane to climb up into, he looked to be quite fit. But Bill Barlow had lost both legs as a result of his Hürtgen Forest adventure and was in a bit of pain today.

Working together, we take our time and he determinedly muscles himself up the wing, swings his legs stiffly into the forward cockpit, and gingerly lowers himself into the seat. Thoughts of Douglas Bader, the legless Royal Air Force ace, cross my mind. We both strap in and I taxi out to runway three-one at Tulare, and run up. The Continental is sounding smooth, so we rumble down the strip, passing the old B-17 gate guard and a dozen odd Stearmans, Ryans, and Vultees that are in attendance for this event. We lift off northward toward our destination, Sequoia Field.

Bill Barlow had taken his primary training at Sequoia Field, and this will be his first visit back since his graduation from primary in 1943. We swing into a low orbit of the field, and he soon has his camera going, a luxury that he was not afforded while a cadet here. Curiously, even after sixty years much of the base remains. Usually at these old primary bases, the buildings, which were temporary, are long gone, plowed under to make way for industrial parks, houses, or agriculture, but Sequoia looks relatively untouched. The cadet quarters are still there, as are the administration buildings, hangars, ramp, and runway. Bill excitedly points to his old barracks. A little paint here and there and this field could be turning out cadets next week.

I cannot imagine the thoughts that must be running through this man's mind as we fly over the field that he has not seen in fifty-seven years. This was where a twenty-year-old kid made the cut, soloed, and moved on to bigger and faster aircraft, including the ill-fated Thunderbolt, *Flak Bait*. This was where he began the most exciting adventure of his young life and the one that resulted in the most pain.

I put the nose down, and the flying wires sing sweetly as we swing in a big arc to line up with the old Sequoia runway, the runway Bill Barlow must have lined up on dozens of times as a cadet. The throttle is against the firewall, and the Stearman is moving along nicely as we level off a few feet above the surface for a low pass. The runway numbers and taxiways and buildings and hangars and flagpoles flash by like a reprise of episodes in a man's life, and we arc back up for a last look. I glance up into the rearview mirror, so thoughtfully provided by the Army to keep track of cadets in the other cockpit, and catch Bill Barlow's eye.

I may not know what thoughts are in the mind of this man, but on his face is the grin of a twenty-year-old kid fighter pilot in a P-47 Thunderbolt. For Bill Barlow, the circle is complete.

# CHAPTER 2

AIR CADET JAMES I. LONGAN

*". . . you can run, but you can't hide."*

# The Beginning

"I'm looking for a James I. Longan who would have been in the Army Air Corps during World War II." So began one of the most interesting and moving phone calls I have ever experienced.

It was a long shot. Out of curiosity, I had sent for the military records on my fifty-five-year-old U.S. Army Air Corps 1941 Boeing Stearman primary trainer, or as the Army called it, aircraft number 41–806. I had owned the airplane for five years and was having a love affair with it as an interesting and exciting airplane to fly. It was a biplane of the type frequently seen at air shows putting on beautiful aerobatic demonstrations of the kind that I could only stumble through. A crowd pleaser and a handsome piece of machinery by any standard, it was an airplane I much admired as a representative of an age long past. The biplane part of it said "barnstormer" and "golden age." It conjured pictures of small midwestern towns, county fairs, and airplane rides for a nickel a pound. It reeked of dope, fabric, leather, noise, and simpler times. But the fact that it was ex-military gave it still another powerful cachet and concealed a past life that I could only guess at. I knew that many of the men who had learned to fly in this very airplane had done some very brave things and had made a difference in this world. Some of those men had undoubtedly given their lives during World War II. By being around this airplane and flying it, I felt somehow in touch with those times and I liked that. It was a thread to the past. Army 41–806 was my time traveler.

The longer I owned it, the more curious I became about its military history. What had this particular aircraft done and where had it been? To my complete surprise, the Army was meticulous about keeping track of such things. The records still existed and they were quite willing to send me a set. As I started to try to decipher the cryptic Army jargon of those records, my eye fell on an entry that read: *"Wrecked 5/13/42. Oxnard, California. Air Cadet James I. Longan. Ground looped upon landing."*

That was clear enough. I was intrigued. Here was a name attached to the airplane. It was no longer just an anonymous machine. This was a person who actually flew the airplane in 1942! He sat in the same cockpit in which I now sit. He operated the same stick, rudder, and throttle and no doubt experienced the same fears and joys I have in flying it. It was a powerful feeling.

I had access to a database of everyone currently living in the United States, and among the many James A's, James C's, and James G's there was only one James I. Longan listed—in a small town in Missouri. I hesitated, not wishing to rake over what could not have been a pleasant incident, but by then the pull of the past had become too strong.

"Well, I'm Jim Longan and I was in the Air Corps during the war, so that would be me," came the prompt reply to my phone call and query. My heart rate increased slightly.

"Mr. Longan, were you stationed at Mira Loma Flight Academy at Oxnard, California, in 1942?"

"Sure was."

More beats.

"Did you wreck a Stearman during your primary flight training there?"

"Oh my God, you can run but you can't hide!" he replied.

I quickly explained the nature of the call before he concluded he was dealing with some overeager Army clerk, determined to extract the Army's rightful due. I told him that the airplane he had "wrecked" still existed, was in wonderful shape, and was hangared less than twenty miles from where he flew it that fateful day in May of 1942. He was stunned. What a call to get after more than half a century! It was debatable which of us was more excited. And he told me his story.

"We were up doing spins and if I recall correctly, that Lycoming R680 engine had the exhaust pipe on the right." (This from an almost eighty-year-old man recalling an incident from fifty-five years ago.)

"Well, the instructor kept me doing spins to the right. Every time we'd roll into the spin, the exhaust would swirl down the fuselage and hit me square in the face. The combination of the exhaust fumes and the rotation of the spins soon had their effect, and I proceeded to get airsick and throw up. The instructor had enough of this and told me to take it back to the barn." But the ordeal wasn't over.

"I was just in no condition to make a landing, and I lost it. On touchdown the airplane bounced, swerved, and neither of us was able to catch it."

"Which wing did you damage?" I asked. The narrow landing gear on the Stearman was very demanding of a straight-ahead touchdown. A crabbed or sideways touchdown, in which the airplane was moving in a slightly different direction from where it was pointed, was an invitation to disaster.

"Both wings. I cartwheeled and got both wings. They took me to the infirmary for a checkup, but I was fine. They told me that my pilot days for Uncle Sam were over, and that evening they had me on my way to New Mexico for bombardier training. No check ride. No nothing." There was a sadness in his voice undimmed by the intervening fifty-five years.

This was typical of the Army. If a cadet damaged an aircraft early in his training, before there had been much of an investment, he would find himself on his way to bombardier, navigator, or air gunner school. If he did it in the more advanced phases, with a very benevolent instructor, the

Army sometimes would swallow hard, dust him off, and send him back up. Jim Longan just had lousy timing.

And so he finished bombardier school, was commissioned late in 1942, and spent the war pounding the Japanese from the nose of a B-24 Liberator as a member of the 344th Bomb Group in the Pacific. He returned in 1945 mostly in one piece, none the worse for wear from his treatment by the Japanese, the Air Corps, or its Stearmans.

We talked a bit of his experiences, and he agreed that should I ever get to his Missouri town with the Stearman, a flight together in his old nemesis would be appropriate. He sent me his old cadet book with the class pictures of himself and all the young men in their leather jackets and scarves grouped around the rows of trainers. I looked long and hard through that book, and it made me realize what a piece of history the airplane and the people who flew it were.

But what about Kelly E. Kimes? Kelly E. Kimes also flew 41–806 in primary training and, like Jim Longan, had the dubious honor of a mention in the records of the airplane. The entry reads: *"Wrecked 1/5/42. Oxnard Airport. Kelly E. Kimes, Air Cadet. Taxiing accident."*

My database revealed no trace of Kelly E. Kimes. There were Kimeses to be sure, but none of them had uncles or grandfathers who had been in the war. What had happened to Kelly? Did he finish pilot training, or did he too become a bombardier or a navigator. And did he come home? Did he live out a peaceful life like Jim Longan, or was his fate a darker one? I guess I'll never know.

But their airplane still exists. It still flies in the same skies and lands at the same fields as it did when Kelly Kimes, Jim Longan, and all of the other young men flew it.

Whenever I was in the cockpit of the Stearman—their cockpit as they trained to go to war—I would think about them and the stories they could tell. Soon I found myself seeking these men out, these pilots of the only "good" war, and listening to their experiences. I was amazed at what I heard.

These men are scattered now, and all are in the twilight of their adventuresome lives. Soon there will be no one left to tell the stories, and that will be a shame. So I began collecting their stories, casually at first, at air shows mostly, with no plan. But an idea grew.

And my adventure began.

I had always had some vague idea of flying the Stearman across the country. Everybody who has an old airplane does. The older the airplane is, the more you want to do it. Of course if it's an old biplane, that just throws more fuel on the fire. It's the classic American road trip that pilots have been doing for years.

But then practicality rears its ugly head and you hesitate. Where am I going to get the time? There is of course the job—that thing that has supported my airplane habit for thirty-five years. It's not about to let me go wandering about the country. In my business there are advertising campaigns to conceive, commercials to make, schedules to be maintained. I'll be asked to check in and probably get as far as Tucson or Las Cruces and have some work crisis necessitate a return. Guaranteed.

A friend of mine, a former creative director at a large advertising agency, tells of a long overdue fishing vacation he once took at a remote lake (pre–cell phone era) in northern Canada. As he sat quietly fishing in his rowboat enjoying the wilderness and solitude, he became aware of the sound of an approaching aircraft. He watched incredulously as a floatplane dropped out of the sky, landed on the lake, and taxied directly to his rowboat with a summons he could not ignore. That was the end of his vacation.

No, a trip across the country should be savored. The mind should be free to focus and enjoy things. It should be endless.

And of course there's the money. For a flight across the country, a set of charts alone is an easy hundred dollars. Thirteen hundred gallons of avgas can't be cheap, nor can the food and lodging. I have done more than my share of sleeping under the wing, but have evolved to the point where camping out now means the breakfast buffet at the Sheraton rather than room service, and roughing it is no grapefruit with my eggs Benedict. Man has his limits.

Finally, the airplane is sixty years old. Surely something is going to break while stressing the aircraft on an eight-thousand-mile, coast-to-coast and return trip. The engine has almost six hundred hours on it and by military standards is already time expired. If I'm lucky, I might have to leave it in some rural weed patch while trying to arrange by phone, from California, for someone named Buford to repair it. Having an airplane repaired is not like bringing your Corolla into a Toyota dealer. The airplane will not be ready by 4:00 P.M. Repairs can take weeks, months, or even years.

If I'm really unlucky, I'll be talking on a cell phone from a swamp in Mississippi. Or worse.

And if I break the Stearman going into the dozens of strange airports at which I must land along the way, then I've destroyed a small piece of American history. Although I am the owner of the aircraft, my responsibilities go far beyond ownership. I must pass this on to the next pilot in better shape than I received it, not as a rolled-up ball of aluminum, spruce, and cotton. I must not damage what good men have kept together for sixty years. Always present with this airplane is the pilots' deepest wish: "Lord, whatever else happens, don't let ME screw up."

Yes, there are a lot of solid reasons to stay home, but as the saying goes, "If you don't take the chance, you don't get to drink the champagne."

Slowly the reasons for doing the trip become more compelling. My other interest, the history of this airplane and the men who flew it, grows. I continue to collect stories from World War II pilots. The talking becomes more formalized with the introduction of a tape recorder into the process as an idea forms in my head. These stories are just too good not to save.

Parker Cole, a former Navy flight instructor tells me a funny story about a collision between his Stearman and a turkey buzzard, and when I call back to confirm some things and say hello a few months later, I find he has passed away. I speak to his sister, who is heartsick that he didn't get to share more. These World War II veterans are passing away at the rate of fifteen hundred per day, so time increasingly becomes a factor. My efforts have now moved from a flyer's casual bull session into a personal collection of oral histories.

Of course you can't just talk to a wartime pilot sitting in a hangar next to a Stearman and not go out and fly it. That airplane belongs to him as much as it belongs to me, and like an aerial martini, a flight in this old bird has a wonderful way of stimulating remembrances and loosening the tongue. I shamelessly use it as a lure to fly with these men whenever I can, and they love it. Age is working its evil ways on them as they peer over their bifocals at the array of switches, instruments, and controls, trying to recall those days. But they smile broadly, because most thought they were going to meet their maker without ever setting foot in one of these machines of their youth, and they are astonished to be wrong. We fly, and for an hour or two they are nineteen again.

I take the airplane to air shows, and it's like a magnet.

"I flew one of these in primary at Thunderbird Field in 1943. Put sixty hours in them," is a typical hello from a youthful old man with steely gray eyes standing at the barrier rope.

He looks at the airplane appreciatively and continues, "Went on to fly Lightnings in Italy. Flew ground support and escort for a year."

Soon he's a guest in my cockpit, and the people in the crowd—or perhaps his sons who brought him there and sense what is happening—smile.

"But I never had more fun than when I flew the Stearman."

"Well, good. How would you like to fly one again?"

And pretty soon we are doing Immelmanns and lazy eights over the Santa Clarita Valley or the Calveras County foothills, and dragging our wheels through the tall grass somewhere. And to a man, they are still excellent pilots fifty-five years later. Then over a Coke in the shade of the hangar they talk. Their eyes grow younger and their speech comes faster as they are suddenly at twenty thousand feet over the Adriatic, or the English Channel, or the South Pacific squinting into the sun for Messerschmitts or Zeros. They easily fall back into the vernacular of that time and talk of *bogies*, and *angels*, and *Jugs*, and *wingmen,* words that haven't escaped their lips for fifty years. And they just unload. For some it's the first time they have ever really been asked what it was like and been listened to. Others tell familiar stories that they cheerfully admit their family has been listening to for years and have grown tired of. Doesn't matter though. It all happened. Or most of it.

And so I continue my callous bribing of these heroes with the Stearman. We talk and we fly and the stories keep coming.

I reread the aircraft records of the old biplane with its list of duty stations where this particular Stearman instructed. Four are in California, and four are strung out across the bottom of the country like pearls on a necklace. That could be my route if I choose to take it. That is certainly the route the airplane flew sixty years ago. I could roll the wheels on every base it was stationed at. Duplicate the trip this airplane made from California to Florida and up into the Carolinas. Then come back. I could talk to even more of these pilots along the way.

Of course the idea of a book is in the back of my head. Many books have been written about cross-country flights in a biplane, almost all are unique, since each pilot has different experiences. But my experiences would be only a small part of the book. I would let the pilots that I have talked to tell their stories during the flight. Hopefully I could stay out of their way.

I am not of the writer's craft, but these stories are just too interesting not to share. I had been in advertising for most of my professional life, enjoyed it tremendously, but know that it is time to say good-bye. The idea has been in the back of my mind for a while and now the timing seems right. I finish my last television commercial of twenty-five years a day or two before Christmas, throw my office pictures and books in a box, and by New Year's Day I'm gone. Now I have the time, the plane, and the reason. I resolve to do it.

So I begin the planning. Soon, charts are on the walls and on the floors. Courses are laid out and highlighted with marker. Availability of hangars, fuel, and good airport coffee shops are critical, so airport diagrams are examined. Weather patterns get a lot of my attention, as this seems to be the year for tornados. I watch the news and it's on tornados. I watch *National Geographic* specials and they all seem to be on tornados. I open a newspaper and the headline is about tornados. My route ultimately will take me through the heart of tornado country, but I hear of only one during the flight.

The Stearman needs a few things done to it for this trip, and soon there are parts all over the workbench. Naturally this effort cannot be confined to just what needs attention, and soon it grows into a major mechanical effort. Everything on the aircraft is checked and rechecked. Aircraft sages and hangar mates are consulted, opinions solicited and advice taken—or ignored. Much beard pulling is done.

A schedule is constructed and, once the flying starts, is tossed. Serendipity becomes my time manager. The only thing I hold to is the departure date.

I use the months that I have before that date to visit the four bases that are in the Southern California area. These are one- to three-day trips, and inevitably I run into more World War II pilots who make more contributions after their aerial "bribe."

Spring eases into summer as the last bolts are torqued down and fluids are changed or topped off. A coat of polish is rubbed on and the Stearman stands ready.

I take a deep breath, and we are off to chase history.

# CHAPTER 3

*". . . the design philosophy of a John Deere tractor"*

The Airplane

Dawn at little airports is usually the best time. In the summer it's quiet and cool and the air is filled with promise. This is the time for a cup of coffee and some quiet reflection, but not too much of either, because we are going flying today. I glance at the windsock. It hangs lifeless. There is normally little or no wind at this hour, so any flight will be rock steady and not filled with the busy little movements an airplane usually makes as it moves through a turbulent air mass. Flying at dawn is like flying through honey.

In the spring there is always a background of birdsong inside the hangar at this hour, because in mimic of their aluminum brothers, these creatures of the air find that airplane hangars make ideal nesting sites. A lot of effort is spent trying to keep them out. They can be troublesome and have been known to build nests in engines, which then ignite once the aircraft is airborne. Fire in flight, as we all know, makes pilots very edgy.

Light floods into the darkened hangar, revealing a large powerful-looking aircraft engine on the business end of a trim silver biplane. The engine, with its beautifully finished copper-clad yellow birch propeller, towers over me. Seven efficient-looking machined black cylinders radiate from a crankcase at precise 51.42-degree intervals and serve as a symmetrical background for the prop. The engine, with its brass, aluminum, and enameled textures, is a work of art just as surely as is a Brancusi sculpture. It's a radial engine, a "round engine" in the vernacular of flyers. It's also an anachronism, an accumulation of nearly sixty-year-old ironmongery that is now of an uncertain metallurgical crystalline structure. Radials were state-of-the-art in the '30s and '40s, and powered everything from airliners to tanks. Now they are found mostly in museums and in the hangars of the odd throwback who never quite got over the fascination of that age.

That would be me.

I glance at the oil pan on the floor. As usual, a few drops of oil are present. These engines leak. Hangar wisdom states that if they stop leaking, they are out of oil. Some leak or use so much oil that the aircraft requires a minor wash down after each flight. Yet they are perfectly safe, just designed to looser tolerances than the engines of today. They can be made to stop leaking, given enough patience and money, but if they are flown hard they are oily.

I pull the chocks and climb up on the wheel of the big biplane. Loaded, the aircraft weighs almost three thousand pounds and, with its fat tires, is a handful for two people to move around. Today I'm alone, so I must use guile. Bracing myself on a strut, I begin to walk on the tire like a lumberjack on a floating log, one step at a time as it rotates underneath. Amazingly the airplane begins to move, gliding quietly and slowly out of the darkened hangar into the sunlight, gravel now crunching under the wheels.

This procedure always leaves me with a smile. It's so perfectly appropriate to an airplane of this vintage. In the back of the hangar is a motorized tow bar for the aircraft, which I am loath to use. With its technology and noises, it will shatter the stillness and mood of the morning. Returning to the hangar after a flight I will use it. By then, I'll be half deafened by the engine and too tired to worry about authenticity.

I grab the pull handle at the rear of the fuselage to rotate the aircraft and align it with the taxiway. This part succumbs only to brute force. It takes nothing less than my full weight thrown against the handle, usually two or three times, before the big biplane will pivot. When the tail wheel "breaks" or releases to allow such a move, it happens all at once, and the unprepared often land squarely on their butt as the fuselage quietly glides over their prostrate form. It is very undignified. This morning, however, I'm too cunning and manage to stay ahead of the swinging fuselage.

My friendly game with the airplane continues. A preflight inspection of the aircraft is necessary to determine whether all is as it should be, that the airplane has all the nuts, bolts, cotter pins, control lines, and flying wires it had when it left the factory. That no new things, such as wrenches or flashlights, are left behind in the fuselage. That everything is working as it should, and that there are no interesting little surprises such as water in the fuel. I usually make it a game of discovery, but it's not a game at all.

"What new trick do you have in store for me today, my friend? And what clues have you left me?" I browse but find nothing today.

Preflights are fairly standard, but on this airplane there are some unique tasks that must be performed. First, the propeller must be "pulled through." Making sure that all switches and valves are off, the propeller is rotated by hand, which in turn rotates all of the engine components. This has the effect of detecting and pumping out any oil that may have accumulated in the lower cylinders, which would cause a disastrous hydraulic lock should the engine start in such a condition. This engine has been a sweet-running thing and, so far, hasn't troubled me with such matters. Conventional wisdom dictates pulling the prop through anywhere from four to fourteen blades, or half revolutions, depending on which expert is consulted. I choose fourteen, hoping to stay out of the overhaul shop.

However, touching any airplane propeller is a dangerous business. They are mysterious. Airplane engines can start very easily, sometimes with only the slightest nudge, and have even been known to start without anyone touching them. This is "Murphy's Law" country. I have witnessed the prop on this very aircraft suddenly and quietly rotate about fifteen degrees on its own, without anyone being near it. I was transfixed and wouldn't have believed such a thing were possible if someone had told me. If the switches had been on . . .

I carefully pull the propeller through and the oil is pumped into the exhaust pipes where, when the engine starts, it will be discharged overboard in great gouts of blue smoke and oil particles splattered on the freshly waxed lower right wing.

Next, the engine must be primed. This is done from the outside of the aircraft by pumping on a small plunger thoughtfully mounted on the engine cowling. Three strokes should do it. If the right combination of valves are open and it's very quiet, one can actually hear the fuel enter the cylinders.

Fully satisfied that the airplane is ready for flight, I now take one last precaution—the parachute.

It's old but airworthy. It's a military chute, and like anything military it is industrial strength, with buckles and webbing that could lift a truck. It's a seat pack, and when properly worn, any walking is difficult. But I'm not walking anywhere today, so I slip it on.

Settling myself in the cockpit, the chute slides nicely into the old bucket seat that it was designed for. I'm comfortable now, but in a couple of hours I know that my butt will be numb from sitting on that hard-packed chute.

Wearing a chute is a debatable issue. Most aircraft are routinely flown without them, even airplanes this old. This biplane, however, is covered in grade A cotton fabric. This is a material from the past. Most fabric-covered airplanes of today use synthetics that last far longer and will not support combustion quite as readily. Cotton burns very quickly. I will wear a chute.

But these thoughts are not in my mind this morning as my hands and feet busy themselves in the cockpit.

Brakes . . . set.

Fuel . . . on.

Mixture . . . rich.

Throttle . . . cracked open one-half inch.

Stick . . . fully back.

Master switch . . . on.

Starter . . . energize.

"Clear prop!" I bellow, and the birds take notice.

This is my favorite part. The old inertial starter begins to wind up. It is nothing more than a heavy, geared flywheel powered by an electric motor. When it reaches a high enough speed, I electrically engage the flywheel into the engine. The results are right out of an old Hollywood flying epic. The prop begins to rotate with that peculiar whine of old aero engines. I've heard the sound in *Dive Bomber, Twelve O'Clock High,* and dozens of other Saturday afternoon movie thrillers I saw as a kid. It still sends shivers as I watch the blades flick by. I pump the throttle once, switch the magnetos on, and the engine coughs to life in a swirl of smoke. It's said that these old engines are never started—they are awakened. This one awakens and smoothes out one cylinder at a time, the exhaust now pumping out clear and invisible except for heat shimmer. The oil pressure snaps into the green range, and I flick on the alternator and the radio.

Alternator and radio! What is such technology doing in this ancient kite?

In 1941, when Boeing rolled this airplane out, it didn't even have an electrical system to start the airplane, let alone an alternator. A ground crewman stationed at the nose plugged a hand crank into an external socket and wound a flywheel starter by hand, in an arrangement that on the surface appeared similar to starting a Model T Ford. But this required far more effort. When sufficient revs had been achieved, he then engaged the spinning starter into the engine by pulling on a "T" handle, making sure to stay well away from the prop arc. After the engine fired he would hand the crank to the pilot, who would stow it in the cockpit. The pilot then simply taxied and took off when he was ready. If there was a tower, which was extremely rare, he looked for a light signal. Nothing complicated. Green meant go. Red, stop. I don't have the luxury of a ground crew. I must use electricity to spin the starter. I must use electricity to power the radio, and I must request permission before I can taxi even one foot.

"Whiteman tower, Stearman five-five-seven-two-one. Blue hangars. Taxi for takeoff." Their reply is equally terse.

"Stearman seven-two-one, Whiteman tower. Taxi to runway one-two. Wind calm. Altimeter two-niner-niner-seven." I set the barometric pressure in my altimeter and lock the harness that holds me to the seat back. With one last look forward around each side of the fuselage, I bring in a little throttle and release the brakes. We're under way.

Taxiing this old bird must be done very carefully. Visibility over the nose is nonexistent. Weaving or S-turns accompanied by a lot of leaning out of the cockpit are the order of the day. I recently spoke to a pilot who, in his words, "tried to push a pickup truck on the taxiway." He had taxied into a parked truck, and the spinning prop turned most of the truck into confetti.

In the run-up area, I once more go through a checklist. This is my last opportunity to catch that one big thing that might ruin my day. I listen carefully as the now fully awake engine is brought up to speed for a magneto check. The quietness of the morning becomes a memory. Denizens of the airport hear the noise, recognize the sound, and know what will happen next. Tools are put down. Conversations trail off. No one can fail to watch one of these airplanes fly.

"Whiteman tower, Stearman seven-two-one at one-two, ready for takeoff. Downwind departure."

Again the cryptic reply, "Stearman seven-two-one, cleared for takeoff, downwind departure approved." That's my signal that I own the runway—all thirty-seven hundred feet of it—though I will only require the first five hundred feet of it to become airborne. Beyond that, the remainder will provide a welcome place to reconsider the situation should the beat of the engine change or the aircraft not respond properly. After that my options narrow. Apartments, houses, industrial yards, and settling ponds await me beyond the runway and are all poor choices. However, there is a railroad track with a rather wide right-of-way. I file it under "Plan B" as I swing the biplane onto the runway.

The throttle must be advanced slowly, as these engines do not like to be hurried. Even so, the effect is amazing. I'm eight feet away from the exhaust pipe, which is pointed straight back at me. A blue flame as hot as a welder's torch is blasting from that pipe. I can't see it in the daylight, but I know it's there, because I have seen it at night. At night it's very sobering to see a one-foot blue flame flickering a few feet away from the gas tank and the cotton fabric. But I dismiss the hazard with the knowledge that it has been there for sixty years without tragedy.

The noise of the exhaust is deafening and creeps around the cleverly sealed high-tech earphones I am wearing. They're one of the concessions to modernity I've allowed myself without a qualm. These engines and airplanes spawned generations of deaf pilots, which I don't intend to join. Authenticity has its limits.

I can't see ahead in this portion of the takeoff run because of the nose.

Nor can I S-turn; so I must trust the tower and my own instincts to detect any errant aircraft that might wander into my path. The airplane is picking up speed now, and the large flight control surfaces are beginning to bite. I push the stick forward and the nose swings obediently downward. It also swings abruptly to the left.

Damn! I know that swing all too well and should have been ready for it. The laws of physics are kicking in. That big wooden prop that's spinning up front, pulling us along so nicely, is also acting as a gyroscope. It's trying to move the airplane in directions that I don't approve of. That's all right. I have other laws of physics I can appeal to. Higher laws. I have, for instance, my friend Bernoulli. He is responsible for the laws of lift. And I have many control surfaces that are now responding to his laws. I easily overpower the dark forces of gyroscopic precession (and a few others that also make the airplane want to turn left) with a foot full of right rudder. We roll straight now, my momentary lapse forgiven. The airplane is balanced on the main gear and is getting light. It leaves the ground with a stately grace, the engine in a deep rumble, not at all hurried by its impatient pilot. It has done this thousands of times before and actually needs very little help.

Just how little help this airplane needs was described to me by an old Navy Stearman flight instructor named Parker Cole, who described a midair collision that he had with a turkey buzzard over the plains of Texas. It was a classic midair, with the Stearman and the bird on reciprocal courses. The bird was the only fatality, instantly becoming turkey ragout, but fortunately missing both the instructor and the student. The bird did, however, take out the plastic fuel sight gauge that hangs down from the fuel tank in the upper wing. This effectively left a one-inch hole in the bottom of the tank, which immediately blossomed into a vapor trail of fuel, drenching both occupants of the aircraft and posing the very real threat of an instant and massive explosion. With one eye on the hot exhaust pipe and the other on the gasoline vapor trail, both student and instructor immediately departed the aircraft and soon were safely swinging in their chutes as the Stearman continued serenely on course, unperturbed by the absence of pilots. Eventually, out of fuel, the unexploded aircraft glided to a gentle landing, upright, in a sod field with very little damage other than to the instructor's image. No one's time was up except that of the turkey buzzard.

I glance at the control tower as I go by. The tower is my "how-goes-it" gauge. If I'm looking down into it, everything is okay. If I am looking up at it, then there must be a problem. Today I'm looking down. I've got a solid rate of climb.

The airplane is rock steady. I can, however, feel the engine pulses through the airframe and into my seat. This Continental engine is not the smoothest of engines. When the airplane first flew, in 1934, it flew with a different engine. A smoother engine with two more cylinders. That engine purrs rather than barks. When the war came, as an expediency the military asked for this airplane to be built with engines they had obtained from a variety of manufacturers. No matter what they hung on the front, it seemed to fly well. Not as smoothly but just as well.

We accelerate to a cruise-climb speed. The coolness of the morning has taken on an invigorating edge as I approach the ocean. I turn up the collar of my jacket and hit the seat release. This allows the seat to slide down a pair of rails and gets me a bit more out of the wind.

I've never much liked the cold, which is a problem if one flies a lot of open cockpit. When I became the present caretaker of this airplane, one of my first tasks was to fly it home. This required an eleven-thousand-foot crossing of the Sierra Nevada Mountains in December and, unprepared for the experience, I nearly froze. In my cold-soaked state, the fuel stop after the crossing was a catalogue of bad landing techniques. But even a fire on the runway would have been welcomed. I was so cold I don't think I would have burned. Since then I have been very careful about where I go, when I go, and what I wear.

I compromise today and take off the chill by slowing down and flying low—about five hundred feet above some orange groves does it very nicely. At this altitude one can easily detect the scents from the ground. Moving through this aerial delicatessen over the groves, the aroma of orange blossoms prevails, after that, silage, then livestock. Once over Illinois in the fall I flew across a small town that still allowed the open-air burning of leaves. In Southern California, where I live, this is considered a crime against humanity. Having grown up in Illinois, which I think of as the home of burning autumn leaves, the passage over the town evoked memories of the pleasant Indian summer evenings of years ago.

Five hundred feet, however, is not a good altitude to be at if there is a problem. Without the engine turning, there is less than a minute between the airplane in serene cruise flight and its certain and panicked arrival on the ground. Choices of landing sites will be both hurried and limited. This does not diminish the beauty of low flight though. It's the flyer's forbidden fruit.

Trimmed out, we are making a comfortable ninety miles per hour. We could go faster, but with more noise and more wind. Besides, why hurry a pleasant experience? However, it wasn't always a pleasant experience for the occupant of this seat. This aircraft was a primary trainer in World War II—usually the first airplane that a cadet had ever been in. Put together with the design philosophy of a John Deere tractor, it was a big, noisy, cold, fire-snorting, honest-to-gosh, ton-and-a-half airplane that was built to take anything a student could give it. In return it gave young men, many of whom had never even driven cars, the beginnings of the biggest adventure of their lives. Plucked from a depression-ridden economy, a nineteen-year-old was given a twelve-thousand-dollar U.S. Army airplane, taught to loop it, roll it, and fly it to places he had never heard of on charts he had never seen before. Heady stuff. Cadets were introduced to the mysteries of aerodynamics, meteorology, and navigation and expected to master these in an incredibly short period of time. Some never made it.

Overwhelmed by the sensations and demands of flight, this pleasant cockpit could become a place of quiet desperation until the experience was terminated by a "down" or negative check ride by an instructor. Four out of ten cadets washed out in primary training. Others found it very natural and learned to give this old biplane a grace it never knew it had. Luck was a big factor. Crosswinds, instructor whims, convenience of the government—all played a role in who made it through the training programs. But anybody who ever flew a primary trainer will never forget it.

For most, it was the airplane that they soloed in. Armed with eight to ten hours of instruction and a curt "take it around, kid," a primary student would take a deep breath, firmly advance the throttle, and way before he expected it (the airplane was two hundred pounds lighter without the instructor), find himself leaving the ground with his fate in his own hands. Getting it back down of course was the trick. But if successful, and better yet, if he could repeat the performance for the next fifty to sixty hours, the student would leave this love-hate airplane behind and move into bigger and faster airplanes that made the Stearman seem absolutely primitive.

But like his first car or his first woman, he would never forget the Stearman.

This aircraft, Army Stearman 41-806, has well over five thousand hours on it. It was built before the war and completed on February 15, 1941, by the Stearman Division of Boeing Aircraft in Wichita, Kansas. From there it was flown to Oxnard, California, to begin its military instructional career, which lasted until the war was over. Many of those five thousand hours were put on in that period. Like anyone in the military it moved around a lot. Its military history looks like this:

March 1941—To Oxnard, CA
July 1942—To Santa Maria, CA
June 1944—To Chino, CA
November 1944—To Hemet, CA
December 1944—To San Angelo, TX
January 1945—To Clewiston, FL
March 1945—To Orangeburg, SC
August 1945—To Bennettsville SC

After the war, Army 41-806, so vitally needed four years before, was declared surplus to the needs of the military, as were most of the pilots that she had trained, and was put up for sale by the War Assets Board. Trainers like this sat in idle, endless rows at soon-to-be-abandoned military airfields, for sale for pennies on the dollar. Take your pick. Many were sold for scrap value and after a trip to the smelter reemerged as cookware or automobiles in the new postwar economy—"Swords into plowshares." But Army 41-806 was lucky. A young man, a decorated former naval aviator, purchased her for $851.90. Her national insignia was painted out and she began a second career as a civilian aircraft. But she was expensive to run and unable to compete with the efficient light civilian aircraft that were then flooding the market, so in 1950, having gone through a couple of owners, her fate became that of many other Stearmans of that era. She became a crop duster.

Dusting, or aerial application as it is now called, turned out to be a blessing in disguise for Stearman trainers. Although dusting went back to the '20s, it wasn't until after the war and the development of pesticides such as DDT that it really became the big business that it is today. The

Stearman was the perfect airplane for postwar dusting. It was overbuilt so that it could take the loads and turbulence of low altitudes. There was an endless variety of engines, some considerably more powerful than the original 225-horsepower engine that could be hung on the front of it. There were a lot of Stearmans around, eighty-five hundred of them having been built during the war. They were cheap, and Boeing had built parts for another fifteen hundred, so parts were plentiful. Army 41-806 easily settled into its new role as a duster in the Mississippi Delta and the Midwest.

Unfortunately, the corrosive effects of chemicals took their toll on these airplanes. Compounds that attacked more than aphids and boll weevils reduced many Stearmans to junk very quickly. Accidents further reduced their numbers. If an airplane is flown low enough, long enough, eventually it will hit something. They were flown into wires, into the trees, and into the ground with astonishing regularity. Wisely, reenforced crash cages were built, which allowed pilots to walk away from these wrecks with equal regularity.

Eventually, worn out and made obsolete by newer airplanes specifically designed for this work, many an old Stearman—Army 41-806 included—were abandoned to corners of forgotten duster strips, left to slowly fill with weeds and return to the earth. In the '60s and '70s, aircraft graveyards in agricultural areas, looking very melancholy with these faded wrecks, were quite common.

But not anymore. Although dusting took a terrible toll on these airplanes, it made it possible for the survivors to linger on long enough to be sought after by private owners as candidates for restoration, often back to their military configuration. Instead of going to the smelter, they were hauled back into hangars and lovingly restored. Again Army 41-806 got lucky and that is exactly what happened to her.

New wings were built up and fitted, new stringers gave the fuselage its classic form, a new front instrument panel and seat were put back into the space formerly occupied by the dusting hopper, and all of the hardware—all of the nuts, bolts, clevises, washers, and grommets that hold an airplane together—were replaced. It was covered in grade A cotton, painted back to its old Army paint scheme, and a freshly rebuilt engine and prop were mounted. It was authentic down to the rubber "Gosport," or speaking tube, that went between the two cockpits, and to the little

Boeing inspector's stamps that approved each major assembly. It could have taxied onto a 1943 Army ramp and been put back to work. It is an irresistible aircraft to World War II pilots.

At a recent air show I met a Stearman cadet who went on to fly B-24s in Italy. His was one of the many aircraft shot down in the suicidal, low-level raids on the Ploesti oil fields, and he spent the rest of the war as a poorly treated guest of the Rumanian government. As we talked, leaning on the wing of the Stearman, his glances at the cockpit told me what was on his mind: he hadn't been in one in fifty-five years—not since his cadet days. Seated in the olive drab cockpit, his hands moved easily over the familiar stick and throttle as his mind moved back in time. Lost in thought, eyes bright and moist, he finally turned to me and with an impish smile said, "You know, it was the best time of my life."

# CHAPTER 4

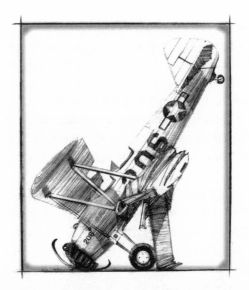

AIR CADET ROBERT POWELL, Mira Loma, Class 43A

*". . . it was not unusual to see ground loops and subsequent
tail-ups during those primary training days."*

Mira Loma Flight Academy, Oxnard, California

I can see Oxnard coming up over the nose and beyond it the Pacific
Ocean, with the coastal fog poised just offshore. Below, the orange
groves of the Santa Clarita Valley give way to million-dollar homes.
This is where it all began for this airplane in March of 1941, when this
valley was all farmland and a million dollars would have bought most
of the valley. This is where she reported for duty, newly minted, fresh,
and shiny that cool February day in 1941, resplendent in Air Corps blue,

with bright yellow wings and tail. Her pilot probably felt the chill and moisture of the onshore breeze as he rolled out on final, her long ferry flight from Wichita now behind her. And here we are, a half-century later, with the same airplane landing into the same cool onshore breeze on the same runway.

I add a little power to get up to pattern altitude, and switch on the radio to collect wind and runway information. The breeze is straight down the runway, and the Stearman floats slowly and quietly over the fence and touches lightly on the runway numbers. *Been here, done that,* it seems to say. *Sixty years ago. You're just along for the ride, kid.*

I tie down in front of the big hangar, on the same ramp it once occupied for a different owner, the U.S. Army Air Corps, and wander through what is left of the old Mira Loma Flight Academy. There used to be two large military hangars here, but now only one still stands, the other having burned down about fifteen years ago. The empty flight operations offices line the side of the remaining hangar, their broken and painted-over windows staring like sightless eyes at the flight line, which was the scene of so many personal dramas.

The barracks are still there. They were built in a circular pattern around a parade ground or inner circle with a flagpole in the center. Today these barracks have become low-income housing. A swimming pool and cabana have replaced the flagpole where the colors were raised and lowered so many times by cadets.

At the time it became operational in July of 1940, Mira Loma acquired the title of "The Country Club of the Air," and for some of the students from the poorer regions of this country it probably was a big improvement on what they were used to. There were two men to a room, and by 1940 standards the rooms were indeed very nice, more resembling college dorms than barracks. But the cadets hadn't come to play golf or party.

# Cadet Robert Powell
# Mira Loma Class 43A

## *". . . you could hear him shouting at the cadet on final approach."*

We had West Pointers who were our upper classmen; they hazed us like plebes at the Point, and "walking tours" around the inner circle at Mira Loma were quite common.

When they got into your face and asked you why you joined the Air Corps, the required answer, while standing in a brace and shouting out, was: "Sir, pa beat ma, ma beat me, the food at home was pee-poor, and my girl and a banknote were thirty days overdue. Sir, that's why I joined the Air Corps, Sir!"

When they asked you if you were familiar with the airplane you flew, the answer went something like this: "Sir, the PT-13B is a two-place biplane powered by an R-680 aircraft engine. Crew: two at two hundred pounds—four hundred pounds. Fuel: forty-six gallons. That's the airplane I fly, Sir!"

When the West Pointers would come around to inspect your rooms at Mira Loma, they would gig you if a drop of water was on the freshly cleaned sinks in our bathroom, and it didn't take us long to figure out how to avoid this infraction. When anticipating an inspection, we would take small pieces of toilet tissue, roll them up, and insert them up into the spigots, thus absorbing any water droplets and avoiding getting gigged.

The Army had hired civilian instructors, and I remember one we had whose voice was so loud that you could hear him shouting at the cadet on final approach. He was darkly tanned, and his face was deeply lined from years of exposure to the sun and wind flying in those open cockpits.

I also remember one cadet, but not his name, who stumbled over his own feet when marching and could never keep in step, but he could fly better than most any of us and was the first in our class to solo.

The brakes on the Stearmans in those days weren't the best. They were very sensitive to the touch, and it was not unusual to see ground loops and subsequent tail-ups during those primary training days.

There were well over fifty primary training bases across the country, the number changing with the Army Air Corps requirements. Avon Park, about sixty miles southeast of Tampa, was one.

## Cadet Arthur Fiedler
## Avon Park, Florida
## July 1943

### *". . . ignorance is bliss . . ."*

Our treatment in primary was in complete contrast to what we had encountered to date at the preflight military bases. Well, I'd better hedge a little and say *almost* in complete contrast, as there were still some instances of "chicken stuff."

The Lodwick Aviation Academy in Avon Park, Florida, was a civilian contract school where we would get approximately sixty hours of flying time taught by civilian flight instructors and be given check rides by Army officers at twenty, forty, and sixty hours. The food was good, and we were housed in a two-story, brand-new building that was very functional. Our days were divided into a half day of flying and a half day of academics.

My instructor was a Samuel Wilbur, who I thought was quite ancient, but later learned that he was just a few years older than we were. I was nineteen at the time. In appearance he was stout; certainly not of military bearing but a fine individual. I guess I thought he was a lot older, as he had fabulous stories. Four cadets were assigned to Mr. Wilbur.

The plane we flew was the PT-17, a biplane made by Stearman, with two open cockpits in tandem, fabric covered, and a 220-horsepower engine. [The Stearman came in a bewildering number of military alphanumeric designations depending on which engine and equipment it had and which branch of service it was assigned to. It could be a PT-13, a PT-17, or an N2S-3, or any one of perhaps a dozen different designators. They all flew pretty much the same and were all just called "Stearman."] It was a good rugged aircraft and an excellent choice for the job. My first flight was a demonstration flight in which I sat in the front seat. All other flights were from the backseat. I remember this first flight very vividly. I was allowed to fly the airplane making turns, climbs, and descents. It was my dream come true and I loved every second of it.

The PT-17 had some interesting peculiarities not normally found in modern aircraft. One was its communication system. Our flight helmets had small brass tubes protruding from each earpiece. When we got into the cockpit, there were two rubber tubes about three feet long, which we slipped over the earpiece tubes. The instructor had a mouthpiece, shaped like a funnel, at the other end of the tubes, and thus he could talk to us but we could not reply—only listen. This device was called a Gosport and was a relative of the old speaking tubes on ships. It left much to be desired. With all the engine and slipstream noise, it was often quite difficult to hear what the instructor was saying. Several instructors were known to stick this funnel-like mouthpiece out into the slipstream when they became upset with the student. The result was a ninety-mile-per-hour airstream blast into your ears and a helmet that would balloon out. If we had not had them fastened beneath our chin, I know we would have lost many helmets. Thank goodness Sam never resorted to this practice.

There was another surprising thing about this airplane. Although the front cockpit had a fairly complete set of instruments, the rear cockpit, from which the students always flew, had only an altimeter, a tachometer, and a combination oil pressure/temperature gauge. Many pilots have expressed disbelief that we did not have an airspeed indicator. And when I tell them that we judged our airspeed by the sound of the air whistling through the wires that braced the two wings, they become even more skeptical. But it is true. The faster we went, the higher the pitch of the sound, and conversely, the slower the speed, the lower the pitch of the sound. In our first ten hours of flying that was one of the things the instructor took pains to demonstrate to us. With my musical background this was a snap for me, but I have often wondered how many tone-deaf cadets washed out because they were unable to relate the sound of the wind whistling through the bracing wires to their airspeed.

Our initial flight instructions emphasized getting off and on the ground safely so that we could solo without killing ourselves. We had something between ten and twelve hours when we were allowed to solo, but I encountered a problem. Although I could take off, fly, and land the airplane very well, for some reason I had difficulty controlling the airplane directionally on the landing rollout, which could lead to a ground loop. This is where the airplane spins around and sometimes the wing on the outside of the turn contacts the ground.

After my first ground loop while flying solo, I had another ride with Sam and—believe it or not—another ground loop! But this time I got a wingtip. Sam insisted that it was not my fault because the tail wheel jammed. However I was getting worried. He reassured me and said that we were going for another ride. He then explained that I was not controlling the airplane after landing because I was not using the rudder properly. He was going to demonstrate to me how this was done.

On my next flight we went to an auxiliary field, and Sam told me he would land the airplane without touching the control stick and use only the rudders to control it. As we got about fifty feet off the ground, he suddenly raised both hands in the air, while the aircraft continued descending until it slammed into the ground and rebounded at least fifty feet into the air. As it stalled, a wing would drop, Sam would kick a rudder to bring it up, we would slam into the ground, and bounce back up again. And so it continued across the entire field, hit, bounce, hit, bounce, until finally it bounced no more. What I was supposed to observe was that as the wing would fall, Sam would bring it up by kicking the opposite rudder, but frankly I was so frightened that the only thought in my mind was that we were about to die. I think this was the most frightening experience I had going through training, and the purpose of his lesson was entirely lost on me. Actually my problem was not how to bring up the wing, but rather how to keep the airplane on a straight course after landing. Following this demonstration, Sam had me make a couple of solo landings, which for some reason turned out okay, but I was still convinced I should resign.

On my next flight I was still apprehensive and had the granddaddy of all ground loops—I not only had a wingtip drag, but I also cracked the main spar of the wing. That was it. I told Sam I was going to resign.

When we got back to the home field, he took me to the head of the military flight group, a Captain Chaffee. He was very pleasant, as contrasted with the rumors, and wanted to know what my problem was. I explained and added it was ridiculous for me to break up all these airplanes; I just wasn't able to handle them. He calmly replied that he thought he could correct the problem. He told me to sit in a swivel chair facing the front of his office, which was one huge window overlooking the flight line.

"Now extend your arm straight out toward the horizon and watch how your hand moves along the horizon when I rotate the chair," he said.

And sure enough, when he moved the chair I could easily detect the slightest movement of my hand along the horizon.

"I know exactly what you are doing wrong. When you land, you're looking at the ground directly in front of the airplane and not looking out at the horizon. Next time, after you land I want you to look ahead at the horizon, and as soon as you see the engine cylinders move either right or left along the horizon just like your hand does in this chair, kick the hell out of the opposite rudder."

And he gave the chair another turn, saying, "It will be just like you see your hand moving along the horizon now."

Instantly it was like a light had turned on in my brain and I knew that this was precisely what I had been doing. In my efforts to level off at exactly the right height to make a smooth landing, I had failed to watch where the nose of the airplane was going.

He then told me to take the airplane that was parked right outside and make three takeoffs and landings while he watched me. Imbued with confidence, I immediately thanked him, saluted, and dashed out to the airplane. I was elated when I made the landings without the slightest problem by following his instructions to "kick the hell out of the opposite rudder" if I saw the nose start to move across the horizon. This lesson was exceedingly valuable, as several months later in advanced flying school we were forced to land on a runway with a very strong crosswind. Although I landed without difficulty, fully a third of the other cadets ground looped. I am certain that if not for the efforts of both Captain Chaffee and Sam, I would not have been a pilot.

After soloing we began cross-country navigation flights, and by now I was convinced I was one hot pilot. We students used to shoot the bull, and I learned one could perform a barrel roll by pushing the control stick to one side or the other, so on my next solo flight I had to try it. My problem was that when I got on my back and the nose started to drop toward the ground, I pulled back on the stick to move the nose back up to the horizon. That was what I did when flying right side up. Unfortunately I was not hot enough to realize that when upside down, the controls are reversed and cause the airplane to react exactly the opposite as when it is right side up. As a result, I did what later I would know as a split-S, which is a half loop toward the ground from the upside-down position. It's a fatal thing if you don't have enough altitude to complete this maneuver. Later I learned that when you are on your back and the nose starts to drop, you push the stick forward—not back—to bring the nose up to the horizon again. Ah well, ignorance is bliss and I survived.

Toward the latter part of primary, we concentrated on acrobatics and learned all the basic maneuvers, which I enjoyed immensely. I recall many times going up and practicing one specific maneuver such as snap rolls for an entire hour. Of all the aircraft I flew, none did a better snap roll than the PT-17. High-performance aircraft usually did a snap roll when one did not want to do one—in a high-speed stall during combat. Otherwise they did not perform them nearly as well as the PT-17.

After completion of our sixty-hour flight check, the survivors of 43-G learned that our destination for basic flying training was Cochran Field, Macon, Georgia. Sixty-three percent of our class had washed out. We knew that a lot had failed, but had not realized that the washout rate had been so high. We regretted only that a lot of fine lads had fallen by the wayside.

I wander back out onto the ramp at the old Mira Loma Flight Academy, my explorations satisfied. 41-806 sits gleaming in the low sun. I can almost imagine the rows of identical trainers she once sat among in the morning light with their cadets and instructors climbing into the aircraft.

But there is a cadet waiting in the tie-down area next to the Stearman. He is the kid who had trouble keeping this airplane straight on the runway a lifetime ago—the kid who broke the spar on one of these airplanes. But they had confidence in him and he did all right. And later when they gave him a Mustang, nine Germans never made it back to their bases. He walks to the cockpit, peers in, and gives me a mischievous smile.

"Good morning, Art. Are you ready for your ride?" Arthur Fiedler, the terror of the Avon Beach, Florida, ground loop, is going up in his old nemesis.

# CHAPTER 5

*". . . a drumstick traveling at one hundred miles per hour"*

Runway 25, Oxnard, California

Birds are strange and entirely too skittish for my taste. They look harmless enough and always get a professional courtesy nod from pilots *(After you, my friend)*, but they are entirely unfamiliar with the rules of right-of-way as defined in the Federal Air Regulations, part 91.111. Most will sensibly avoid aircraft in flight, but every once in a while, one, or an entire flock, will act totally irrational and decide to take on a three thousand- or a three-hundred-thousand-pound airplane, often with serious consequences for both parties.

I think the only person birds have ever truly frightened is Tippi Hedren, but when finding a bird closing on an airplane at say, one hundred miles per hour, serious reflection on past misdeeds is appropriate, for judgment is often at hand.

They are deceptive. Seeing a bird approaching in flight, instinct refuses to believe they could be a threat, even though the mind knows better. They certainly look harmless enough. A few ounces to a pound of well-engineered, low-density mass with a nice cushion of feathers—who could get hurt? But imagine getting hit in the face by a drumstick traveling at one hundred miles per hour.

Dusters are faced with them constantly. Flocks will rise out of fields and collide with these all but armor-plated aircraft, usually to the detriment of the birds. I'm told that after a big duster bird strike, there is often the pleasant smell of poultry cooking in honey coming from the hot engine. The honey aroma is there because the birds eat bees and the ag aircraft eat the birds.

But as I turn onto runway two-five at Oxnard airport and bring power up to return from my visit to Mira Loma, I'm not flying an armor-plated ag aircraft, and my smiley face—thanks to the vertical seat adjustment on the Stearman—is well above the windshield frame.

That's when I notice the birds.

I'm not sure what kind they are, but the flock arrives out of the blue about four hundred feet ahead of me and well off to one side of the runway, in the grass. I make a mental note and continue my takeoff roll.

At about two hundred feet they all abruptly decide to relocate to the runway. They rise as one, travel to the runway at Mach 1, and land directly in front of me, as though they had been planning this move for weeks. By now the tail of the aircraft is up and I have a good head of steam. Swerving is out of the question, since there is nowhere to go. What I should do is to try to stop. That has its risks, but the impact speeds would be less.

I elect to try to go over the little buggers, and I'm also betting they will just as abruptly fly off when they notice what is coming. About fifty feet before impact, I do my normal rotation and the only smart thing so far: I put my head down.

I don't really see much of the incident while looking at my shoes, but when I rise back up I am aware that there have been visitors—and the results are spectacular. Our ETAs at that place on the runway have coincided. The windshield is now covered with a brown glutinous mass. There are feathers and bird parts all over the flying wires and "N" struts, and a spray of brilliant red blood covers everything from the center section of the upper wing to the tip. In short, the airplane is a mess.

I'm climbing well though and a check of controls and instruments reveals no problems, so I head out for the San Fernando Valley. I'll deal with things when I land.

I'm alarmed when I hear on the radio the next takeoff behind me reporting what looks like tire casings on the runway. This gets my immediate attention, since I can't see my tires from the cockpit. I call the tower and tell them about my little episode and ask them to check out the tire casings, which they do. The casings are, of course, dead birds.

I am lucky and the damage is minimal, but the cleaning goes on for months. When a bird goes through a propeller and into a radial engine with all of its cooling fins exposed, the results look like the Attack of the Ginsu Knives.

Curiously, there is an incident reporting form with the National Transportation Safety Board for bird strikes. I guess that the birds have a powerful lobby in Washington. As for me, I now sit quite a bit lower on takeoffs.

So I had my little surprise on the runway. Flying is often full of interesting little surprises, and they frequently occur on runways. One of the biggest surprises to any group of airmen, ever, nothing like my quirky little bird surprise, came to the crews on a routine flight of B-17s to Hawaii in December of 1941.

After spending eight years in the peacetime Army, Lt. John Compton had his reverie shattered that morning by having one of the most unfortunate ETAs in history. There was something on his runway that day and it wasn't birds.

Lieutenant Compton was puzzled over a place referred to as PLUM. He had helped draft the operations order for his squadron but still didn't know where PLUM was. All he knew was that it was overseas and they were going there as part of a plan. Although as yet there was no war on, America, the sleeping giant, was beginning to stir.

Each crew had brand-new airplanes, B-17Es with oxygen and superchargers—the first American heavy bombers so equipped. The crews had evaluated them at altitude to determine their performance, fuel consumption, and maximum ceiling, but were uneasy about the aircraft. At thirty-two thousand feet the handling appeared to be sloppy.

## Lt. John Compton, USAAC
## Hawaii, 1941

### *"They won't let us go! There is no war declared!"*

> We were told that there would be no problem if we ever fought the
> Japanese. They could not see well. We were told that their aircraft
> wouldn't come anywhere near our airplane, that we could out-fly them,
> out-altitude them—everything. So we were pretty well convinced.

In early December Compton and his squadron deployed to Hamilton
Field, just across the bay from San Francisco and made last-minute preparations. Their next flight would be a takeoff for PLUM.

> We knew our first leg was to Hawaii. At that time, that was all we knew.
> We knew Hawaii wasn't our final destination, but we didn't know even
> then what that destination was. PLUM was the Philippines.

A general at Hamilton briefed them.

> "You are going to war and it's going to be sooner than you think. You
> can take your civilian clothes with you if you have them packed, but
> you'll never need them. You're going to fight a war." I didn't feel particu-
> larly scared. But in looking back at it after all of the investigations that
> came after Pearl Harbor to determine who was at fault, this man told
> us things that convinced me that they knew what was going on. They
> didn't know what day or how—but they knew we were going to have
> to fight a war.
> And of course the buildup is indicative of that too; the relaxation
> of the college degree to become a pilot, the building of new aircraft—
> everything was being geared up. I am convinced that the president and
> everybody in the War Department knew what was going on.

The E model of the B-17 had no nose turret, not that it mattered. They
had nine machine guns on board the B-17s, but no ammunition. The only
weapons they had were their Colt .45 sidearms, and only the officers had
those.

There were nine aircraft. One had mechanical problems and couldn't make the takeoff. Eight got off and one turned back. Seven B-17Es set a course for Hawaii that evening and flew for thirteen hours over the Pacific, maintaining radio silence all the way. With a qualified navigator and celestial navigation, the trip over water was uneventful. The seven B-17Es were scheduled to arrive over the Hawaiian Islands at eight o'clock in the morning on Sunday, December 7, 1941, and they were on time.

> When we came in over the island, we saw airplanes in the air but did not recognize them as Japanese airplanes. Close to Oahu we saw a lot of antiaircraft fire going on. Well, I had been to Hawaii and knew there was an artillery range up along the mountainside. My first assumption was that they were having maneuvers there.

But as the B-17s came over the harbor at three thousand feet they saw the carnage of the ships burning in the harbor.

> I saw a ship go down in the harbor . . . I believe it was the *West Virginia*. The *Arizona* was on fire and burning with a whole lot of smoke.

They could see planes and hangars burning at Hickam Field, their destination. Although they were unable to raise anyone in the control tower, they could easily tell the wind direction from the fires at the field, so they knew which runway to use.

> Did we realize the place had been bombed? Yes and no. I think it was such a shock; it takes awhile, I think, for something like this to sink in. Now we knew it had to be the Japanese. We knew this wasn't normal. We knew that something drastic was happening. We began to get scared.

They tried to find a runway on which to put the B-17 down. Hickam was in flames. A flight over to Wheeler Field found the same conditions. All of the hangars were burning and there were burning aircraft on the runways. They briefly considered flying to Kauai and landing at the municipal airport there, but they had been in the air for thirteen hours and fuel was critical. The wind was most favorable at Hickam, so Hickam it was going to be.

> We came across Pearl Harbor and the channel to land. Everybody was hollering that we had a Japanese fighter on our tail on final approach. We had no bullets in our guns, but the guys were shooting from the side windows with their pistols.
>
> I heard a crackling sound on final approach. This part I will never ever forget. I was on final approach to the runway, down to maybe two hundred feet, and it sounded like the airplane was on fire.

Compton started to turn to ask the crew chief if they were burning, but then decided that it wouldn't make any difference. He continued the approach.

> I looked out and the people on Hickam Field were shooting at us. The Japanese fighter followed us all the way in.

They had ten minutes of fuel left, so they had no choice. They dropped the flaps, gear, and pulled off power. They were down.

> I looked out the window to the left, and I saw the American flag flying on the flagpole and was very happy. I remember being very elated about that.
>
> About halfway down the runway there was another B-17 landing in the opposite direction. We dodged him. It was a squadron mate who had decided to land there at the same time we did.
>
> We got out of the airplane and ran off into the revetment area. The Japanese airplane that followed us in was circling and strafing the crew. I remember telling the crew to fall down every time a fighter came over.

The men made it to the revetment area, all the while shooting at the fighters with their pistols. The Japanese made two more passes and left.

> Of course we went back to the airplane. We found that we had twenty-two or twenty-three holes in the ship. We had self-sealing fuel tanks, and there were several holes in the fuel tanks that had sealed up, no problem. The only basic problem we had—one bullet had hit a prop. When a prop is out of balance, it is no good.
>
> Four crews had landed at Hickam. Frank Bostrom had landed at a golf course. Knute Chiffen and Dick Carmichael had landed at a little fighter auxiliary field with a two-thousand-foot runway—how I'll never

know. But they did and had no problem. Bostrom was out of gas when he landed on the golf course.

Their senior officer in charge, Major Brandon, gathered the crews together. He had an idea where the Japanese attack came from and was ready to go to war.

They've got to be out there in carriers. Now's the time to go get them, because their airplanes will all be getting back and landing.

He went in to headquarters to get permission to go after the Japanese.

We got busy and changed our prop. We dropped our bomb bay tanks that we'd used for the long-range flight, loaded our bombs, and were ready in less than two hours.

Brandon came back and said, "They won't let us go! There is no war declared!"

They knew where the Japanese were. They had the bearing from the radar operator who had spotted the incoming flight and an estimate of the distance. It would have been a simple matter to fly out the bearing and search.

We were scared to death, but we were ready to go. Going out there would have been the greatest thing that could have happened. We could probably have gotten a ship, although from high altitude on a bomber type of mission, there's no way to know for sure.

But we did not get permission!

# CHAPTER 6

LT. ROBERT C. HANSEN, Tuscaloosa, Alabama, 1943

*". . . God, I think I've seen manuals for operating a toaster with more instructions than I got for that P-40."*

Hemet Ryan Field, Hemet, California

The Stearman rumbles smoothly in the chilled early morning air, and as usual, I'm cold. I huddle down behind the windshield to hide from the wind, but it does little good. A sip of the hot coffee that I brought along helps, but with the wind chill at this altitude I know the coffee will have a thermal half-life of just a few minutes.

Just off of my left wingtip, rising abruptly from the valley floor, the San Gabriel Mountains sit brooding in the morning haze. I can't be more than a half mile laterally from the peaks, and it feels like I can reach out and touch them. Five thousand feet directly below me are the busy San Gabriel Valley streets of La Canada, Arcadia, and Rialto. These mountains are steep; the San Gabriel range curves inland from the sea near Ventura, California, gets progressively taller as it works its way east, and builds to a spectacular climax at Mount San Gorgonio, just outside of Palm Springs, where a single peak reaches 10,900 feet, almost straight up from the valley floor. Base to top, it's the tallest peak in the lower forty-eight.

Off to my right, westbound through the center of the San Gabriel Valley, an endless procession of Boeing, Douglas, and Lockheed heavies stream into position for the long final approach into LAX. This is why I'm shouldered up against the mountains and out of their way. I'm flying upstream in their downstream world, and it just wouldn't do for a Jurassic Stearman to be run over.

But it wasn't always like this. Almost sixty years ago this valley was thick with these biplanes. Chino, Banning, and Hemet launched hundreds of them each day, and on good days as many of them returned as went out. The last time this airplane made the flight down the San Gabriel Valley to Hemet, it probably bored right through the center of the valley, having to dodge only other Stearmans or perhaps a Ryan trainer.

Stenciled neatly on the side of this airplane in a proper military manner is a legend that says:

### HEMET FIELD
### U.S. ARMY PT-13B
### AIR CORPS SERIAL NO. 41-806

Hemet Field is where this airplane was stationed in 1944, and Hemet is where we are bound for today. One of the instructors at Hemet Field during that time was a young man by the name of Warren Magnuson. Magnuson frequently flew 41-806, but it probably never meant more than a logbook entry to him, and their ways soon parted as the Stearman headed off to San Angelo, Texas, and Magnuson flew whatever airplane came along.

Years rolled by and in 1979, Magnuson, looking for a restoration project, bought the rusting hulk of an old Stearman in Oklahoma. Later, checking the Army serial number against his logbooks, he was pleasantly surprised to see that he had indeed flown that very airplane at Hemet in 1944. It was Army 41-806. He restored it over a ten-year period to look pretty much as he remembered it. Sadly, once restored, he flew the airplane very little and then passed away. It sat in a hangar for a number of years, essentially unused, until I bought it in 1993. I've flown it to the point that a second restoration will be in its future.

I swing the nose to the south to pick up a highway that I know will take me directly to the little San Gabriel Valley town, and lose some altitude to slide under the commercial traffic. As I pass over Hemet Field, I can see vestiges of the wartime appearance. The huge ramp, with its four large military hangars, is now filled with general aviation aircraft and dozens of civilian T-hangars. A neat, well-marked four-thousand-foot runway has replaced its much shorter military predecessor. I can see why they picked this location for training. In almost every direction there are grass fields on which a student could land in an emergency, and to the south are lovely little valleys, protected on both sides by mountains, in which aerobatics could be practiced. Surrounding the field in those days were five auxiliary runways for takeoff and landing work.

The Stearman settles into the pattern. This will be another one of those landings where I find out if machines have a memory. It has been fifty-four years since this aircraft has flown in this particular patch of sky, slid down the final approach, and rolled its wheels on the runway at Hemet Field. Fifty-four years since nineteen-year-olds did clumsy lazy eights, turns on a point, and sweated out crosswind landings in this ship. However, the aircraft gives no sign of recognition as I line up with the runway. I know that if I get too sappy over the occasion of this visit and quit paying attention to the landing, the airplane will eat me alive—so I'm all business. The runway numbers pass under the gear as I feel for the ground. The tail wheel touches, followed by a nice chirp of the mains as it rolls out straight and true without a wobble. I have not disgraced myself at Hemet.

A small crowd mills around one of the big military hangars as I taxi up. Mostly old men, well up there in years, with a lot of white hair showing, they are nonetheless generally trim and fit and have an accomplished look about them. They should, for these are former U.S. Army Air Corps pilots who took their training at Hemet Field during the war—Ancient Mariners of a different sort. I've purposely timed my arrival to coincide with their annual reunion. What could be more appropriate than reuniting the men and their planes at the field of their youth? There aren't many though—fifty or so. Five years ago at this reunion there were close to five hundred people and almost fifty aircraft to give hops. But five years ago most were in their early seventies. Time is taking its toll. This year there are only two airplanes to do the honors.

At the dinner that evening, the head of the reunion committee is forced to face up to a reality. "In view of our dwindling numbers, do you guys want to continue these reunions?" asks Maury Soles. Soles, who learned to fly in 1931, had instructed for the entire war at Hemet. He is a barrel-chested man, who does not look his eighty-plus years and no doubt could still fly any airplane that needed flying. With his dapper little mustache, he bears an uncanny resemblance to Clark Gable.

There is a shocked silence for a couple of beats, then an overwhelming reaction as that idea is shouted down. No, these guys aren't ready to quit yet.

## Lt. Robert C. Hansen, Tuscaloosa, Alabama, 1943

### *"I'm alive and I'm flying"*

The first day that we were going to fly, I walked out to the first airplane I'd ever been near, the first airplane I'd ever touched, and it was the first airplane that I ever flew with an instructor. It was a PT-17, a Yellow Peril.

This is what I still find a little bit hard to accept today. My parents had never been in an airplane. Their brothers and sisters, my aunts and uncles, had never been in an airplane, and I don't know if my parents even knew anyone who had ever been in an airplane. This was in 1942. My dad was a milkman and had a high school education. My mother did too. But somehow, I didn't think it was too unusual that I was going to fly. I was thrilled beyond words to have gotten as far as I had. I remember saying to myself, "If I can only get assigned to pilot training. If I can only just fly." Then after I flew I thought, "If I can only just solo."

Our instructors were civilians and each one had about six students. There was some bad chemistry between my instructor and me; he seemed to write me off from the beginning. I didn't get very much flying time. I was the runt of the litter. That only added to the natural tenseness one had in a strange situation.

I was on the road to washing out and I'd lie awake at night. Yet the flying I did was so beautiful. And lo and behold, a fine little Italian man came back from leave. He looked like an old man to me: He was probably thirty-five. He wasn't the Smilin' Jack or the John Wayne hero type like my first instructor was. My first instructor thought that he was God's gift to the world and that only great people should be pilots—because he thought that he was great.

Anyway, the little Italian came back and had to be assigned some students. Obviously, each instructor gave him his dog. He must have known that, because he took five or six of us to stand underneath the wing of an airplane and said, "I want to tell you boys one thing, and let's get this absolutely straight. You are not going to wash out. I'll make pilots of you." And he did. But over half of the rest of the class washed out.

I felt relaxed with this man and had absolutely no problems. I was a good student. I feel like I was one of his best students. The man saved my neck. He was just a beautiful man.

I ended up going to Newport, Arkansas, the exact opposite of the pretty little base from which we'd been flying. It was carved out of the raw clay of Arkansas and had tarpaper shacks for barracks. That's where we flew the BT-13. [This was the next step up from a Stearman. A low-wing aircraft manufactured by Vultee, it had an enclosed cockpit, was twice as powerful, twice as heavy, and considerably more sophisticated than the Stearman. It was a modern aircraft for the time.] Once again I had a little second lieutenant as an instructor I didn't get along with, but I guess I was lucky there.

I remember one particular flight when I had a three-legged, night cross-country. The wind had changed. All of the students, about thirty of us, were up and we got scattered across Arkansas. We were supposed to go in one particular direction for about forty-five minutes and pick up a heading from there.

Well, I did. I thought that I was at the right place, but I wasn't, and I ended up taking off in the wrong direction. I was absolutely lost and resolved to land at the first opportunity.

I saw some flashing lights on the ground, called in, and entered the traffic pattern. I landed and taxied up to the transient parking area, which at that time was always underneath the tower. On the tower you'd see the name of the base and the elevation. It was Newport, my home field, but I have no idea how I got there.

So I kept going past the transient area, went to the parking area, and pulled in. And there was that mean little instructor of mine. He looked at his watch, he looked at me, then made some smart-ass remark like, "Hansen, for Chrissake, of all the stupid cadets—you're the one I'd least expect to be here on time."

I saluted and strode confidently off. Of course there were new problems the next day, but I graduated.

Then I had a great, great second lieutenant in advanced training. I did extremely well with him. I did very well in gunnery. Some P-40s had just been brought on base, and it had been decided that the cadets would be given ten hours in them. You've got to remember that six or eight months previously, I was riding a bicycle and delivering telegrams. I didn't even have a driver's license. I turned nineteen in July when I was in basic, and graduated in October of 1943.

I was barely one or two months over nineteen and didn't have a whole lot of AT-6 time. Somebody had to start flying those three P-40s, and in order to give everybody ten hours in them, the Air Corps couldn't afford to wait until we all had sixty or seventy hours in the AT-6. So I was the first of my group of three to fly the P-40.

That was a thrill. The P-40 was a tail dragger, with a long nose and one thousand horsepower. After a very brief cockpit check and reading the manual—God, I think I've seen manuals for operating a toaster with more instructions than I got for that P-40—we were out at the plane the next morning. And the instructor said, "Hansen, you might as well go first." I jumped on the wing and the instructor got up there.

That plane made a tremendous noise. It snarled, crackled, and I was both scared and excited. That long nose went out to infinity—all those dials—but you have confidence. I started to taxi out, touched the brakes, and the nose dipped. It felt like I was going to go over on the nose. When you get used to that feeling, it doesn't bother you, but every time I touched the brakes—oh, my God. My heart was beating wildly by the time I got out to the end of the runway.

You're supposed to check the mags at eighteen hundred rpm. I ran the engine up and it made far more noise and vibration than an AT-6. That engine was just roaring! I just couldn't force myself to bring the engine up to the rpm that it was supposed to turn. The tower started hollering at me, but I was sure the engine was going to wrench itself loose.

I finally got the engine up to eighteen hundred rpm, checked the mags real quickly, and pulled the throttle back. I lined up on the runway, locked the tail wheel, and started down.

We'd been told that there was a lot of torque and that you had to trim the airplane. We'd been told about torque, but I was just not prepared for this. I kept putting in my right foot and putting in my right foot. You have to watch this and stay in the middle of the runway. I got the tail up, and I guess we're doing one hundred miles per hour and the plane is making all this noise, but I pulled back on the stick and off we went. I was level, straight and level, and I pulled the gear and milked the flaps up.

I said, "I'm alive and I'm flying." And I checked everything to make sure. Throttle back. Set propeller rpm. I checked the manifold pressure gauge, got all calm, and took a deep breath.

And I was lost! Honest to God, I was lost!

I'd been watching that I didn't run into anybody, but I wasn't paying any attention to the ground. I had taken off—and instead of going 120 miles per hour, I was doing 160 miles per hour. I had gone into a gradual climb to the left. When I first looked out of the plane, I thought I was about four miles off the airstrip to the south we'll say, but I was really eighteen or twenty miles off of the end of the strip and to the east. I had become disoriented.

By the time I had calmed down, I was another twenty or so miles farther away. I was supposed to be up for an hour and go up to eight thousand feet, where I was to put down the gear and flaps. First I was to approach a stall with the gear up, just to feel how the plane flies at slow speed. Then I was to put the gear and flaps down and practice with that so that I could land the airplane. It was kind of a primitive method of teaching a kid to fly that plane.

I finally got oriented, but I really did spend about half the time just finding where the hell I was and getting calmed down. So I very briefly did the exercise I was supposed to do. Then I had to find the base and land.

I was at eight thousand feet and looked down. There were AT-6s in the pattern, and I just poked the nose down. All of a sudden I was going about 350 miles per hour entering the traffic pattern with AT-6s whizzing by me. I said, "Oh, my God!" You just can't conceive the difference between our trainers and the much heavier airplane. I had pulled back the throttle a little bit, I'm sure, but nowhere near enough.

I didn't say anything and the tower didn't say anything, so I did a 360 and entered the pattern again—downwind. It was the most beautiful landing in the history of the P-40. The P-40 was a rotten little airplane. I didn't like the plane and nobody I ever knew liked the plane. But I'd made a beautiful three-point landing. I just greased it in, barely knew I was on the ground. I got to the end of the runway and turned off, but my knees were shaking so hard I couldn't taxi.

It took me a few minutes to compose myself, then I taxied back to the flight line. This was the only P-40 in commission; the others weren't ready yet. Two students were standing there waiting for me. "How'd it go? How'd it go?"

"A piece of cake!"

On October 1, I graduated from flying school. My mother and dad came down. It was a very proud moment for me. The last time my parents had seen me, I was a runny-nosed kid on a bicycle.

I had a ten-day delay en route to Mitchell Field. I got home and asked my dad if I could borrow his car, a '41 Hudson. That was a pretty nice car. He said, "Gee, Bob, you don't have a driver's license."

I said, "Well, Dad, the government lets me fly its fifty-thousand-dollar P-40s. I ought to be able to drive your nine-hundred-dollar Hudson." Of course, he let me drive the car.

I reported to Mitchell Field and was assigned to Richmond, Virginia, for P-47 training. We were treated pretty much as we had been as cadets. We were all brand-new second lieutenants and thought that we should have been treated more as officers and gentlemen instead of like nineteen-year-old kids. We thought such treatment mortifying. After all, we had such vast experience in flying.

# Hemet Ryan Field, 1943

## *"We don't know where you're stationed Ed. . . ."*

Every primary training class published a graduation book full of pictures and thoughts of the students' experiences. These were not unlike the high school yearbooks we're all familiar with and in which most of these young men had appeared in only a year or so previously. They had colorful names such as *Crosswinds* or *The Eagle,* but instead of rows of photos of awkward high school kids, these were photos of glamorous pilots in sheepskin-lined leather jackets and white silk scarves. For many it was the most exciting and the best time of their lives. For some it was extremely stressful. And for a small but relentlessly predictable number, it marked the end of their lives.

Learning to fly an airplane is a wonderful and magical experience, but it also has a dark and savage side. Many cadets learned the hard way of the consequences of any inattentiveness, inability, or neglect. Or just plain bad luck.

Ed Hutchinson of Wisconsin was such a man. No one knows exactly what happened to him or his airplane that sunny day over the San Gabriel Valley. He was found lifeless in the wreckage of his once-beautiful silver Ryan trainer. He was never to appear in his graduation book.

But his classmates did not forget him. And this is the letter that they wrote to him in that book.

> Dear Ed:
>
> Just a line to let you know how things have been since you left. It's kind of hard to believe that we're actually through primary. You know how it is while you're in the swing of things. It gets pretty rough sometimes and you wonder if you'll ever make it, but when it's all over it seems so easy.
>
> Remember how you used to stick up for Wisconsin? The battle of the states still rages but not quite so merrily as when you were in there pitching. Ed, you had a knack for really chasing the blues away.
>
> We really enjoyed our graduation banquet with our instructors. You know that they turned out to be nice fellows after all. If they were harsh with us sometimes, it was for our own good.
>
> Wish you could join us for a coke at the canteen, a game in the recreation room, or another bull session in the cabin. We wish you could be with us through our days of training, our days of fighting, and share with us our day of victory.
>
> We don't know where you're stationed Ed, but we salute you and wish you happy landings.
>
> Sincerely:
> Your fellow Cadets and Instructors
> Hemet Field Class 43C

Ed Hutchinson was nineteen years old.

# CHAPTER 7

*. . . the Grumman F4F Wildcat fighter, an airplane with a landing gear that looks like it belongs on a roller skate and is even more of a challenge to land than a Stearman.*

C al-Aero Academy, Chino, California

The Army records on 41-806 say "12 July, 1944. Airplane is assigned to C.P.S. (Contract Pilot School), Cal-Aero Academy, 3045th Base Unit, Major C. C. Moseley, operator, Ontario, California." At the time of the assignment the Stearman had a total of 1,577.4 flying hours since first being commissioned. It had been wrecked and rebuilt twice and had flown many cadets.

Contract pilot schools were an innovation of Army Air Force chief Gen. Hap Arnold and a handful of civilian aviation pioneers such as C. C. Moseley, Tex Rankin, and Bevo Howard. The budget restraints of the '30s had left the military in bad shape, and by 1939 the U.S. Army was the eleventh largest in the world. The U.S. Army Air Corps was able to turn out fewer than a thousand pilots a year, and seeing war on the horizon Arnold set up a program of civilian flight instruction. Using military aircraft and military check pilots, civilian schools were set up by these men and provided the first sixty-plus hours of flight instruction, known as "primary." It was so successful that the United States was able to train pilots faster than it could build airplanes. The Air Corps actually had to begin winding down pilot training in late 1943 with the end of the war in sight. The Japanese and the Germans, on the other hand, were never able to replace their pilot losses.

But a visit to this field is not something that I'm looking forward to. Ontario Airport has since become a major passenger hub in the Los Angeles area, and I know that there can't be much left of whatever was there in 1944. A 12,200-foot runway sits on top of most of it anyway, so I'll only be going through the motions.

Any landing at Ontario Airport is not going to be a casual thing either. There are lots of heavy jets there, and my spruce and cotton dinosaur is not going to be happy with the wake turbulence they create. Nor will Ontario Approach Control be pleased with me upsetting the rhythm of their arrivals with my seventy-mile-per-hour approach speed and scratchy radio. So, although it is only about thirty minutes away, I put off the visit to Ontario for a long time. And then the aviation gods intervene.

## Lt. Julian Kahn
## Van Nuys Airport
## July 1999

### Chicago to Spearfish to Kunming and back

Time had not recently been kind to Julian Kahn. When I first met him he was impatiently pushing a walker around the tarmac of an oppressively hot Van Nuys, California, air show. Spotting the Stearman in the display area, he stopped to study it. His voice, affected by a stroke a year previously, was tremulous and high-pitched, but when we started talking airplanes, a focus came into the voice and it got younger, almost belonging to someone else. His eyes laughed, and as I listened to his stories I could easily see this man pushing a C-47 around the world and over the "Hump" into China.

Julian Kahn had enlisted in Chicago and, with the logic only the Army is capable of, was sent to Spearfish, Montana, to begin his flight training. He started in a sixty-five-horsepower Aeronca trainer and nine short months later drew his first military piloting assignment. As a newly minted aircraft commander of an equally new crew, he was to pick up a factory fresh Douglas C-47 transport and deliver it halfway around the world to China. Of course there were a few events along the way to that assignment. He shared some of them.

> I took my primary at Cal-Aero Academy in Chino, California, in a Stearman. And the first solo I had was in a Stearman. I still to this day remember the downwind leg and thinking to myself, *My God, I must be nuts up here all by myself.* But I got through it okay. And I landed okay, and my instructor waved me around again and I did another flight.

His retelling of the solo made him as excited as if it had happened yesterday.

> When we flew from Cal-Aero Academy—we used to get terrible smog in those days—we'd go up to Victorville and fly around up there and have a great time doing aerobatics, loops, spins, and everything. We would go out and pick watermelons and take them with us in the Stearman. Then we'd dive-bomb the cattle and throw the watermelons at them—in the Stearman. God Almighty! 1943! I was twenty-two!

He went on to basic flight training and flew a unique version of the Vultee BT-13 trainer. It had a wooden fuselage and wing skins instead of the customary aluminum. The country was running out of critical materials and was experimenting with substitutes. The airplanes flew reasonably well, but they were restricted to straight and level flight. Aerobatics, the stuff of life to a military pilot, were not allowed. It was rumored that the airplanes weren't strong enough. Julian didn't know it at the time, but he was already on the track for training as a transport pilot.

He went to Lemoore and trained in UC-78s, known more casually as *Bamboo Bombers* because of their wood and cotton structure. Also called *Useless 78s,* they were never a popular airplane and always a downright dangerous one on a single engine.

> From there I went to advanced training at Wahata, Colorado, and I flew, would you believe, B-25s. I was a cadet flying B-25s. What an

airplane! My God, how that thing flew. I can still hear them in my sleep. I'll wake up and say, "That's a B-25." There's one at Van Nuys Airport that flies every now and then.

From B-25s at Wahata I went to Bergstrom Field in Austin, Texas, and transitioned into the C-47, then went on to Fort Wayne, Indiana, and picked up a brand-new airplane. And from Fort Wayne our first stop was Syracuse, New York. From there they routed us to Manchester, New Hampshire—that was our port of embarkation. They outfitted us there in Manchester, and from there we went to Gander Lake, Newfoundland, and we stayed there about four or five days waiting for the weather to clear, which it finally did, and they headed us out over the Atlantic Ocean.

Their aircraft flew alone. Formation flights invite collisions. If they were lucky they were able to see clouds over the mountains of the Azores from eight hundred miles out. This simplified navigation. Some weren't lucky and were never heard from again.

I think back on it and I think, "My God, we had gall." We had more balls than you can imagine to take off over the Atlantic Ocean like that in a twin-engine airplane that really wasn't that sophisticated. All we had was ADF navigation. [Airborne Direction Finders give the direction to a signal from the ground such as an AM radio station. In the early '40s they were very problematic, especially in the middle of the Atlantic.] We had nothing else. No electronic navigation gear at all.

I was the aircraft commander. I had a copilot who lives right here in San Fernando. I had a navigator who didn't know how to find his ass in front of a mirror. I had a radio operator who was pretty good and a crew chief who was very good.

We had eight hundred gallons in the wing tanks and four hundred gallons in fiberboard cabin tanks. We went to the Azore Islands from Gander, nonstop, landed in the Azores, stayed there overnight, fueled up, and took off the next morning. Flew to Marrakech in Morocco. They finally gave us orders to proceed to Karachi, India, by way of the North African coast, but we had to be careful because the Germans were jamming our ADF frequencies. We were cautioned not to use it. We flew along the north coast of Africa and stopped at Bizerte, which was an emergency landing, as the weather had turned crappy and we had to land. We found this big beautiful runway at Bizerte, fired the flares of the day through the roof of the cabin, went in and landed and said, "Where are we?"

They continued on to Benghazi and Cairo.

> We stayed in Cairo about four days. We had a bad autopilot and whenever I wanted to delay my next flight I'd say, "Fix the autopilot," and I knew darned well that they didn't have any parts, because it was a brand-new airplane. And they'd say, "Well, that will take us a few days," and I'd say, "That's okay! That's okay!"

Their final destination was Dinjan, on the Brahmaputra River in northeast India, just over halfway around the world from Spearfish, Montana, where Julian had flown his first airplane just nine months before.

They took his brand-new C-47 away from him and put him back in the copilot's seat for five hundred hours. When he finally checked out again as aircraft commander, he went to the bottom of the pecking order and got the most beat-up aircraft in the squadron. It required twelve degrees of aileron trim just to fly straight. Julian was not pleased, but it happened to everyone.

He hauled rice, troops, mules, gasoline, and trucks into Kunming and Chen Yi. A six-by-six truck was too big to carry in a C-47, so it would be cut up with a torch, the parts stuffed into the airplane and welded back together in China.

> There were missions to overfly Chinese positions where crewmen would kick rice sacks out of the open double doors of the C-47 to the waiting troops. There was an incident that we had heard about where when we first started dropping sacks of rice, a Chinese soldier tried to catch one. Of course it drove him right into the ground. Only once. Only once.

On one flight, as Julian put his foot on the step to board the aircraft he noticed that it was lower than normal. He pointed it out to the crew chief, who dismissed it as a low tail-wheel strut. Their takeoff, however, used up the entire runway, and the aircraft would not climb above five hundred feet. When they got the airplane back on the ground, the shaken crew discovered that their load included three complete field hospitals, only two of which were on the manifest. They were eight thousand pounds over their normally overloaded gross weight!

So Julian flew. And flew. A thousand hours in six months. Over the Nara Hills into Burma and across the Himalayas into China. And when the war ended he went back to Chicago, his two-year odyssey over. Chicago to Spearfish to Kunming. And back.

Julian did not fly again for over twenty years. But finally in 1967 he got a single-engine private pilot's license. His military license was no good, as it was for multiengine only. I asked him if he ever again flew a C-47. He laughed and said he did once. "My God, it flew like a truck."

About the time I met Julian Kahn, I was rebuilding the cockpit of 41-806. The aircraft had two entirely different instrument panels, obviously the result of some casual repair sometime in the last fifty-five years. The front instrument panel had seven instrument holes and the rear one had eight, configured entirely differently. They were from two different models of the Stearman. One was correct, but without drawings or photos I had no way of knowing which. Right on cue, in the course of our conversation, Julian pulled out a faded photo of a smiling young Air Cadet Kahn at Chino Field, sitting proudly in his PT-13B, the exact same type as 41-806. Plainly visible was the seven-hole panel. Thanks for the photo, Julian.

So the Stearman had been stationed at Cal-Aero Academy at Chino Airport, and not Ontario. In those days, Ontario was the nearest major town and that's how the military records referred to it. Chino was a great airport and an entirely different proposition. I was very familiar with Chino.

## Chino Airport, July 1992

### "What insurance?"

"How does a guy learn how to fly one of these?" I asked a question destined ultimately to give me huge amounts of satisfaction and cost me great bags of money—yet worth every cent.

I had struck up a conversation with the pilot of a maroon and silver Stearman who was refueling at the Chino fuel island. Hartley Folstat, the owner and pilot of this beautiful airplane gestured to the wing and said, "Sit on the wing walk. We'll taxi back to the hangars and I'll tell you." And so my flying life changed.

We went back to his hangars, where he had no less than five maroon and silver Stearmans. Hartley was a busy man. In addition to his day job as a DC-9 captain for American Airlines, he flew an air show aerobatic act, The Silver Wings, with three of the Stearmans and a wing walker, Margee Stivers. He offered Stearman flight instruction in the other two.

Finding someone who actually instructed in a Stearman surprised me. It was like finding a stagecoach driving school. No one actually used these airplanes for instruction anymore for a lot of reasons. First of all, they aren't really relevant to the type of airplanes being flown today. They're a dead end, an anachronism, and far too expensive to purchase and maintain to risk with a student pilot. The liability insurance alone on a Stearman rental aircraft would eat you alive. Insurance companies are loath to get anywhere near these airplanes, mostly because of their landing characteristics, which are "interesting." A look at the National Transportation Safety Board accident records reveals all. Almost everywhere that there is a Boeing Stearman Model 75 accident listed, the cause is inevitably the same: "Pilot failed to maintain directional control on landing." And these accidents involved owners who flew them regularly.

But here it was. Instruction. If you were a reasonably competent nose wheel pilot, there was a ten-hour minimum checkout for insurance purposes and then, the most incredible thing of all, you were free to rent one of these beauties and fly to your heart's content.

Everywhere I looked in this hangar complex there were Stearmans or parts of Stearmans under construction or repair. Three of the airplanes had the big Pratt & Whitney 450-horsepower engines in them. These were the air show aircraft and were also available for instruction. On the wall were painted the names of people who had been checked out and soloed in the aircraft. They were the graduates of the Hartley School of Time Travel. It was like finding the Lafayette Escadrille squadron alive and well in Southern California. I thought I had died and gone to heaven. I couldn't get my name on the schedule fast enough.

And so the entry on my logbook says, "July 7, 1992, Boeing Stearman Model A-75. One-hour familiarization flight, turns, climbs, glides, takeoffs, and landings. Carter Teeters, CFI." Carter was my assigned flight instructor. A genial southern lad, he quietly suffered through my crashing arrivals for ten hours without ever once grabbing the stick to save his life. He earned his money.

Instruction at Hartley's was fascinating. Ground school was mandatory and consisted of watching the very same training films that World War II cadets watched. There were both Army and Navy films. Robert Taylor, a major Hollywood actor of sixty years ago, who I had always thought of as Ivanhoe, had become a naval aviator and an instructor, and was the narrator of the Navy films. They were intelligently put together, informative, and I ate them up. Here I was going through the same training, at the same field, in the same type of airplane that the cadets once flew. What I didn't know was that I would soon own one of those airplanes.

Carter was, to my benefit, charmingly merciless. Almost the entire ten hours of instruction was taken up in takeoffs and landings. I think that if Carter could have figured out a way to just do the difficult landings without the easier takeoffs, he would have. The runways at Chino were laid out in an "X." If the traffic was light enough, we would take off on one leg of the "X," immediately turn and land downwind on the other leg of the "X," add power to take off again, turn and land upwind on the original leg of the "X," and so on. The flight path became a huge figure eight with the wind and landing conditions always changing. The pressure was relentless and the instruction superb. I loved it.

Soon, in spite of all of my many attempts to wreck the Stearman, Carter climbed out one day and said, "Take it around a few times and when you're tired of that, bring it back to the hangar." He walked off across the ramp without a look back, probably uttering a silent prayer. I did what he asked and flew well. He had done a good job. It was one of the most satisfying flying days of my life, and soon my name went up on the wall with the immortals.

I still see Carter occasionally to get a flight review, one of the rituals every pilot must go through. The last time I saw him he was flying the Confederate Air Force Grumman F4F Wildcat fighter, an airplane with a landing gear that looks like it belongs on a roller skate and is even more of a challenge to land than a Stearman. There is a constant worry with these old airplanes. Some are almost too rare to risk flying. But the Wildcat couldn't be in better hands.

Eight years later I flew 41–806 out to Chino to revisit its old home. Hartley was still there in the same hangar, surrounded by Stearmans and parts of Stearmans. One of his airplanes had been replaced. An engine failure had brought it down and Hartley had gone with it into the woods. The airplane had been demolished, but Hartley had walked away. Thankfully the Stearman has an extremely strong airframe and will protect its pilot well in the event of a mishap.

We talked for a while and he told me that he still did the aerobatic act but no longer does the flight instruction or the rental.

"Insurance costs getting too much for you?" I asked.

"What insurance? We never had any insurance."

"But you told us that the insurance required a ten-hour checkout."

He just smiled.

# CHAPTER 8

*. . . Hancock Field frozen in time.*

Hancock Field, Santa Maria, California

In July of 1942, after a year at the Mira Loma Flight Academy in Oxnard, California, 41-806 was reassigned to Hancock Field in Santa Maria, about eighty miles up the coast. She spent the next two years there and they were better years for the trainer, because unlike her initial assignment in Oxnard, everybody kept it straight on the runway and nobody wrecked her. There would be no more trips to the Glendale Air Terminal repair facility for new wings.

In the 1920s, Santa Maria was a sweet little agricultural town nestled among the coastal valleys halfway between Los Angeles and San Francisco. Allan G. Hancock, a California industrialist, had purchased a ranch in the area, and his subsequent interest in aviation soon prompted him to put an airstrip on the property. In 1929, as a business venture and an investment in the town, he developed this into an air academy designed to train pilots and mechanics. It was intended to be the West Point of the air and was in fact a semimilitary operation with a cadet system and uniforms. It graduated many highly skilled technicians and pilots before the war and was perfectly positioned to be a major contributor to the coming war effort. During the war years, Hancock geared up and ultimately graduated over eighty-four hundred pilots.

My flight there from Oxnard is scenic, though quick, even for the Stearman. Much of it is along the California coastline to Santa Barbara and then east through the San Marcos Pass in the coastal range. The old Southern Pacific tracks run right along the beach, and it's here I'm told many a cadet raced the mighty Union Pacific Starlight Limited with his Stearman. They were well matched, because they both cruised about the same speed.

I begin my letdown over Solvang in the Santa Maria Valley and head for the large municipal airport southwest of the city. This airport, though graced with the perfect triangular set of runways in the classic military tradition, is not the Hancock Field of sixty years ago. This airport was a P-38 fighter training base during the war and sent many fighter pilots to Europe and the Pacific.

## Lt. Everett Farnham, USAAF
## North Africa, 1943

### . . . of '38s and '39s

I had five hours in the P-40 at Luke Field before I graduated and then went down to Florida and flew P-39s. I got about eighty or ninety hours in the P-39 and became fairly familiar with it. It's an interesting airplane. It's different from anything that you've ever seen, with the engine behind and the cannon shooting through the hub of the propeller. Because of that it has an odd weight distribution and could even get into a tumbling condition. It could actually go head over tail and fall through the sky that way, and it stalled out strangely but was a fun airplane to fly. I don't think that it was ever very effective in the war, and that's probably why they gave most of them to the Russians.

Then they sent us overseas. We got into North Africa and ended up at a base just outside of Casablanca, ten or fifteen miles out in the sand. It was the middle of July and hotter than hell.

All they had there were Spitfires and P-38s. None of us had ever flown multiengine airplanes or been at the controls of anything multiengine, so it was going to be a major transition. The P-38 is a big hunk of airplane with those two engines on it. It was just so different than anything we had been around.

They were using the P-39 for coastal patrol up and down the edge of the Mediterranean, and if we wanted to fly them we could, but it wouldn't be a combat tour, because practically nothing happened. It was a two-and-one-half-year tour.

I had just turned twenty-one, and when you say "a two-and-one-half-year tour," it sounds like two lifetimes, so we said, "God, no. We don't want to do that."

They replied, "Well, you can get checked out in Spitfires, but we're not sure what they're going to be using them for—and we also have the P-38." Everybody I was with said they wanted to fly the P-38.

They had established a base at Bertoux, Algeria, and that's where we ultimately got checked out in the P-38.

Normally when you get checked out in any airplane, you read the tech manuals and then sit in the cockpit to familiarize yourself with it. You talk to somebody who has flown it, or hopefully you go up for a ride with someone who can show you its characteristics.

Well, very little of that happened when we were checked out. First of all, these were war-weary planes that had been left behind to use for checkouts because they weren't in the greatest mechanical condition. We saw a number of accidents happen—probably pilot error, but you never knew. Anyway, it was kind of a frightening experience checking out in this thing.

The operations officer took you out to the plane, and he would give a cockpit check so you pretty much knew where everything was. You didn't know what everything did though. And of course your biggest concern getting into a big, very-powerful-for-its-day, twin-engine aircraft was, "What happens when you lose an engine on take-off?" Of course, you've got the counter rotating props, which were wonderful.

They were smooth and eliminated torque. All you did is get to the end of the runway and run the throttles up until you couldn't hold the brakes anymore, then release them, and away you went. It practically took off by itself.

But you knew that you really had ahold of a big piece of equipment the first time that you flew one. You were twenty-one years old, you've had about 240 hours of total flying time, and there were no piggyback aircraft there to give you your ride or to demonstrate anything for you. You were on your own.

I went out and flew the thing about three times and it scared the hell out of me. I just wasn't familiar with a plane like that. I'll never forget it. [He laughs.]

I came into the operations tent after about my third flight, and told the lieutenant, "I don't know what I'm doing in this aircraft. I'm afraid that I'm going to go out there and kill myself if I don't learn this thing pretty quick. I'm not sure that I want to fly it after all."

The lieutenant said, "I'll tell you what. Why don't you go back to your tent and think about it. And think about the alternatives—about what you're going to do. Are you prepared to go to that P-39 squadron and fly coastal patrol for two and a half years if you decide you don't want to fly the P-38?"

So I sat around and thought about it, and the next morning I went over to operations and said, "I'm ready."

I flew them for 750 hours after that and never had a serious incident. Wonderful airplane! Wonderful airplane! And it felt so good having two fans out there turning, especially when you were three to four hundred miles behind enemy lines and knew that you had to get home some way. It was the Cadillac of all fighter planes in those days and a wonderful airplane to fly.

I think in the beginning, when I got up to the group in Italy, I had a total of about twenty hours in the airplane in North Africa, one practice dive-bombing with a hundred-pound bomb and one ground gunnery flight where we fired at a ground target. That was my total experience with the airplane. On about the first five missions that I flew, I was really more afraid of the airplane than I was of the Germans. But luckily for me I didn't see any Germans for the first five missions. I think it was on the sixth mission that we ran into some fighter opposition. My mind-set at that time was that I really needed to learn more about this airplane so that I'd be more comfortable. As I got a little more time in it and flew a few more missions, I got to feeling more comfortable with both the airplane and the fact that I was in combat. And at that point you say, "This is my job. This is what I'm here to do. And I'm going to do the best I can with it." It was not really fear. It was a nervous anticipation.

I'm landing at the municipal airport simply because the old Hancock Field no longer exists. Typical of many airports built on the edge of little cities during the '20s and '30s, the town of Santa Maria had expanded and swallowed it up. So I put the Stearman down among the Jetstreams and Metroliners and, armed with a street map, drive into town to find the old Hancock Field.

At first I can find no trace of it. The site had become a pleasant campus, the Allan G. Hancock College, and students milled purposefully between classes. Circling the school once, I look in vain for some evidence of its past and, finding none, park the car for a more thorough search. While getting out of the car, I happen to glance into an industrial park across the street from the campus and know instantly that I have found what I have come for. Almost hidden from the road is the unmistakable shape of a good-size military hangar. It sports a bright yellow paint job, and a look inside reveals hay bales stored to the rafters, but there's no concealing its original purpose. And like a Polaroid slowly developing, I can also see that many of the other buildings in the industrial park are also former base hangars. Instead of Stearmans, they now house all manner of businesses from body shops to boat builders. The parking lot where I am standing had once been the flight line of Hancock Field. 41-806 no doubt stood daily on this very apron. Comparing with period photos, I can see that the old runway, just a few feet away, now holds a row of apartments. Walking down what would have been the old flight line, I can see that many of the buildings of the base still exist as college administration buildings, though they now wear California jonquil, peach, and turquoise paint. This time swords had been painted into plowshares.

Of course, with fifty years of building on the site, my picture of the base is not as clear as it could be. However, a passing conversation with a local resident soon changed that. "Well, you know, Hancock Field was used in the filming of *The Spirit of St. Louis.*"

*The Spirit of St. Louis,* with Jimmy Stewart, is a classic aviation film. It chronicles the crossing of the Atlantic in 1927 by Charles Lindbergh.

Made in 1957, the movie is full of charm, excitement, reasonable authenticity, and is delivered in the "aw shucks" manner that Stewart does so well. I'd seen the movie many times but didn't recall any scenes that resembled what I was now looking at. Instead, the movie depicts Lambert Field in St. Louis, Randolph Field in Texas, Roosevelt Field on Long Island, and Le Bourget in Paris. And although I had never been to any of those airports, the movie was quite convincing to me.

So, I rented the movie . . . and indeed saw Hancock Field frozen in time.

The front of the big yellow Hancock main hangar had been painted to read "Lambert Field, St. Louis." There's a great shot of Lindbergh landing at Lambert (Hancock) Field right after a rainstorm and taxiing in. In the movie, a coffee shop is part of the main Lambert hangar. It was in this coffee shop that the flight was first discussed and its progress tracked. It is still there. I almost want to go back and see if Jimmy Stewart is still at the counter or on the phone. But today it just stores more hay. The administration offices and flight line of Hancock must have posed as the cadet flight line during the scenes at Randolph Field, Texas. Two smaller hangars looked like they were used for the eve of Lindbergh's departure from Roosevelt Field, and the Roosevelt runway surely must have been the Hancock runway. The movie is so convincing that I had never thought to question what eucalyptus trees were doing growing at the end of a Long Island, New York, runway. The trees that were reaching for the landing gear of the "Spirit" as it barely cleared them on takeoff had a distinctive California feel.

So Hancock Field, the field that trained thousands of army pilots in hundreds of old Stearmans, hasn't disappeared entirely. It still lives on, not in some musty inaccessible historical society library, but in a beautifully filmed story of a different chapter of aviation history.

# CHAPTER 9

CAPT. JOSEPH C. PIMENTEL, Thunderbolt pilot, France, 1944

*". . . a gusting thirty-five-mile-per-hour crosswind in blowing snow."*

$\mathbf{S}$an Fernando Valley to Kingman, Arizona, August 7, 2000
The journey begins.

Climbing out through the Mindenhall Pass on the northern edge of the San Fernando Valley, all seems right with the world. The engine, with its fuel/air mixture enriched by the cool dense morning air, beats a smooth, powerful tattoo on the steep canyon walls surrounding us. My passenger on the first part of the flight, Dennis Law, a very old friend who has never been in an open cockpit biplane before, sits enthralled by the spectacle. We go back many years, all the way to high school, and have a history of these little adventures. He's chosen to throw in his lot with me and ride along for a first-class view of the desert between Los Angeles and Midland, Texas—a brave man.

Although it's called a pass, Mindenhall is nothing more than a steeply walled, dauntingly narrow slot in the San Gabriel Mountains with a reservoir at the bottom. When the Santa Ana winds are up, it becomes a venturi, accelerating the winds that come pouring down from the higher elevation deserts to the north. At such times it's not a place to be in an airplane. I've tried it and regretted it. But when it's calm, as it is today, I can sneak through its narrow corridors with impunity.

Coming out of the pass, I alter course to the east toward Kingman, squint into the morning sun, and sip reflectively on my coffee. Now that we're in the air, I can relax, because the preparation phase for this flight is officially over. Whatever I've forgotten will stay forgotten. The hours of flight planning are done and a complete collection of seventeen up-to-date sectional aeronautical charts rest in my flight bag, stacked neatly in their order of use. They'll take me all the way across the country and back. Course lines are laid out, compass headings noted, and mileage marks are penciled every ten miles between destinations. A Boeing 767 would cover those mileage marks at the rate of one a minute. The Boeing Stearman will take seven and a half minutes between each. From Los Angeles to the Atlantic, touching down at the four remaining bases, the course lays out across the southern extremity of the United States. The return route is a bit more northerly, getting up into Tennessee and possibly up into Missouri. So in addition to the four fields in Southern California, which I've already touched down at, there are Goodfellow Field, San Angelo, Texas; Clewiston Field, Clewiston, Florida; Orangeburg, South Carolina; and Bennettsville, South Carolina, yet to be visited. It looks to be an eight-thousand-mile round-trip.

That's a lot of flying for a sixty-year-old airplane. But it's running well and every item has been checked and rechecked. I've made Dave Bowerman, a very skilled round engine mechanic, who has maintained this engine, crazy with nitpicks about magneto timing and carburetor adjustments. In the last two years we have fitted no less than four carburetors on the airplane until we found one that ran perfectly. The prop has had a static and dynamic balance. Every flying wire has been checked and adjusted for tension, every moving part lubed, and every ounce of fluid in the aircraft changed or replenished. Instruments have been rebuilt, and the airplane has been brought kicking and screaming into the year 2000 with the installation of a modern set of disc brakes and an electrical system. I'm confident of the aircraft.

I have a perfect old biplane under me, and most of the summer and fall ahead of me. Hell, even the winter if I need it! I have stories to hear, people to meet, and at this moment I feel like the luckiest man alive to be able to do this.

Denny and I arrive at the airport at 4:00 A.M., load the airplane, and are ready to go at 5:30, but after five consecutive crystal-clear mornings, it chooses to be foggy on our departure day and remains so until 9:00 A.M. This of course just gives me more time to think about things that I had forgotten to do. But at the first sign of blue poking its way through the fog we are off the ground, and as I pick my way through the low stratus clouds in the San Fernando Valley, I catch a glimpse of the 405 freeway and its bumper-to-bumper traffic sliding by underneath. After twenty-two years on that road there will be no more morning commutes for me.

But as we cross the San Gabriel range and enter the Mojave, near Palmdale, I watch I-40 point out across the desert toward Kingman, and the irony is that I'm still using the highways—this time as a navigation tool, and in an emergency as a very handy airstrip.

When President Dwight D. Eisenhower signed the interstate highway system into law in 1956 it was called the National System of Interstate and Defense Highways. From his point of view, after his experiences in Europe, the emphasis was probably more on the defense aspect of the highways. He had no doubt noted the Germans' use of the autobahn during the war and particularly their use of it as an airstrip. In fact, toward the end of the war, when Allied forces were overrunning Germany, our own aircraft were occasionally assigned stretches of the autobahn as emergency fields. Urban legend has always held that one mile out of every five on U.S. interstates must be straight for possible aircraft use, but that is a myth. Nonetheless it is comforting to see all of that concrete down there coming and going along our course. It certainly makes navigation simpler when there is a nicely drawn line pointing directly at your destination. Just get a little altitude and follow the yellow brick road.

## Lt. Bill Phipps, F6F pilot, USS *Enterprise*
## Great Marianas Turkey Shoot, 1944
### *"That was our bible."*

Navigation? Each of us had a plotting board that we took with us on the flight. Every mission, we would go into the ready room and the flight leader would tell us where we were going and what we were going to do. We'd plot out the wind direction, our airspeed, our groundspeed, courses for the flight out and its return on the plotting board. But what are you going to do if the carrier has to change course while you are out on a mission? Where are you going to go?

Well, Navy pilots always built an error into their navigation. If you fly to where the carrier is supposed to be and he is not there, you won't know whether to turn right or left to find her. If you turn left and she is to the right of you—you're dead. So you always program in an error, and that is something that you learn from the start. You never try to hit the carrier's position exactly. You try to make an error in one direction or another so that you know which way to turn. If you've done your navigation properly, you're not going to see the carrier when you get to that position, but you'll know which way to turn.

We didn't use our radios for navigation. We weren't about to tell the Japs where the carrier was going to be. We had radio silence. Every flight we made we had that plotting board. That was our bible.

I relax and enjoy the Mojave Desert. From a car the Mojave has to me always resembled a huge vacant lot with mountains in the distance. A Philistine point of view perhaps, because I know that it teems with wildlife and vegetation, but I prefer the larger view from the air. From an aircraft the Mojave tells an amazing and violent story. It is filled with volcanic craters and near the Cajon Pass, the strata tilts at impossible angles. At one time the Mojave must have been a hellish landscape of lava, smoke, and fire. Craters with their sides blown out attest to the violence that wracked this part of the world. One can easily see how over time these volcanic cones that rim the Mojave have eroded and provided fill material for the alluvial plains of the desert floor.

The Mojave is also home to part of the San Andreas Fault, which is plainly visible from the air, and the whole area is a hotbed of seismic activity. For forty years I have lived just on the edge of it and been literally knocked about quite a few times by its temblors. I have sat in the cockpit of the Stearman, amazed as it danced across the hangar floor during one of the aftershocks of the Northridge quake. This is a geological battleground.

Kingman appears just over the nose now, with the Colorado River and that curious phenomenon of Laughlin, Nevada, directly below. Speed-boats with water-skiers arc across the Colorado River in defiance of their parched surroundings, while the city huddles against the green of the riverbank. I can see by the riffles on the water that there is a big wind blowing down there.

I check with Laughlin tower for winds and, yes, I have picked up a twenty-five knot tailwind. Terrific! This should be an interesting landing at Kingman. The Day-Glo windsocks are sticking out absolutely rigid as we overfly Kingman, but the runway gods have been good today and landing on runway two-one should put me right into the teeth of this wind. I turn base and can feel and see the aircraft sliding sideways across the ground at an alarming rate as we fly across the wind.

Technically this should be a very simple landing, but my antennae are up for any threat to this airplane. Under normal circumstances I simply wouldn't be flying in these winds. It's not worth the risk to this old bird, but today I have little choice. I turn final and the airplane slows to a crawl. It's gusty and those gusts are probably thirty to thirty-five knots. I'm indicating seventy miles per hour, so we are crossing the ground at not much more than thirty miles per hour and I have to add considerable power just to make it to the runway. At this low altitude the effect is startling and not unlike flying a helicopter. But the Stearman comes floating down, hovers over the runway, and settles with a big squawk that makes me look like a pro. Taxiing to the ramp is a major trial of brake dragging, ruddering, and power as we resist the wind's determination to weathervane the aircraft and lift a wing. This plane will easily fly in ground effect at forty miles per hour, so we are in a gray area here. Old rules about control positions are recalled and applied as we inch our way to a tie-down. It's a bit like sailing a boat. On the ground it has two wings as big as sails that want to catch the wind. I park and shut down into the wind and stay in the cockpit working the stick as Denny jumps out and chains the aircraft down.

Well, we wanted some excitement.

I had the wind straight down the runway. Had it been a crosswind, I wouldn't have landed there. I would have found someplace—a ramp, a taxiway, a road, whatever it took—where the wind was more favorable. But sometimes you don't have that choice.

# Capt. Joseph C. Pimentel, Thunderbolt pilot, France, 1944

## *". . . the jug started oozing a trail of black smoke."*

This all happened during the beginning of winter 1944, just before Hitler's counterattack in the Ardennes, otherwise known as the "Bulge." On this particular day the weather really stank—subfreezing OATs [outside air temperature] in the midst of a windstorm and random snow flurries. Snow and ice covered the landscape.

The mission that day was to attack a Kraut-held airport, strafing any aircraft on the ground and delivering five-hundred-pound demolition bombs on runways, ramp hangars, and buildings.

As was true of most major Luftwaffe layouts such as this one, the airfield was heavily defended, therefore a tough one against low-level attack. Early on, my wingman got shot out of the sky by a direct hit from an eighty-eight-millimeter antiaircraft gun. I continued my attack, delivering my two five-hundred-pound bombs, then concentrating on pounding a flak tower the Krauts had built out in the middle of the airfield. I succeeded in silencing the two thirty-millimeter cannon slots in that tower, but took a lot of hits myself, one of which tore up something in the engine.

The Jug started oozing a trail of black smoke and running sour, so I headed for friendlier territory. It soon became clear that I couldn't get all the way home, and I started nursing the Jug toward whatever nearest friendly airstrip I could find.

Mind you, the weather still stank, with windblown snow, lousy visibility, and iced landscapes in all directions. This is the way it was when, to my great relief, I found the airport at Nancy showing up ahead.

Nancy, at the time, was occupied by a Ninth Air Force Mustang group, and I could see a lot of their birds parked in snow-covered revetments. I could also see a few wrecked aircraft in the banked snow bordering the airfield's runways.

I got on the radio and tried to raise Nancy's control. Their reply was to advise that the field was closed due to extreme storm conditions and iced runway surfaces. I told them I was battle damaged and barely airworthy and intended landing straight ahead on whatever runway I could find, ice or no ice.

I got a "Roger, Wilco" from them and a green light, plus an advisory that I would have a gusting thirty-five-mile-per-hour crosswind in blowing snow. Sure enough, that's the way it was, but at least I had it better than bailing out. That dear old 3350 [Pratt & Whitney] was still delivering, although also still trailing smoke and overheating into the red line. Well, I crabbed the Jug, dropped gear and flaps, and three-pointed the old girl onto their runway. That's when the fun began.

A convoy of emergency vehicles was tearing along following me—an ambulance, a couple of jeeps, a command car, and a fire truck. There must have been just enough crab left in my landing that the Jug, with no grip on that ice, started into a majestic, counterclockwise rotation as we hurtled down the runway. She slowly turned end-for-end at seventy miles per hour or so, giving me this changing view of the landscape, swapping a look at the crowd following for a look at the banked snow and trees at the approaching end of the runway.

Mostly out of self-preservation, but admittedly with a hint of cocky bravado, I wondered if I could brake the Jug with the engine when it came around backward. So I tried it. Well, it worked! Between the torque and the thrust, lo and behold, the Jug slowed and finally eased backward into a snow pile. I hadn't killed the engine, so I simply taxied back to their parking ramp.

As you can probably realize, as I taxied away from the runway in my still-smoking Jug, the "self-preservation" theme sank out of sight, but not the "hotshot-cocky." I waved to the audience of Mustang jocks who had watched my magic performance as though it was just part of a day's work.

# CHAPTER 10

PRESIDENT LYNDON B. JOHNSON

*"You mean to tell me that some ignorant peasant in a vintage
MiG shot down three of our best fighters?"*


Kingman to Tucson, August 9, 2000


Denny and I have an early start and are off the ground by seven. The Stearman doesn't want to climb today, and as we swing southeast we're moving into rising terrain. The lack of climb can be attributed in equal parts to elevation (takeoff elevation is 3,450 feet above sea level), heat (it's ninety degrees even at this hour), load (we are easily at gross weight), and the airplane (it's old). Maybe a brand-new Continental engine would be making the fully rated 220 horsepower, but this one is sixty years old and has 550 hours on it since its last overhaul, which was over twenty years ago. During the war the military would overhaul these engines at 500 hours. Often the instructors would feel that they didn't need an over-haul and would plead with the engineering section to leave a well-running engine alone, but they were ignored and the engines were done to a schedule. Instructors weren't thrilled with having to deal with a freshly overhauled engine. Better an old, good-running engine than something just out of the shop that might have a few surprises.

The good news is that our rate of climb exceeds that of the terrain, but I stay low just to observe the Arizona desert. It's beautiful at this hour with its long shadows. The Big Sandy Wash is underneath us, with the Hualapai range on the right. The little village of Wikieup is on the nose. Our destination is Gila Bend. If you didn't know you were in the west, you do now by the names alone.

The trip down the Big Sandy Wash is uneventful and soon Wickenburg, Arizona, slides under our wing. Just south of Wickenburg is a mountain that abruptly rises from the valley to about thirty-six hundred feet and falls off steeply on all sides. At its peak it has a little cradle just a bit bigger than the wingspread of the Stearman. It's too inviting to resist in the exuberance of the morning. I raise the wing and peel off, heading for it. The pitch of the flying wires changes up as the airplane builds up speed. Speed in this instance has to be qualified at 120 miles per hour, or just slightly faster than your maiden aunt's thirty-year-old Buick will do if she really puts her foot into it.

Denny is silent, but I know he's always been game for just about anything, so I'm sure he'd approve. We flash close by the peak and I rack it around and dive through the cradle. It is exhilarating. We're both grinning as I straighten us out and climb back up to altitude, my little frolic done. Some things you've just got to do.

Breaking the chain of colorful names as I get farther south is a range on my left called the White Tank Mountains, and just on the other side of them is Luke Air Force Base. Nearly sixty years ago when it was called Luke Field and was an advance-training base, the White Tank Mountains offered a place out of sight of the field to experiment with an airplane. A place to possibly see how many turns an AT-6 could be spun. And no doubt there are still little pieces of that AT-6 out there.

# Cadet Joseph C. Pimentel
## Luke Field, 1942

*". . . that old girl lurched and went flat!"*

I never had to bail out under combat conditions, but I did have a bad training episode at Luke Field. It was a strange circumstance in a way, I guess.

Each airplane type probably has one area where it might be marginal, or at least subject to improvement. For example, the BT-13 basic trainer might snap roll if you stall it while trying to make a turn onto final landing approach with the nose high. A couple of my friends were killed that way. The airplane will snap roll on you and you've got no altitude for recovery.

The AT-6's problem was that anything more than a three-turn spin could get really rotten, but I had an instructor at Luke Field who was convinced that recovery from a four- or five-turn spin ought to be taught to aviation cadets.

West of Luke Field there is a mountain that juts abruptly out of the desert floor. I think that they called it White Tank Mountain. Well, it was just the right height, the right position, and reach in a north-south direction so as to be a barrier of concealment for anybody who is flying around and wants to do something that nobody can see. That's what led to this happening.

The instructor was fair enough to talk it over with me beforehand. He said, "We won't do this unless you accept the idea." And he didn't want to use the term "volunteer," but that was the essence of it. I'm sure that you know what an aviation cadet's viewpoint would be. You could reply, "Yes, sir," "No, sir," or "No excuse, sir," but as far as I was concerned, I liked the idea anyway, because I was curious why they were so bloody touchy about spin recoveries. The AT-6 recovers beautifully from a one- or two-turn spin, and at that stage of my training I had no reason to worry about the rest of it.

Well, we got up there behind the White Tank Mountain and made two or three spinning descents, counting the turns, recovering from the spin, and then we'd climb back up and he'd have me do the same. At length he climbed on up to ten thousand feet and put the airplane into a four-turn spin. We had used up about half of the air when the AT-6's spin started to go unstable. It would lurch and he had to go through two spin recovery efforts before he got it out, but he did get it out of the spin.

He said "Climb it back up, Pimentel." And so I did.

"Now you do a four-turn spin, but be ready to kick it out of the spin immediately if I tell you to."

So I did a four-turn spin and my spin didn't develop this lurch, and it turned out to be a pretty normal spin recovery.

He then said, "Well, we've got a problem here. It doesn't repeat, so maybe we'd better try one more." [Joe says this with a broad smile.]

Well, he tried it again, but he let it go to five turns, because it didn't lurch on four, and I think that he was really pissed off that I got out cleanly on four and he didn't, but we'll never know. So he went beyond four and that old girl lurched and went flat! It was doing a real unstable lurch with every turn, and the altimeter was really unwinding on us.

I heard his hatch slide back, and he came on the intercom and yelled, "Bail out!" He didn't even suggest that I try the spin recovery; he just said, "Bail out!" As you know, the pilot is to stay with the ship until everybody else is out.

But I couldn't get out; the centrifugal force was too great. I had the seat belt off trying to get out of the goddamn airplane, and was busting blood vessels from pushing. I had both feet on the edge of the bucket seat and was straining with my legs and pushing with my arms on the coaming. I wasn't talking to him; I was just trying to get out of the airplane. Then, all of a sudden, I'm an s.o.b. if he didn't bail out first!

In a way it's lucky that he did, because the momentary change in the center of gravity when he left altered the impetus of the spin. The airplane made a big funny heave, and I was pushing so goddamn hard that I came out of there like a champagne cork when it gave me that chance. I think there was less than a thousand feet left when I pulled the ripcord on my parachute. The impact was just soft enough that I didn't hurt myself, but the wind was blowing aplenty.

The instructor got out sufficiently high so that in the blowing wind I never did see him again. All I did was hit the goddamn ground hard in that desert behind this White Tank Mountain, where nobody knew anything about where we were or what the hell we were doing.

I ended up with a sore backside from being dragged through the rock and sand and gravel and cactus and God-knows-what-all for a quarter of a mile until I finally managed to dump the air out of the chute.

So that's the story of my bailout, and it didn't make me ever want to bail out again.

The instructor got transferred, and they talked to me man-to-man and suggested that it would be prudent to forget the whole episode. That was all right with me, because all I wanted to do was graduate and get the hell out of there.

The White Tank Mountains and the remains of Joe Pimentel's AT-6 lie behind us as I start looking for Gila Bend, our next fuel stop. At 177 miles, or two hours and twelve minutes since takeoff, it is not at the end of our range, but it is a good distance into it. The airplane will stay in the air about three hours and thirty minutes, but I don't like to have to sweat gas.

Gila Bend is in front of us now, and I slow things down and search the airport for a windsock. The sight that greets us is very strange. There are no airplanes at this airport. The ramp is empty and the field looks abandoned. There is a sock and the runway looks okay, so I land and taxi to the fuel pit, which is a mess. The pumps are smashed and the 100-octane sign is on the ground. I walk over to the pilots' lounge, and it's just as bad, full of graffiti, trash, and in a general state of decrepitude. Curiously, out by the road sits a rather nice USAF F-101 Voodoo as a gate guard. And there's hope. There is a sign scrawled on the wall with a number for fuel. I call the number and the city hall answers.

"Oh, we haven't had fuel out there in a long time," a voice says brightly. "Are you out of gas?"

*Well, I sure didn't stop for the fine facilities,* I think to myself. "The flight guide says that this is an attended field," I mention pointlessly.

"Well, we can send you some fuel," she adds. I breathe a sigh of relief. "Be about fifteen minutes," she adds.

So Denny and I go out and lean on the airplane—for an hour. My second phone call reveals that the gas we are waiting for is coming from a gas station. And it is not avgas. The Stearman does not like car gas, and I've had a threat of bodily harm from Dave Bowerman if I ever use it in this engine.

"Thank you, but never mind."

So now it is time to get busy with a chart. The nearest fuel is back up at Buckeye, thirty miles north of here. We'd passed it coming down and heard a lot of traffic using the airstrip. I looked at the gas sight gauge. This is a simple, clear-acrylic tube projecting from the bottom of the fuel tank. A cork bobs up and down on the surface of the fuel inside of the tank, and a plastic indicator rides in the tube and tells you how you are doing for fuel. The tube is crudely marked "3/4," "1/2," "1/4," and "E." This was 1934 technology at its finest, but it works—usually. I had recently replaced this tube because of leakage, and the replacement seems to indicate on the low side, or that there is really more fuel in the tank than indicated. But you have to be a believer. The gauge shows a quarter tank, more than enough to get thirty miles. To be sure, I do the math. Let's see. This bird will stay in the air about three hours and thirty minutes. We have just flown about two hours and twelve minutes. It will take us just under a half hour to get to Buckeye. No problem. I'm not even into my one-hour reserve yet. Okay, well then why is the tank gauge sitting on one-quarter full? Something doesn't quite compute, but no matter how I do the math we should have enough gas, so we go.

The thirty-minute flight allows me to watch the gauge sink toward "E" all the way. I wonder if I've really done something dumb. Should I believe the math or the gauge? Buckeye creeps over the horizon in slow motion, and the float is bouncing on the bottom of the tank when we land. We taxi to the self-service pumps, and I climb up on the upper wing and start the fill-up. This should be interesting. How much fuel will it take? For some reason, halfway through the fill-up, the pump quits and I have to go and reinsert my credit card. Denny looks at the counter and says, "You just took forty-four gallons," and I'm stunned. I have a forty-six-gallon tank! Was I flying around with two gallons in the tanks? Then it occurs to me that I hadn't reset the counter on the pump from the last customer. I finish filling and we do the math. We took a bit over thirty gallons, so I had plenty of fuel but a very pessimistic gauge. Better that than the other way around.

Fuel gauges lead an insecure existence on small aircraft and are only rarely believed. Most wise pilots take the distance of their journey, convert that into time, factor in the winds, and then multiply that time by their fuel burn in gallons per hour. And you had better make sure that you do the math right. But that will only be as good as the winds allow it to be. And winds can be capricious.

# Lt. George Middleton, P-51 pilot, 328th Fighter Squadron Bodney, England, 1944

## *". . . nothing but water down there."*

We had no long-range navigational aids at all, so we flew time and distance, paying attention to winds aloft. When the group came back from this particular mission there had been a 180-degree wind change and we had gotten blown out over the North Sea, which we didn't know, because there was always two or three layers of clouds under us. They did have some DF [direction finding] stations on the English coast, but they had a very limited range and you had to be in very close to get them at all. We tried sending one or two aircraft down through the overcast, but there was nothing but water down there. Then we tried sending them up to altitude to pick up a DF station, which was unsuccessful.

We had an exchange pilot from the Royal Navy Fleet Air Arm flying with us, which they did occasionally, and he finally decided that from his experience we should be heading off in a particular direction, which for lack of anything better to do, we did. By that time everybody was starting to get very low on fuel.

Well, he was right. He may have saved the whole damn squadron, because we finally did pick up a weak direction finding signal.

Shortly after that, three of the aircraft ran out of fuel. When you went into the North Sea, you probably wouldn't even be able to get out of your airplane. And if you bailed out, you wouldn't have more than a minute or two in the water before you were so numb that you wouldn't be able to unbuckle your chute. Those three pilots were never heard from again.

Just about the time that we sighted the English coast, another four aircraft ran out of fuel and went down. Two of those pilots were picked up by British patrol boats just off the coast, and the other two made landfall but their aircraft were damaged on landing.

My wingman and I got to the coast and were looking for any place to land. We were all ready to bail out. We had all the straps off and were throttled back as lean as we could be when we saw this strip that turned out to be an RAF field that wasn't in use. We made a pass to get in there as quickly as we could, and they started shooting flares at us to keep us out—to go someplace else.

Well, we weren't about to do that. We did land, and we got about three-fourths of the way back to the control tower and my wingman's engine quit. I went a little farther and mine quit too.

I don't know how anything could have been different, because we had no way of knowing about the change in the wind direction. There was no ground reference to indicate that anything unusual was happening. We lost three pilots, five aircraft, and two damaged that day.

We're on the way back to Gila Bend again and then on to Tucson's Ryan Field, only now we're getting batted around by thermals. Our little fuel excursion has wasted a lot of time and we're edging into the afternoon turbulence.

I'm having trouble with charts. An aeronautical chart, when unfolded, is about five feet by two feet and will blow out of the open cockpit in a heartbeat if not watched carefully. Holding one of these in an eighty-mile-per-hour slipstream is an art form. Sitting in the back cockpit, which I normally do, there's an area down near the floor that allows me to unfold a chart and refold it to a new section, something that must be done regularly as one moves across the countryside. But in the front cockpit, where I currently reside after having recently discovered that it's quieter, the aerodynamics are a bit different. There's a considerable airflow up from the floor and out of the cockpit. Unfolding or refolding a chart takes on all of the aspects of a Keystone comedy as the chart wraps around my face and my hands while I try to manipulate it. Simply opening and refolding it takes about ten minutes of extreme concentration as the airstream tries to pluck it free.

I hold the stick between my knees, bend over, and go to work. If successful, after what seems like an eternity of wrestling with the chart, I usually discover that we are now off on some new and highly inventive heading. Stronger solutions are in order, so I proceed to give Denny some rudimentary flight instruction on stick holding while I deal with these more prosaic chart-folding matters. This seems to work as we chart-fold our way across the country.

I used the term "floor," but there is no floor in a Stearman, only a couple of floorboards to rest one's feet on. These are on each side directly under the rudder pedals. If you drop something, it falls to the bottom of the airplane, totally out of reach, into an area I refer to as the bilge. This is an area frequently inhabited by pencils, washers, screws, cotter pins, and the general flotsam of maintenance. Drop something down there and often it's gone for a long time, particularly if it's nonmagnetic and can't be reached by the long magnetic tool I have for such contingencies.

Charts have been known to find their way down there while in flight. There is nothing more frustrating than being unsure of one's position and gazing longingly at a chart lying just out of reach at the bottom of the airplane.

After a very bumpy ride, Tucson comes into view and we are soon taxiing to the tie-downs, our work for the day done. I'm looking forward to my much-delayed breakfast.

Tuscon's Ryan Field is a former primary training base and got its name from its then owner, T. Claude Ryan. His company ran the civilian school and built the trainers that flew out of here during the war. Ryan trainers were elegant little low-wing monoplanes that were also used by both the Navy and the Air Corps. The Navy used them for formation trainers at Pensacola, perhaps because they were configured most like the fighters then in use, while the Army used them at Tucson Ryan, Hemet Ryan, Tulare, and a number of other California bases for primary flight training.

Ryan trainers were a little more demanding to fly, with a stall/snap-roll characteristic similar to a Vultee, and were perhaps not quite as tough as the Stearman, but this can and will be debated endlessly by the cognoscenti of each. Ryan is an ancient and honorable name in aviation, and only twelve years before the war the company had built a trim little high-wing aircraft for a Mr. Charles Lindbergh, who did some amazing things with it.

While tying the airplane down, I am soon engaged in a conversation with one of the local pilots. This is one of the very enjoyable aspects of the Stearman. It almost outweighs the negatives of chart folding. Everybody loves these airplanes and loves to talk about them, none more than me.

Gregg Horrell is a hopeless aviation addict. A former F-16 crew chief and twenty-year Air Force veteran, he now runs Ryan Aero Service at Ryan Field. At his invitation the Stearman was soon safely stowed inside of a large hangar, out of the way of any weather that might be passing through. After a long examination of the Stearman, he gets a mischievous look on his face and asks if I would like to see his little project.

Expecting to see some lovingly restored antique Fairchild or Waco, we walk over to his other hangar and step inside. An honest-to-God MiG-17, still in its Polish, Communist bloc paint job, lives in this hangar. It is beautiful but ominous. This was one of the airplanes that had given so many headaches to U.S. pilots during Vietnam. Although an old aircraft even during that war, it was an airplane that you didn't mess with and certainly didn't want to dogfight with. When three MiG-17s jumped five F-100s early in that air war and shot three of them down, Lyndon Johnson bellowed, "You mean to tell me that some ignorant peasant in a vintage MiG shot down three of our best fighters?" Yep.

Ironically these MiG's are now being imported from cash-poor former Communist bloc nations who have no further need for them. They must be gone through carefully. Then it helps if you were a former military fighter pilot and own a Jet A fuel farm, because they do suck up gas. But they are an exciting and beautiful aircraft. However nasty the Russians were, they did know how to design a good airplane. Gregg's jet is a work in progress with panels removed and parts out on the bench. On one side of the aircraft, just below the cockpit is Russian Cyrillic graffiti. Russian generals, on inspection trips to Davis Monthan Air Force Base to confirm the destruction of B-52s in compliance with the SALT Treaty, somehow discovered that there was a MiG-17 in the area. They made it a point to drop by to visit their progeny and were bemused by the fact that this MiG-17 had found its way to the Arizona desert and into the hands of a former American Air Force crew chief. They just can't quite figure out how civilians can own fighter planes, but are good humored about it and have autographed the aircraft. The airplane is actually owned by an airline pilot, Pat O'Kelly, in a working partnership with Gregg, but that doesn't matter. You can see the passion that Gregg has for this airplane.

We spend a couple of hours over lunch "hangar flying" and having a few laughs. About the time I'm starting to think about where we might be staying this evening, Gregg instantly makes arrangements and Denny and I find ourselves quartered in a wonderful Santa Fe style bed-and-breakfast, which being off-season, is incredibly reasonable. And just in case we don't feel welcome enough, one of the airport workers volunteers to pick us up in the morning.

I start to wipe the airplane down. Gregg gives me a can of solvent and helps. Rags? He gives me a bundle. Places to land? He recommends three along the route where he has friends that will take care of us. This man can't do enough for us.

The next morning as I'm stuffing the airplane with all of our luggage, rags, and polish, Gregg asks me if I have room for one more thing. Puzzled, I'm a little hesitant, as I can barely get the baggage door shut. He hands me a notebook and a small index-card-sized file box. I open both. It's a complete set of engineering drawings of every part of the Boeing Stearman Model 75 on microfiche. The notebook contains an index. Want to see what that instrument panel should really look like? It's there. The throttle knob? It's there. The intercom box? It's all there, every part and every detail of the airplane. This is like the Rosetta Stone of Stearmans! No more guessing on how things were built.

I'm speechless. I can't believe that somebody would just give me such a thing. I am touched and thank him repeatedly. I wish there were some way or some part that I could contribute to make his MiG fly. I resolve to keep an eye open.

And to show my gratitude, I fly off with his hangar key!

# CHAPTER 11

LT. WARREN CHRISTIANSON, in a B-17 over Vienna

*"We were spinning down and, hell, part of the engine
had fallen off and the fire with it."*

Tucson to Las Cruces, New Mexico, August 10, 2000

We're off early this morning. It's smooth and the engine is quiet. One would think that the sensations of flight in an open-cockpit airplane would always be the same, but they are not. Lift off of a runway at dawn on a sixty-five-degree calm morning cruise at fifteen hundred feet, and it's a rare sensory experience. The engine rumbles quietly and the airplane seems to fly itself. The aroma of the land is sweet, the breeze on the face is refreshing, and the whole experience, sublime.

The same airplane at two in the afternoon becomes a raucous bone-shaker that because of turbulence wants to go three directions at once and must be constantly fought with. Sixty-five degrees has now become ninety-five, and the heat comes back off of the engine in waves. The sounds of flight are deafening, the headphones heavy, and the goggles are giving a massive headache. And finally, all the bouncing around brings on the urge to go to the bathroom.

I come off of the runway pointed straight at the "Class C" airspace of Tucson International Airport. I must either call them immediately before entering their airspace or alter course to the south and work my way around it. It's time-consuming to do the latter, but I'm just not in a talk-ative mood this morning, so I elect to give the radio a rest. Besides, I have my new GPS (Global Positioning System) toy with its moving map that I want to experiment with. I stay low over the desert floor and fly a big arc around Tucson as if I am on a string that pivots on their airport. The GPS shows me exactly the extent of their airspace and it's easy to give it a wide berth. Soon I fly a tangent course off of the arc and follow the more prosaic interstate eastward.

My choice now is whether to fly a straight line to Lordsburg, my refu-eling stop, or follow the highway, which does a lot of meandering. It all comes down to how much I trust this engine.

The logbook entries on the engine are rather sparse. Twenty years ago it was overhauled with new bearings, rods, pistons, cylinders, and valves. The newly overhauled engine was run in for five hours, then pickled and not run again for five years until it was installed in 41-806. This is not good for an engine. Engines should be run. If they are left idle, gaskets dry up and unprotected metal rusts. There is a signature on the logbook entry by the man who did the work. His name was E. F. Brockman. I have no idea who he is or where he worked. He has vanished into time, and I must trust that he knew what he was doing. There are no receipts from any of the highly accomplished shops that do this kind of work. No neat logo on the crankcase from a premier engine rebuilder. There is also no previous history of the engine in the logbooks. As far as the logs are con-cerned, the engine just appeared, magically, in 1978. It's a rather bare pedigree for an engine, but it's all I have. Just E. F.'s signature attesting that he did the job right.

On the other hand, it has never let me down in the five hundred hours of flying behind it. The compression is always up, it uses almost no oil, which is unusual—no, make that almost unheard of—for an engine of this type, and it runs almost ridiculously cool. It gets cranky periodically if I don't take care of it by leaning it out during taxi, or if I leave the carburetor heat on too long. It will then let me know its displeasure by loading up the plugs and stumbling on the next takeoff. But that is pilot error and not the fault of the engine.

If I want something to worry about, I can always worry about the engine bearings.

In the heart of this big Continental radial engine, down where the engine oil lifeblood pumps through steel arteries and capillaries, live a pair of devices known as main bearings. These are ball bearings much like those found on bicycle wheels, but on a much larger scale, because they must take much larger forces. They support each end of the massive crankshaft that spins under the repeated hammer blows of seven pistons the size of coffee cans.

These bearings have a dark history and are the Achilles heel of this particular make of engine. Crop dusters first noticed failures of the rearmost bearing under the harsh usage of their trade. After enough engines had failed, resourceful mechanics simply put stronger bearings of a different type into the engine and the problem went away. This was an effective but illegal fix, since the old Bureau of Flight Standards had never certified the engine to use any but the original bearings, and they were very picky about such things. For the dusters, the issue of whether to fly safely or legally was an easy choice. For the bureaucrats it caused a great deal of angst.

The knowledge of this little fix was passed on furtively down through the years and applied on the q.t. by knowledgeable mechanics and pilots who didn't want excitement in their lives.

A main bearing failure in flight is an exciting event. The first message of distress from the engine is a quivering of the oil pressure needle. From this point on, your time left in the air is measured in minutes. If you missed this symptom, don't worry, as there'll be more and they'll come quickly. A few spots of oil will form on the windshield, then a few more, and then a whole lot. And while you are busy wiping the hot oil off of your goggles and face, there will be smoke as the oil cooks on the exhaust manifold. Smoke in a wood-and-fabric airplane is not a welcome thing. All of this will take less than a minute, so it's good to have a plan for where to park the airplane in a hurry.

What is happening is that the broken pieces of the failed bearing are plugging up the delicate little oil circulation ports and the oil is being blown overboard. In addition to smoking and spewing, the engine will begin running very rough. Run it long enough and it will come to an abrupt halt. Better to shut it down before the big pieces break. This engine is having a major heart attack, and unless you happen to be very lucky, you're looking at an off-airport landing—always an exciting event.

One Stearman pilot had his crankshaft break in flight while in the traffic pattern. The propeller, attached to one end of the crankshaft, screwed itself out of the engine, flew back, hit and broke the main spar of the wing. The wing collapsed and the airplane plunged into the ground, killing the pilot.

With the passage of time, the attrition of mechanics who really knew these engines, and the rise of litigation in aviation repairs, most engine rebuilds come with the original certified, though sometimes troublesome, bearings. Inspectors can sign off on them with a clear conscience, and most of these bearings spend their life happily spinning away without a problem. But every once in a while, one lets go. This airplane has the original bearings. That fact becomes just another consideration in the constant decision-making process that is called flying.

So the prospect of the possibility of losing the engine in the New Mexico/Arizona desert is a daunting one, and coming down twenty miles from a highway in August could be lethal, so I prudently stick to the roads. Seven thousand miles later, returning over this same route and full of confidence in the engine, I fly a straight line. It's a curious business, because what you are doing essentially is betting your life on a sixty-year-old engine.

Loss of an engine on some World War II aircraft was considered the supreme test of airmanship. The Martin B-26 Marauder was an airplane that when introduced into the Air Corps inventory quickly earned a reputation as a dangerous airplane plagued by engine failures, a variety of mechanical ills, and therefore accidents. Its Curtiss electric props could malfunction, go into flat pitch, and bring the airplane down like a stone. Its wingspan was deemed inadequate for its power and weight, giving it a high wing loading and critical approach speeds, and both its wingspan and vertical stabilizer area were ultimately increased in later models. This was an airplane that gave rise among airmen to the old adage, "Never fly the 'A' model of anything," but most of all this was an airplane that had a learning curve and had to be flown "by the numbers," which were rather high and new to the Air Corps.

As a result, the airplane was not initially popular among aircrew and was approached warily by student pilots. Loss of an engine in flight was considered to be unmanageable by all but the most skilled. But the most feared situation with this airplane was the loss of an engine on takeoff. It was commonly held, particularly in the early days of this airplane, that this usually resulted in fatalities. And of course if it happened on a student's first solo in this aircraft, those results were certain.

## Capt. Fred Foster, B-26 Marauder pilot
## Dodge City, Kansas, 1943

### "They don't fly on a single engine."

I was in Dodge City, Kansas, and we were in transition from UC-78s, Bamboo Bombers, to B-26 Marauders. We flew "war wearies," straight "A's," with no armament and empty bomb bays. I would rehearse single-engine procedures at night sitting in a chair, but it used to be if you lost an engine you bailed out. That was standard operating procedure.

I got so many hours in and it was time for solo, meaning you fly the ship with a crew but without an instructor, so Captain Brockhouse, my instructor, said, "Okay, tomorrow morning, you've got the whip."

I got this tall six-foot-four skinny guy from another squadron—never met him before—as a copilot, and we were going out to fly formation. The joke was that we flew formation so that if anybody dropped out we knew where to pick up the pieces.

On takeoff, up came the gear, and we got to four hundred feet and lost the left engine! Bang! First solo on a B-26! They don't fly on a single engine. I looked out and there was a stream of oil coming out of the left engine about two inches thick.

If you lost the left engine, she would pull to the left because of the asymmetrical power, so you must push in on the right rudder pedal, and I pushed hard. I reached for the feather switch, saying, "Right is good. Right is good. Right is good. Right is good"—and I hit the feather switch for the left engine. If I had feathered the right engine we would have died, as B-26s had the glide angle of a rock. I spun the coffee grinder—

the trim for the vertical stabilizer—and held 150 miles per hour. We were still flying, heading for the tops of the trees, and we might have picked up a few leaves, but she climbed. Gradually.

Then I realized that my shoulder hurt, and by this time we were up at three thousand feet turning to the left. They say *never* turn into a dead engine, but you can—about a three-degree-per-second turn. The flight engineer, whom I had never seen before that morning, felt the turn and was hitting me on my right shoulder, yelling, "Single engine! Single engine!" and I never heard him.

This flight engineer, who had three thousand hours in B-26s in Dodge City, was as white as a ghost. As a flight engineer he flew every day, eight hours a day, but he was scared, and the copilot and I were too dumb to know how dangerous things really were.

We got a few miles out, and I called in and they gave me the runway, but the runway had changed and we now had gusts from the left at fifteen to twenty-five knots.

So we were flying straight and level, trimmed and stable, and I turned to my little crew and gave them the option of bailing out, but they elected to stay.

We came in and I had it crabbed, but it kept pushing me, and I thought, *If I don't set this s.o.b. down, it's going to go off the runway into the mud.* I got it down and I'll bet you—I never checked it—that I was six or seven inches off of that runway. But the fire and the emergency trucks got to go home.

They brought me up to the flight line to my senior instructor, Captain Brockhouse, who said, "Foster, you'll do anything to get out of flying formation. Take my ship and go out and meet that formation, right now." So I turned around and I said, "Red, come on," but my flight engineer was walking away. I heard later that he went to his squadron commander and asked to be relieved. He was never going to go up in a B-26 again. He quit.

So my copilot and I get back up, and he says, "Are you going to try and find that formation?"

I say, "Are you crazy?"

We kept it at five thousand feet, straight and level, for an hour and a half. I was in no condition to fly formation after what I'd gone through.

The next day I was told that Colonel Oldfield wanted to see me in his office—right now! Well, I'm telling you, I was scared. So I went over and gave him the best salute I could, and he said, "Relax, lieutenant. Do you know what you did?"

"No, sir, I don't."

"Well, since we started instructing in B-26s here, you are the only one who has ever taken a B-26 off, lost an engine at four hundred feet, and flew it. And you are the only one here to ever land a B-26 on a single engine and not kill somebody." All of the instructors were there in the room.

"Not one instructor has ever had what you've had who didn't crash the ship and die. Now I want you to relax and tell these instructors everything that you did from the time that you got in that ship to the time that you got out of it. Tell them what you did and what your airspeeds were. They've never experienced it. You have, and you lived."

There were three Congressional investigations into the B-26 program, including one chaired by Harry Truman, and attempts to eliminate it. Curiously, once "fixed" and flown properly, the B-26 achieved the lowest loss-per-sortie rate of any twin-engine bomber in the USAAF.

# Lt. Sam Ed Brown
# The Adriatic, 1944

## ". . . glide until the ice melted."

I had an engine failure coming back from the trip to Russia. The engine quit fifteen times, but I was always able to get it started again. We never did find out what caused the problem.

The P-47 quit on me once over the Adriatic up by Venice, but at that time we were having problems with carburetor ice in the P-47 under certain conditions. It was a very quiet situation to have that big engine quit and be up there just gliding along over enemy territory. You'd have to chop everything and glide until the ice melted. Then you could turn things on and the engine would start up again.

We had one pilot who was coming back alone one day and his engine quit on him. But he knew what it was and he was at twenty thousand feet and knew he had plenty of time. There were four Me-109s in formation, coming head-on at him. He pulled the nose up, even with no power, and fired a burst that got one of them. Two of the Me-109s broke together and exploded in the air; the other one went home.

The American started his engine and came home with three victories. That was an unusual sort of thing, but it actually happened.

## Lt. Warren Christianson
## In a B-17 over Vienna

### *". . . Warren, we're losing a lot of oil."*

We were bombing Vienna. I had five missions over Vienna and four over Ploesti. I never got out of Vienna without some holes in my ship somewhere, somehow. On this particular trip we got pretty badly shot up. I was flying at the time. It was pretty bad.

Flak had knocked out one engine completely and knocked the supercharger out of a second. In those days that meant you were limited to atmospheric pressure—at twenty-five thousand feet you effectively had no power. We lost altitude fast. Then another engine got a shot through either the propeller head or the engine and was leaking oil very, very badly. The ball turret gunner kept calling and saying, "Warren, we're losing a lot of oil."

We were over the target and there were fighters in the area. I had to make a decision whether I would feather or continue to use some power until we got away from the fighters. The decision was not to feather, which is what caused all the trouble.

After a while I tried to feather and couldn't. As a result the engine got hot and then caught fire. Things were getting kind of tight. The plane started to vibrate very badly, and I knew that the propeller was going to come off. I ordered the bombardier, navigator, and the top turret gunner to the back of the aircraft. I figured there was a good chance that when the propeller came off, it and maybe part of the engine would go through the cockpit. But I figured that if it didn't go through the cockpit, we'd still have one and one-half engines and maybe we could get home.

We were doing about 135 miles per hour, just above stalling speed, but the vibration of the ship was such that it destroyed the airfoil characteristics of the plane. It stalled out, went into a spin, and fell. I got on the intercom and told everybody to get out. I found out later that they had already gone. I was going to bail out too.

I figured the thing was on fire and was going to explode. The configuration of the B-17 is such that the pilot is supposed to go out the navigator's escape hatch. I pulled the emergency release, the door fell off, and I looked out. We were spinning down and, hell, part of the engine had fallen off and the fire with it.

I thought, *Well, blazes, man, I can pull this thing out.*

I went back to the cockpit and there was a loose parachute bouncing around in my seat, so I got in the copilot's seat. I was pretty excited and kind of overdid it. I dumped the stick too far forward. The plane was in a semi-inverted position . . . about ten to fifteen degrees off vertical . . . going straight down like hell. I pulled the power off and started pulling it out. I didn't want to pull the plane out too fast and pull a wing off. The airspeed indicator on a B-17 has a redline at 305 miles per hour, but I didn't even notice what the airspeed was until I was already into my pullout and going up. At the bottom of my dive I was about one thousand feet above the ground.

I pulled the ship out, and once I got to where the airspeed was down around three hundred or so, I put full power on—whatever power was available to me. I was on the wrong side of the Alps, and I wanted to get as much altitude as I possibly could while I still had all of this speed.

I got it up to about seven thousand feet, but the Alps are higher than that. Well, there are passes. The navigator had taken his charts with him, and I didn't know if anyone was in the back or not. I got the ship squared away and was pulling forty-six inches (takeoff power) on one good engine and as much as I could on the other. I had about sixty inches altogether. Fifteen inches per engine is considered as good as nothing, so at the altitude I was flying I had essentially a little more than one engine. When I got lower I had a bit more power.

I thought, *Well, I might as well take her home.*

I trimmed the ship up as much as I could and tried to put it on autopilot, but that wasn't working very well. I trimmed the ship with the trim tabs and made a quick dash to the after section to see if anybody was back there, but nobody was. I tipped the ship up again when I got back in the cockpit, because it was in a slight dive by that time.

I dashed very quickly down into the navigator's compartment. I knew, generally speaking, where I was. We had been given an escape kit that had a map of Europe from southern Sweden down to North Africa and it helped some. I decided to try to go down the Yugoslavian coast, east of the Doric Alps, as they were a helluva lot lower. I thought I'd watch my altitude, and if I saw a pass I'd cut through it.

I started losing altitude, so I thought I'd experiment. I put a little bit of flap in and flew between 110 and 115 miles per hour, barely above stalling speed without full flaps. I wanted to get the most possible lift and lose the least possible altitude. I was down to fifty-five hundred feet.

There was a big valley and I could see a good-sized river coming out of it. I thought, *That river has to be coming from a pass, so I'm going to take a chance and go up that valley.* I went through, scared stiff that I was going to see ground coming up at me. As I got closer, I could see that I was going to make it, but I was about 150 feet above the ground at the treetops.

There was a woman and a Yugoslavian mountain house on the right side of the pass about 150 feet above. I just sort of thundered in front of the lady's front porch, and she came out and waved a towel or something at me.

Once I got over the pass, things were all right, but I gradually continued to lose altitude. I got down to the Adriatic and was able to hold my altitude at four hundred feet, where the air was thicker. I had thirty inches on one engine and was still pulling forty-six on the other one.

About that time I got on the air and called Big Fence, the rescue homing beacon. I identified myself and took the heading Big Fence gave me, but gradually lost more altitude until just before I hit the Italian coast.

I didn't have very good visibility ahead at my altitude. I knew the ground fairly well, but usually from much higher up. I stayed on the same heading and saw a fighter field and thought, *To hell with it, I'll land on that field.* Then I thought, *Nope, I'm going home.*

I lost about another one hundred feet of altitude, but then it held. I was over a fairly low plain, and when I got close I called the tower.

I dragged it in and made my landing. I didn't realize it, but my tires were shot up and the ball turret guy had left his guns down when he bailed out. Clankety, clank, clank. I ripped up some steel mat runway and came to a stop pretty quick. I was sure glad to get back.

I counted eighty-eight holes in the ship. One of the crew chiefs said later, "You didn't count them all."

No, I just counted the big ones. There were 424 holes in that ship.

Lordsburg soon crawls into sight and I put the airplane down for fuel. It's not exactly a booming airport, and the manager is happy to have the company. The wind is blowing and it's a sullen, gray day. The manager offers up coffee and we all shoot the breeze for a while and then launch for Las Cruces, which is barely one hundred miles down the road. That leg is a nonevent, done at low altitude across the desert, and we are quickly on the ground. The sun is now out and it is glorious. It's taken us four days to get here. The last time I flew across the country—in a different airplane, forty years newer—I made Las Cruces on the first day.

# CHAPTER 12

CAPT. FRED FOSTER, B-26 Marauder pilot, Germany, 1944

*"One-fifty, not one mile less. If you get slower, you will roll that thing over and land on your back, two hundred yards short of the runway."*

Las Cruces to Midland/Odessa, Texas, August 11, 2000

High altitude takeoffs on hot days can mean big trouble for airplanes. Aircraft manufacturers provide detailed charts and graphs so that pilots can figure out how much runway they will need, or if in fact they will be able to get off the ground at all. When flight planning for this trip a very logical route was through Flagstaff, Arizona, and Albuquerque, New Mexico. But Flagstaff is 7,011 feet above sea level, and on a hot day, when the air is thinner, it can have a pressure/density altitude of 11,000 feet or more. That means that as far as the airplane is concerned, it is being asked to take off from a theoretical elevation of 11,000 feet above the ground. That is very close to the ceiling of this airplane. On a hot summer day, it's very easy to look at a long 7,000-foot runway, knowing your airplane needs only 500 feet at sea level to fly, and go for it. But the woods beyond the end of the runway at Flagstaff are filled with scraps of aluminum from airplanes that didn't quite make it. Since this was August in the Southwest, where one-hundred-degree days were routine, I avoided that route in favor of the more southerly course through Tucson, Arizona, and Las Cruces, New Mexico, where the field elevations are not quite so high. We didn't need the trouble—on a really good day the Stearman is not noted for its climb performance. In fact there are those who claim that the only reason that it climbs at all is due to the curvature of the earth.

And this was not a really good day here in Las Cruces.

We are up early this morning, but by the time we rustle up our sleepy ride to the airport and load the airplane, it's pushing 9:00 A.M. We're very late and it's getting very hot. In addition, Denny and I either have more baggage than we started out with, or the baggage bay is getting smaller. The airplane is getting heavier. The field elevation here is 4,454 feet above sea level, and I know that this is going to be an ugly, labored takeoff.

A departure to the west should give me some slightly descending terrain to coax the Stearman into flight, so I start up and taxi to runway two-six. Then a left turn out will point me southeast toward the Rio Grande and El Paso.

I know of two ways to fly this airplane off of the ground. It can be lifted off in the three-point tail-low attitude, which really just gets you flying in ground effect just above the runway before the airplane is ready to do any substantial climbing. Or the tail can be raised when it is willing and the airplane allowed to roll on the main gear until flying speed is attained. The aircraft is then rotated into an immediate and positive rate of climb. Since it's going to be a long trip down the runway, this latter method offers the added benefit of letting me see where I'm going for the better part of a mile. With the altitude here plus the extreme heat of the morning, there is no way I'm going to let the airplane stagger into the air in a tail-low attitude.

I bring in the power. Predictably, the Stearman accelerates slowly and takes a long time before the tail wants to come up at all. Once up on the main gear, we roll. And roll. Halfway down the runway I tug gently on the stick, but she is not quite ready to fly. I keep a little aft pressure on until the Stearman, tiring of all this, finally does a little dance, gets light on its wheels, and with me talking nicely to it, allows itself to be coaxed off of the ground. The runway numbers at the departure end, 6,069 feet from where we started to roll, flash by us just a few feet below. We do a sweeping turn to the southeast, examining closely the flora, fauna, and beer cans of the desert floor, before eventually attaining a decent cruising altitude. I relax my grip on the stick and throttle and unbite my lip. We have flight.

## Capt. Fred Foster, B-26 Marauder pilot
## Germany, 1944

### "We are going to fly them out of here."

We cruised that airplane [the B-26 Marauder] at about 220 miles per hour. On landing, we would circle to the left, hit 170 on the downwind, 160 on base, 150 on the approach. One-fifty, not one mile less. If you get slower, you will roll that thing over and land on your back, two hundred yards short of the runway. If you were a student and you let it get to 149 instead of 150, you were washed out. We landed at the same speed that the B-17 cruised at. I can still feel it. I was part of that ship and I loved it.

There was one .50-caliber in the nose; four forward-firing .50-calibers—two on each side of the fuselage, two fifties in the tail; two in the top turret; and one fifty in each waist position. Eleven guns firing. Practically the same as a B-17. It was a formidable weapon.

It had two, two-thousand-horsepower R 2800-43 Pratt & Whitney radials with Curtiss electric props. It had a four-thousand-pound bomb load and carried six men. It would take more punishment than any ship in the ETO [European Theater of Operations] and still come back. Best ship in the Air Corps. I volunteered to fly it for selfish reasons; I wanted the "best" around me.

My ship would fly off of the ground at 123 miles per hour, though sometimes we didn't have that much runway.

On one of the last missions of the war—it must have been in March or April—I was leading a flight that was coming back into Belgium from Germany. I asked my navigator/bombardier, "Is that the Rhine?"

He said, "Yes."

I said, "What town is that over there?"

He said, "I hadn't noticed it." Then, after checking his charts, "That's Frankfurt."

"Frankfurt! What the hell are we doing flying over Frankfurt?" Just then, *boom, boom, boom,* and we get a dose of "friendly" flak. So I peeled my flight off to the south.

I said, "Give me a heading to Trier, Germany." That was our designated auxiliary field in case we got into trouble with gasoline. We also had eight thousand feet of autobahn designated as an auxiliary if we were in that sector, but we went to Trier. If you flew in one of our formations, the requirements were demanding on all, but particularly the numbers five and six men, who were burning up all of their gasoline trying to hold position. My numbers five and six needed gasoline.

So we come up on Trier and begin descending. Instead of 160, hell, I find that I'm doing 180 on the base leg. I've picked up twenty miles per hour. Trier is down in a valley and I didn't realize it. And now I'm doing 165 or 170 on the approach, and I called to the other aircraft and said, "Watch your airspeed. This is in a valley and it's a short runway!"

I landed with my feet standing on the brakes. Why I didn't blow the tires I'll never know. There was a P-47 sitting a hundred yards off of the end of the runway, which had landed long. I got the airplane stopped, turned it around, and found that I had to taxi back up the runway because there was no taxi strip. Well, here comes one of my B-26s landing from the other direction, and we passed each other on the runway! His eyes were as big as saucers. I taxied off onto the ramp, and my copilot, Jack Hanley, and I just looked at each other. By this time, everybody was down and they'd made it!

And here came a jeep with the tallest major I had ever seen.

I said, "Hello, I'm Captain Foster with the 344th Bomb Group . . ."

But he was mad as hell, cuts me off, and says, "What the hell are you doing coming in here? See that ship out there, that P-47? It couldn't even land here, and here you are bringing in B-26s! I don't want you here for the rest of the war! How in the hell are you going to get your ships off?"

I said, "Just like I got them in here, Major. We are going to fly them out of here."

Well, everybody on that airfield came out to watch. Cooks, clerks, people on jeeps, everybody was out there lining the runway watching us take off, because they didn't think we were going to get off.

We had already dropped our bombs. We didn't need any gas except for my numbers five and six, who needed only to pick up only one hundred gallons each, because we were not that far from home, so we had empty ships. We didn't even get anything to eat. I told my crews that we were going to take off in reverse order. They asked why and I told them, "Well, I want to pick up your dog tags myself when you crash."

"So here's how we are going to take off. We're not going to take off like we do at home base with two on the runway, one halfway down and one releasing brakes. No. I want your mains right on the end of the asphalt with your tails hanging off. I want you to bring up those throttles, lock them down, and hold the airplane until it won't hold anymore. Then release brakes and after the takeoff roll, at the far end of the runway, the copilot goes from one-fourth to one-half flaps, and you'll pop up. Then 'wheels up.'" Of course right at the end of the runway at Trier there are church spires, but we got off okay.

Everybody joined up on me and I circled back toward Trier. Jack said, "What are you thinking about?"

I said, "Well, I want to say good-bye to them at Trier."

When we came down we must have been doing almost three hundred miles per hour right down that runway. It occurred to me afterward how close my number five and six men must have been to the ground, because I was flying low! I'll bet you they damn near took the asphalt off of that runway.

When we got back to our base in Florennes, Belgium, the colonel called me in and said, "I've got to apologize, Fred. I gave you the wrong auxiliary landing field. It wasn't Trier. Trier has a short runway."

I said, "You're telling me it was a short runway. It was thirty-two hundred feet."

"Well, I want you to tell all of your flight that I'm sorry that I sent you in there. But before you go, I have something else to tell you. You're court-martialed." But he was grinning.

I said "What for!"

He said, "For buzzing the field. That major had a court-martial request in here before you landed. We'll give it to you under the 104th Article of War—company punishment. You can't fly until tomorrow. So if we have a night mission tonight, you're grounded!"

"Thank you, Colonel." Later on I found out that we were the first B-26s to land in Germany.

El Paso is twenty miles to the south, and although I want to go east, I'll have to detour two huge military restricted areas that bar our path. I don't mind though. Those areas also contain the nine-thousand-foot Organ Mountain range that would take me fifty miles of climbing to get over. This way I can do an end run and follow the lush vegetation along the Rio Grande River south to El Paso, where I can swing east. The gate to Texas will be open and it's all downhill from there. However, there is a curious scarcity of airports and fuel in this area, so I'll have to drift back up into New Mexico for a fuel stop in Carlsbad before we hit Midland/Odessa.

The run from El Paso to Carlsbad is quite flat until forty miles west of Carlsbad, where the Guadalupe Mountains rise abruptly two to three thousand feet from the desert floor. At the point where we cross them, they resemble more of a sheer wall that instantly puts us just above the trees that stretch for miles. But once over the sixty-five-hundred-foot peaks, we are on the back slope and the terrain begins to fall away. We're over the hump and there will be no more high and hot flying for many miles.

Carlsbad, now just over the nose, was a bombardier training base during the war and greets us with a maze of runways to cover every possible wind condition. Bombardier training at Carlsbad was done in AT-11s, which were a twin-engine, twin-tailed Beechcraft with a glass nose. Generally, pilots hated an assignment here, seeing their role in the war as nothing more than truck drivers for students.

The buildings that made up the base are mostly gone except for a couple of the big hangars. There is a nice museum display in the terminal, with photos of the base during the war and an honest-to-gosh Norden bombsight, the premier tool of the bombardier's trade. This was America's secret weapon early in World War II and never went anywhere without an armed guard. However, the first B-17s and B-24s that fell in Europe and the Pacific quickly delivered copies to all concerned. This bombsight had its faults, but was capable of some remarkable accuracy.

On my visit to the Hemet Field, California, cadet reunion, I gave a ride to Bill Blair, a former copilot on the B-24 *Red Headed Woman*. Fifty-four years before, Bill had visited Cavite Naval Base, then owned by the Japanese, on at least two occasions as a member of the "Bomber Barons" of the Fifth Heavy Bombardment Group. The conversation got around to just how accurate the famous Norden bombsight really was. Bill showed me three remarkable strike photos from those visits.

"I always felt that we did real good with it," he said, "but there's a book that is quite critical of the bombsight. The author said that it was one thing to bomb targets out here in the deserts of New Mexico and Texas under ideal conditions and quite another to bomb targets where you're undergoing attacks from enemy fighters and flak in adverse weather. But the Norden bombsight was always touted as being able to put a pickle in a barrel from twenty thousand feet, and I think that we did some pretty good work with it."

To make his point, Bill pulls out a series of strike photos of the raid on Cavite Naval Base. The base is on an oddly shaped geometric island, about three-quarters of a mile wide and about four miles long on the south side of Manila Bay in the Philippine Islands. It's connected to the mainland by a causeway, which leads to a tightly packed urban area that supplied a labor pool and services to this major U.S. base prior to the fall of the Philippines. Cavite was damaged during the invasion of the islands, but it was quickly repaired by the Japanese.

The strike photos are amazing. The first photo shows a completely built-up Cavite, with fabrication shops, wharves, docks, cranes, and hangars, just starting to take bomb hits. The second photo, taken after the raid, shows the peninsula transformed into a cratered lunar landscape. Two buildings, seaplane hangars with an aircraft parked in front, have escaped damage though. These hangars apparently rated the attention of a follow-up raid. In the photo from the second raid, the hangars are obliterated and concealed under a cluster of bombs that have arrived to within a two- to three-hundred-foot circle, zeroed in on the hangar. Poof! The hangar is gone and very little else has been touched. What is equally amazing is that the Philippine-populated urban areas, a few hundred feet away from the Japanese naval base, show almost no sign of damage.

"Would you like to see a Norden bombsight?" Bill asks, as if just about everyone had one of these lying around. At his house I follow him out to his deck overlooking the sunny, peaceful hills of Pasadena. Among the outdoor furniture, plants, and bird feeders sits a small cart about the size of a barbeque, but incongruously supporting what turns out to be a Norden bombsight with the appropriate instrumentation, switches, a power supply, and a belt-driven moving map display. He has collected the bits and pieces of this intricate and complicated machine from other collectors and aeronautical antique dealers. He then overhauled it and built his own private simulator.

"I fired it up, found that the gyros ran fine and thought that it would be fun to set this thing up and demonstrate it."

He shows me an old Army Air Corps picture of what looks like a fifteen-foot-high motorized scaffold on wheels being steered by a pilot and with a bombardier hunched over a Norden bombsight. These training devices were used to supplement actual bomb dropping.

"I remembered the trainers that we used out at Muroc [now Edwards Air Force Base]; we had a whole hangar full of them. The bombardier would look through the sight and sight on the little bug, though they called it a crab. It's a little motorized bug that goes across the floor and simulates either a moving target or drift from wind, crosswinds, and so forth. He synchronizes on that, drops, and then there was a piece of carbon paper that left marks on the target if you were fortunate enough to hit it. It left dots. So then you'd kick the thing into reverse, back up and do it all over again. Much cheaper than burning two hundred gallons of gas per hour in a B-24. Well, I wanted something more compact, so I came up with the idea of building this."

Bill turns the bombsight on and its gyros softly wind up to their designed rpm. He shows me how to operate it and I give it a try. I look through the eyepiece, and suddenly I am in every World War II bomber movie I have ever seen, as the terrain moves through the crosshairs of my 160-mile-per-hour B-24. I make adjustments, and the bomb strikes, which appear as little red laser pinpoints on the moving map, reveal that today I have killed many fish by salvoing my bomb load into the ocean. Bill demonstrates the proper technique, neatly walking a stick of bombs across an airport runway intersection. It makes me glad that he was on our side.

"I got a letter from an instructor and five students at Chester Nimitz High School in Houston, who chose to do a research project on the bombsight for a science competition on a national level." Bill brought the device all the way to Houston and demonstrated it to the students.

"They were setting up the Norden bombsight as the hero of World War II. Their point was that it was used strictly on strategic targets, which is a little bit of hogwash," he laughs. "Part of their diorama showed the German way, where they bombed indiscriminately." The kids won the district and the state championship.

Okay, so these kids never heard of Dresden and Hamburg or the American incendiary raids in Japan, which in addition to being very effective were a long way from precision bombing. They'll have an entire lifetime to become disillusioned. But to a couple of thousand Philippine citizens living next to Cavite Naval Base, whether they know it or not, on that day in 1944 their lives were spared by the Norden bombsight. And by guys like Bill Blair and the crew of the *Red Headed Woman,* who knew what they were doing and risked their lives to do it properly.

The visit to Carlsbad is uneventful; I refuel and Denny and I are on our way, grinding across the featureless Texas landscape at a doddering ninety miles per hour. Occasionally a road drifts by to indicate progress. About halfway to Midland, oil pumping rigs begin to put in an appearance, first in tens, then in hundreds, then to the horizon. We can smell the petroleum and gas at forty-five hundred feet.

Midland gradually creeps into sight and we set down. Ground control is effusive in their comments on the appearance of the Stearman. I approve of their good taste, chat with them, and then proceed to get lost on their taxiways. Twice. There is some construction going on here and one of the taxiways is closed, so I wind up taxiing through what feels like a small town before I arrive at my destination.

The Midland/Odessa Airport is the new home of the American Airpower Heritage Museum of the Commemorative Air Force, and I plan to spend quite a bit of time in their research library. The facilities are spectacular, and I'm able to roll the Stearman into the museum, where it nests like a small bird under the wing of an old Curtiss C-46 Commando, out of the Texas thunderstorms and sun.

The Commemorative Air Force is a wonderful organization. Dedicated to the preservation and care of vintage military aircraft and history, it is obviously in the middle of some major growing pains, not the least of which is changing its name from its original identity as the "Confederate Air Force." Having matured from a regional bunch of independent "good ol' boys" and their airplanes to a national organization with assets, budgets, schedules, and reliant on corporate sponsorship, their former name became a political liability, and in 2001 they became known as the Commemorative Air Force.

It is a fascinating facility to walk through, their air shows are spectacular, and where else can you walk into a hangar and find a bunch of guys spending their Saturdays patiently restoring a Japanese Zero or a Grumman Bearcat.

We stay in Midland for the next five days, and at the end of our stay Denny departs for his home on a different Boeing, a 737. He's been a big help and we've had a lot of laughs as we have reviewed the folly of our youth. It is a wonder that we got through it. I'll miss him.

# CHAPTER 13

CADET ARTHUR FIEDLER, Basic Training, Vultee BT-13s
*Of Screamers and Knee-Knockers*


Midland/Odessa to San Angelo, Texas, August 16, 2000


I arrive at the Midland/Odessa field just as the sun is streaking the eastern sky, making an overly dramatic backdrop for the Stearman. I almost expect credits to roll. I had awakened at 4:30 A.M., misjudged the sunrise hour, and strolled outside into inky blackness at a quarter to six. Rethinking things, I sit down and have coffee and a bagel in the airport cafe.

"Well, at least this fits Carter Teeters's definition of an early departure," I muse. Carter, who had checked me out in the Stearman ten years ago, had cautioned that on any transcontinental trip the time to fly is between dawn and noon—advice I had followed with some success.

"Hit the starter switch just as the sun ball breaks the horizon, be back on the ground by noon, and ye shall live long and prosper," he advised with some wisdom. This gives a silky-smooth early morning flight, followed by a refueling at about nine-thirty, then a slightly bumpy ride that usually ends with an uneventful landing just after twelve. A day's work done, one can relax at poolside with a hamburger and a beer and watch the thunderstorms explode all afternoon, making life miserable for other pilots not as perceptive or fortunate in their choice of flying hours.

So I spool up the starter on the Stearman and while the engine warms call ground control for taxi instructions.

"Your departure control frequency will be 124.6 and your squawk code will be 0306. Please advise your climb-out heading and altitude," is the reply. Whoops, they caught me off guard. I'm at an international airport and they are going to want to follow me out of here, even at this hour. But I know that it is all to the good. I fumble for my chart to get the heading and trade this information with ground. They let me taxi to runway one-six right, dodging a waddling Southwest 737 along the way.

The flight from Midland to San Angelo is unremarkable; the terrain an unchanging pattern of sagebrush and oil pumping rigs nodding their little heads off. These taper off a bit as I put distance between Midland and myself. There are no section lines to steer by and only an occasional road to place myself on the map. Section lines are a great aid to navigation. These are the man-made lines on the earth that one sees from an aircraft and that define the patchwork quilt of crops, roads, and property lines. Most are laid out to true north and follow lines of latitude and longitude. Once established on a compass course that cuts across these lines at an angle, or even paralleling them, navigation becomes quite easy. A pilot needs only to continue cutting across the section lines at the same angle to maintain a reasonably accurate course. The lower you are, the better it seems to work, as it's easier to gauge the angle down low. The horizon today is offering no distant points such as mountain ranges to help steer by. I can also steer by the rising sun as long as it's low, keeping it in the same relative position to the aircraft, but the longer the flight, the less accurate that method becomes, because the sun is both rising and arcing horizontally across the horizon. These are all rather crude methods of navigation, but so is chasing a bouncing magnetic compass.

Nearing San Angelo I see the attractive pattern of lakes that surround the city and head for them. They are the most water that I have seen in

Texas to date and exist due to a confluence of rivers in the area and reservoirs to contain them. They look refreshing in this arid countryside.

I soon spot the object of this flight, Goodfellow Air Force Base. It lies nestled in the southeast corner of the city, and I head for it and fly in lazy circles above. Although the 41–806 was assigned here late in the war, its tenure was brief. It arrived in early December 1944 and was gone by the following February. Throughout the war, Goodfellow was a basic training field and the BT-13 Vultee was the aircraft used for that function. It was only at the end of the war, when Goodfellow became a primary training base for South American pilots, that this base started using the Stearman. The Vultee was a far more modern aircraft and truly prepared cadets for the more complex aircraft they were soon to fly.

## Cadet Arthur Fiedler
## Basic Training, Vultee BT-13s

### Of Screamers and Knee-Knockers

We learned to fly the BT-13, nicknamed the *Vultee Vibrator,* a low-wing aircraft with an enclosed cockpit and a 450-horsepower engine. Also new was the ability to change the pitch of the propeller to either a high or low setting. At low pitch and high rpm, which were our climbing and landing settings, the propeller made a tremendous racket. High pitch was used in cruising. In contrast to primary, all the instructors were military officers, with a sprinkling of British pilots who had flown combat in Europe.

For many of the cadets the BT-13 was a surprise, but not a pleasant one. It was much larger than the PT-17, and whereas the Stearman had only a couple of cockpit gauges, it seemed the BT-13 had scores of gauges, levers, switches, and handles. It was a real task for some of the cadets to learn the purpose of all the instruments plus memorizing a whole series of checklists. There was the exterior preflight check before you entered the cockpit, the cockpit checklist, the prestart engine checklist, the start engine checklist, the after-engine start checklist, the pretaxi checklist, the taxi checklist, the engine check procedures, the pre-takeoff checklist, the takeoff checklist, and the after-takeoff checklist.

As is evident, there was a lot of memorizing to do—far too much for some as it turned out.

Here we encountered instructors who were known as "Screamers" and who felt their job was to make life as stressful as possible to ensure you could cope with combat. Personally, I thought at that time, and still do, that there was no correlation. Other instructors were "Knee-Knockers," who when dissatisfied with a student's performance would slam the stick from side to side. More than one student had black-and-blue knees.

I was fortunate and experienced none of these types. However, Andy McDerby, one of the three of us who had been instructed by Sam Wilbur in primary, had a screamer who berated him constantly. Our procedures required that after takeoff we climbed at 90 miles per hour, flew the downwind at 110 miles per hour, the base leg at 100 miles per hour, and the final at 90 miles per hour. If Andy let his airspeed waver a hair off the required airspeed, for example on final approach, his instructor would scream, "90 miles an hour! 90 miles an hour, not 89!" And if Andy forgot one item on the checklist, as we all did occasionally, he made Andy repeat the checklist over and over. It got so that Andy could not sleep at night, and finally despite the efforts of Al Merz (another of Sam's students) and myself to keep him in the program, he turned in his resignation. I learned later that he went to the South Pacific as a B-24 gunner and, thank goodness, survived.

The BT-13 was a relatively easy airplane to fly, with a very wide landing gear and thus little tendency to ground loop. The major complaint of most was the enclosed cockpit. After the PT-17, we felt confined and complained that the canopy hampered our vision. And I guess if the Plexiglas was not absolutely clear and unscratched, it did, but I am sure the real reason was that we missed the feel of the wind on our faces that was always present in an open cockpit.

This was also the phase where we began instrument flying and thus learned to fly from under a hood in the back cockpit. The hood prevented us from seeing outside the airplane, and we had to rely on the flight instruments to perform our maneuvers.

Several weeks into basic, we had a most unfortunate accident and a cadet was killed. He was practicing formation flying with two other airplanes on a day of considerable clouds. As they flew close to a cloud, another BT-13 suddenly emerged from the cloud and struck his aircraft.

For some reason, he did not bail out, and was killed in the resulting crash. Speculation was that the instructor in the other airplane was flying in the clouds to give his student some real experience in instrument flying. We were not privy to the results of the accident investigation.

During primary, I had one flight at night and my landing attempts had been unmitigated disasters. I am not sure why Sam took me up, as night flying was not in the normal primary curriculum. In basic we officially began programmed night flying . . . and therein lies another tale.

I can look back on it now and chuckle, although it was far from laughable at the time. After learning to fly the BT-13 during daylight hours, we had to get a night checkout. This was the only flight I had with the British instructor. He met with us at noon and explained we would be checked out for night flying by making three landings with him in the backseat, and then three solo landings. This seemed reasonable at the time.

Late in the afternoon we flew several airplanes to an auxiliary field that had two huge floodlights set up on the approach end of a grass field. This was the only lighting there was. As soon as you passed the threshold of the field, there was only the light from your landing lights and inky blackness ahead.

As soon as it got dark, the instructor called, "Let's get going," and off we went. My three landings were terrible. The grass was about two feet high, and once past the area lit by the floodlights it was extremely difficult to judge your height above the ground. After we completed the third landing, he told me to taxi to the tee, where he jumped out and told me to make three more landings. I protested vigorously that I was not ready to go solo, but he replied that he had survived the Battle of Britain, but sitting in the backseat of a BT-13 while cadets were trying to learn to make night landings was not his idea of how to live to a ripe old age. With a great deal of trepidation (scared as hell), I taxied to the floodlit area, requested takeoff permission and off I went—not at all happy.

On the final approach to my first solo landing, I was astonished that I was losing altitude so slowly that I passed right over the field a couple hundred feet high and had to go around. For a few moments I was absolutely terrified and thought I was doomed to fly around that night until I ran out of fuel.

Abruptly a droll voice came over the radio, "I say, old chap, if you want to get down tonight, take the power all the way off on the next try." It was my instructor, with good advice. We always made our landings with the power off (throttle at idle), but in my anxiety I had failed to retard the throttle completely. With partial power, the rate of descent was much less, and I would have landed in the woods on the other side of the field if I hadn't gone around. This time everything worked out fine, and I made a decent landing, at which time the instructor said, "Jolly good, take it around again."

And so it went for two more landings, at which time he instructed me to taxi over to the tee and let another student have a "whack" at it. This went on until about 3:00 or 4:00 A.M., when several of us were told to fly an airplane back to Macon solo. I was given a course to fly and told it would take about fifteen minutes. This was no problem, but after landing, as I was getting out of the cockpit, I saw and heard a BT-13 fly directly over the field and keep going. I could hear the tower calling him, but for some reason he did not respond. We all proceeded to the hangar, where it was found that a cadet by the name of Schram was missing. Several of the instructors then went up to search for him. We learned later that Schram, realizing he was lost, had cut the mixture control back as far as possible until he located an airfield just after dawn. When he landed, the bird had over five hours of flight time logged. His feat may not be fully appreciated unless one knew the airplane carried fuel for only three hours and thirty minutes when fully fueled, but he had coaxed over five hours out of it. Because he had used such good judgment to cope with this situation, he was not washed out.

After our night checkout, we still had to make night cross-country flights plus many additional takeoffs and landings. Control of so many airplanes at night around an airport posed an interesting problem. Imaginary north-south and east-west lines would be drawn through the airfield, which established four quadrants. One would be designated the climb quadrant. The quadrants were about five miles in radius, and when you took off you would be assigned initially to a quadrant and an altitude; for instance, northeast quadrant at five thousand feet. One would take off, climb in the climb quadrant until reaching the assigned altitude, then head directly to and circle in the assigned quadrant. After checking in by radio, each pilot would continue circling until directed to descend. Thus, one quadrant would be clear for climbing and the other three quadrants would be filled with airplanes at one-thousand-foot intervals from two thousand to about seven thousand feet.

Control of the aircraft in these stacks was relatively simple. The three aircraft at the two-thousand-foot level in each of the three stacks would be cleared to enter the traffic pattern and shoot landings. As soon as they reported being established in the traffic pattern, the aircraft at three thousand feet in each of the stacks would be cleared to descend to two thousand feet and report reaching that altitude. Then the next higher aircraft would be told to descend one thousand feet until everyone in each stack was circling one thousand feet lower than he had been. When the aircraft in the pattern had completed their landings and takeoffs, they would return to the ramp and three more aircraft would enter the pattern for their turn.

It was boring flying in small circles, often for up to two hours, before getting an opportunity to shoot your landings. In the wee hours of the morning it became difficult to stay awake after a full day of flying and academics. One night it got to be too much for me.

As I recall, I was at four thousand feet in one of the stacks and it was between 1:00 and 2:00 A.M. I was having a dickens of a time trying to stay awake and realized that I needed to do something drastic to stay alert. Turning off my running lights, I dove to about two hundred feet and headed directly toward Macon, a couple of miles away. Doing some 220 miles per hour with the prop in full low pitch, I went screaming across the entire town at low altitude producing an ear-splitting thunderous roar. Immediately I zoomed into a climb and returned to my altitude in my assigned quadrant. When in position, I again turned on my running lights.

The sound must have awakened a lot of irate citizens, as a couple of minutes after returning to my position we were called from the tower and one by one we had to turn toward the tower and flash our landing lights. This was to see if anyone was missing and thus identify the culprit. Needless to say, I was able to stay awake the rest of the night. Discretion being the better part of valor, I decided I would not tell even my best cadet friend of my escapade.

Two additional types of flying received a lot of attention during basic. These were formation flying and precision acrobatics. Although we had considerable acrobatics during primary, there was much greater emphasis on it during basic. We learned all the normal acrobatics such as loops, rolls, Cuban Eights, Immelmanns, Chandelles, lazy eights, plus precision spins. We also surreptitiously used to get into mock combat with other students during solo flights. Sometimes a cadet made the mistake of bouncing a bird in which an instructor was aboard. Since individual combat was prohibited, some interesting things happened in these circumstances. The plane doing the bouncing usually did it from a higher altitude and thus had greater speed. When he saw two people in the airplane and there were clouds anywhere near, he would immediately head toward them hoping to lose the pursuing instructor in the clouds. Some would immediately climb toward the sun and hope the instructor would be unable to follow them in the glare of the sun. The problem with this tactic was that we did not have enough power to climb very long if the sun was high in the sky. The instructor would climb to the side until the fleeing plane stalled out, and then get the number. Others would head full speed for the field and hope to get lost among the airplanes trying to land. The more intelligent flyer *first* made sure that there was no instructor in the airplane before he bounced it.

At the end of May 1943, we completed our basic flight training. We heard several figures as to how many cadets had washed out in this phase, but the general impression was that we lost between 6 and 10 percent.

I was elated to see I would go to Marianna, Florida, for single-engine advanced flight school. At the same time I was saddened to see that a considerable number of my friends had been assigned to multiengine advanced flight school, which meant that we would likely not meet again.

The runways at Goodfellow AFB have been officially closed since 1975, so a landing there is out of the question. I fly some lazy orbits above the base and then head five miles south for a landing at Mathis Field, formerly San Angelo Army Air Field, a bombardier training base.

Having lost my passenger, Denny, in Midland/Odessa, to the relative luxury of a 737, I now fly from the backseat. It's noisier and windier, but the aft center of gravity is a little friendlier to the airplane on landing by helping to keep the tail wheel, the steerable part of this contraption, firmly on the ground. The airplane can be flown from either the front or the back, depending on how it is equipped, but if I were to remain in the front, a few sandbags would be a prudent addition to the rear cargo bay and these I don't have.

While I'm here I elect to have the compass swung. Coming from Midland I had noticed some minor disagreement between what the front and rear compasses were telling me, and this needs to get resolved.

Maintenance on any airplane is a tricky business, but this airplane is twice as old as anybody likely to work on it, and most mechanics have never even seen a Stearman up close. Manuals are hard to get and Stearman specific tools are rare. Even though it is tractor technology, I have found that on this airplane it's in my own best interest to know the aircraft as thoroughly as I can. I find an excellent mechanic here at Mathis and soon I'm in good shape.

Federal air regulations spell out just exactly who may work on an airplane and who may not. Most work is restricted to licensed airframe and power plant technicians and their supervisors on the food chain, aircraft inspectors (AI). Pilots are allowed only very limited participation in the maintenance of their own aircraft and in most cases rightfully so. Aircraft maintenance is complex, requiring years of training, and the consequences of a simple mistake by an untrained hand can range from inconvenient to tragic.

I enjoy working on the Stearman and have done a lot of supervised maintenance on it. Through the years I have repaired and rebuilt many components on the airplane and am proud of that work. Yet sometimes mistakes can happen.

It's the simple things that can bite you. Once, while fueling the Stearman, I noticed that the seal on the fuel cap was deteriorating. It was an uncomplicated device, almost exactly like an automobile gas cap, so I ordered a new one. This was certainly nothing to bring to the attention of a mechanic. After all, by regulation I can fuel my own aircraft—removing and replacing the gas cap each time. Who cared if I put on a new one?

The cap arrived two days later from a Stearman parts supplier and, unlike the cap I was replacing, this was an original Stearman part. I was pleased. The only thing that stopped its immediate installation was that it was painted the wrong color. It was black and should have been red, so it went on the bench for a while until I could get around to painting it. I was tempted a couple of times to put it on, but my anal instincts, this time about color, were on my side. It was a ticking bomb.

The closest it came to installation was the day that my wife and I had been invited to Edwards Air Force Base for Armed Forces Day as a display aircraft. On that day I actually climbed up to the tank (it is in the upper wing) and started to put the cap on, but was interrupted. Out of time, I put it back on the bench and we left.

When we got back, I took some time and painted it. That is when I noticed that the cap was unvented. A fuel system *must* be vented to the atmosphere (there must be a hole in it somewhere) to allow the fuel to draw. If there is a vacuum, fuel won't flow. It's the same principle that won't allow you to suck out the contents of a Coke bottle without letting in some air.

So the replacement, the original equipment, was an unvented cap. But that was okay, because I knew that the tank itself was vented out of a tube that was routinely checked on every preflight. This tube comes out of the front of the tank and is routed through the inside of the wing to the trailing edge. I could plainly see the tip of this vent tube. But I felt uneasy.

*Why* had the previous owner put a vented cap on this airplane, which already had a vented system? There could be one big reason. The engine wouldn't run without it!

I took off the metal fairing that covered one of the gaps in the upper wing and examined the hidden vent tube. Here was my answer. The vent tube had been disassembled and masked for the painting of the aircraft. Masking tape still covered the ends of the tube and it had never been reassembled. The tank was unvented and had I put the correct gas cap on it; very likely it would have run just long enough for me to get off of the ground and win the "smoking hole" award just off the end of the runway. All for a simple gas cap. You can bet that the reassembly and the new cap were thoroughly inspected by an AI.

Then there was my friend John Kinsman.* A young man of considerable accomplishment and promise, John was one of the newer pilots at our local airport, and we had spent a bit of time in each other's hangars and airplanes. In his early thirties, he was an accomplished musician, playing the cello in a local quartet; a champion competition swimmer; and of all things, a rocket scientist working at NASA's Jet Propulsion Laboratory. He was also a very good and cautious pilot who owned a mint-condition, forty-year-old Ercoupe that he constantly fussed over. I had flown with John in the Ercoupe and watched how careful he was in his approach to aviation. We had flown close formation for air-to-air photography, and the shots taken from his airplane line my walls. His piloting skills and the care he lavished on his aircraft were remarkable.

John was getting ready to fly the Ercoupe to Florida to watch the

---

*Not his real name.

launch of the Cassini spacecraft, a project he had worked on for five years, when he began to have intermittent battery trouble. He would come out to the airport on a Saturday and find a dead battery. Battery installation is one of the things a pilot may do to his own aircraft, so this is what John did. A new battery fixed things for a while, but soon the electrical troubles returned. Thinking that it might have been a defective battery, he made another replacement. The problem persisted. His airplane was now talking to him, but he couldn't hear. It had become his ticking bomb.

One beautiful Saturday afternoon John and his young girlfriend got in the Ercoupe and took off for a weekend trip. He was off of the ground less than a minute and had just turned crosswind when the tower called to say that they had observed smoke on climb-out. He acknowledged and declared an emergency, but within thirty seconds the Ercoupe had plunged, inverted in flames, into a garage one-half block from the edge of the airport, killing the young woman instantly. John lingered for a week, and then he too passed away.

Postcrash investigation revealed this sequence. Years previously, the Ercoupe had been reengined with a more powerful but heavier engine. To counterbalance the weight of this engine, the battery was moved aft into the cabin and the wiring was routed through the firewall. That wiring over the years had chafed and was intermittently shorting out where it passed through the firewall and draining the battery. It finally welded itself to the airframe and caused the fire—and there was a gas tank directly above it. The dead batteries weren't the problem; they were the symptom. John had done nothing more than what most of us would have done.

But his ticking bomb had gone off.

# CHAPTER 14

DON CARRELL, L-4 pilot, Europe

*"At five hundred feet someone could throw a helmet through your prop."*

San Angelo to Burnet, Texas, August 18, 2000

Once again I have to go high-tech. It's 0700 and the tower is now officially open for business, so I must call them to depart. Yes, that's right—control towers have business hours just like dry cleaners and doctors. I was hoping to leave before the tower opened, but didn't quite make it. I was hoping to walk out to my old airplane and just climb in and fly away, without talking to anybody on the radio. There is something very pure about doing so and that makes it more desirable. You are alone with your thoughts and there are no distractions. The bond between the pilot and aircraft is stronger, and it allows one to focus on the process of getting an aircraft airborne. I've just awakened this big machine. It has a lot of parts that are flying about, and I want to concentrate on what they're telling me. Are the brakes squealing? Is that a rocker arm tapping in the engine? Is the idle smooth? Too many pilots have gotten into trouble flying the radio instead of the airplane.

But I call ground control as required. Except for mine, there is not an engine running on the field or an airplane in the sky. The sun has just made its appearance.

"Seven-two-one, your squawk code is oh-two-oh-one and departure control is one-two-four-point-six."

Departure control. They are going to follow my progress out of here. Of course it's to everybody's advantage, but it's just one more link to the ground that I'd rather do without. They'll track me for forty miles, and if I vary my heading or altitude to look at something and don't mention it, they'll get all tense and want to discuss the situation. It's a freedom that you give up by flying into certain airports.

"And say again type of aircraft?"

I love this question. "It's a Boeing ST-seven-five." I give them the proper designator and am greeted by silence from ground as they try to figure where that fits in among the Boeing 727s, 737s, and 747s.

I smile to myself as I think of the apocryphal story of the Stearman pilot who reported in as a "Boeing, three miles out, coming in on one engine." The tower guys were not amused.

"It's a Stearman." I try and simplify but am greeted by more silence.

"You say a Stinson?"

"No ma'am, a Boeing Stearman Model A-seven-five." More silence as the pages of books are turned. Mathis Field was a training base sixty years ago and was bracketed by at least two others within twenty miles. There must have been hundreds of Stearmans in these skies. Now it's as if they never existed. But we soon get it all sorted out to everyone's satisfaction and the FAA makes me a neat entry into their system, hopefully with a correct name.

I roll onto the runway and lift off into the early morning liquid air, taking up a heading of one-zero-zero degrees on the compass. Staying low over the featureless sagebrush countryside, in the middle of nowhere I pass over an old military auxiliary airstrip. It was probably used by students out of Goodfellow during the war. No buildings, just the runway with a lot of tire marks at each end, decomposing back into the earth. I'll bet it could tell some stories. The terrain soon changes, gradually rolling into hills with lovely little mesquite groves. I stay low and follow the contours of the earth. It's magic. At this hour the shadows are still long, the hills gold on the sun side and blue on the shade side.

It is truly a treat to fly low, the Stearman gently rising and falling with the terrain-induced lift. The cows grazing on the hillsides pause in their ruminations to contemplate the rumbling sky creature that passes over-head. If I were in a 747 at thirty-five thousand feet, these hills would merely be an interesting interlude during the beverage service. If I were at thirty-five hundred feet, they would be pretty. At one hundred feet they are spectacular. If heaven exists, it is at one hundred feet—not at some vague altitude beyond the jets.

The hills give a vertigo effect as they quickly drop away and then rise. It's like repeatedly stepping off the edge of a building, the pit of the stomach sending that primordial "you're falling" message each time.

In the constant game of *Where will I land this airplane if the engine quits?* the choices are going to be hard because of the limited time for selection. I'll have about five seconds at most. Fortunately, for every small hill there is a small valley, and a quick turn into one of these valleys will offer the safest course. (Who am I kidding?)

Although no one has ever asked them why, cows seem to prefer to congregate in these valleys, presumably because of the shelter they provide from the wind. (I see no cows on the hilltops.) There is even aviation folklore that says that cows will put their fannies into the wind when it is breezy. For pilots, this becomes the bovine equivalent of an emergency windsock. However, cows I have met have apparently never heard of this rule and always seem to graze aimlessly. Whether a cow would be motivated to move out of the way of a silently descending Stearman is highly problematic and when a one-and-a-half-ton airplane and a half-ton cow meet, the results are going to be ugly.

I give a quick glance at the chart to make sure no one has built a tower on my course, but see none. The trees get thicker and the hills become forested. I crest a ridge and there is a lake in front of me about eight miles across. Now I can really get low. I've never heard of a tower in a lake.

The morning fishermen are out, quite a few actually. They are standing in their little boats, which are very full and appear to be top-heavy. It must be a local fishing method—or a social technique. If it were me, I'd be lying in the boat with a good book and a cup of coffee, not caring if the fish bit. I give the fishermen a wide berth, get low, and cross the lake like a kid in a new Corvette, loving every minute of it.

One group of pilots whose job was to fly low was the World War II liaison pilots. They performed reconnaissance and directed artillery fire from what were essentially slightly modified civilian airplanes. These were aircraft that were generally known as "Cubs," even though they might be Aeroncas or Stinsons, Taylorcraft, or indeed, Piper Cubs. They were the "L," or liaison, aircraft. To employ these aircraft as we did was a brilliant decision. This was the American genius of improvisation at it's finest. They were available, expendable, cheap, could be built quickly and in great numbers. Many civilian versions of these types were pressed into service with some quick modifications and an olive drab paint job. No other army used them quite the way the U.S. Army did. They became the eyes of the artillery, and their combat arena was between the treetops and fifteen hundred feet. American artillery, probably our most effective ground weapon of the war, was feared by both the Germans and the Japanese, and the liaison pilots made it even more accurate and devastating.

## Don Carrell, 8th Armored Division
## Europe, 1944–1945

### ". . . you rolled it over and got down below tree level."

Don Carrell was an L-4 Cub pilot, an artillery observer in Europe. He began his training as an enlisted pilot.

> I went to Stillwater, Oklahoma, to take sixty-five hours. That was the initial part of the course. I was flying in a Porterfield aircraft, single engine and a real small aircraft.
>
> From Stillwater, I went to Fort Sill and went through this fabulous short field school run by a bunch of bush pilots. We were given fantastic training for operating out of fields and off of roads.
>
> The training had never been done before. The instruments in the plane were all covered except for the oil pressure. You had to fly the airplane by feel. In fact, they went so far as to put what I'd call Indian

moccasins on your feet so you'd feel rudder pressure. All feel. We'd fly over barriers and make the landings shorter and shorter. We landed on curved roads. We'd do ninety-degree takeoffs. If you've got a field that is too short and you can run around a corner—you learned how to take off that way.

We could never have a school like it again. To get students into this particular type of flying was dangerous. It destroyed a lot of airplanes. Only the government could supply that many airplanes.

Piper, of course, was part of it. They supplied four or five aircraft down at the Louisiana maneuvers in '41 to show how it could be done. It had never been tried before. Everything was Air Corps, bombers and fighters.

So when the value of the Cub was proven, the program started. That's how the Fort Sill school came to be. Their job was to teach pilots how to get out of barnyards, baseball diamonds, off of roads, and everything else. We had no runways. We took what we could get and we were taught how to do it.

The Cub is a fantastic airplane. I've operated out of cornfields that just weren't big enough to get anything into. The approach needed for that is called a power stall. You stall the airplane all the way to the ground, with power to get the shortest possible landing. We used to carry a roll of toilet paper. When we'd go into a small field, we'd go in as short as possible. But the takeoff was always a longer run. You'd walk it if necessary and use the toilet paper to mark the various stumps and whatever else could be in your way.

I've landed in a baseball park on home plate and stopped before I got off the infield. Of course I did that in Louisiana and then had to take the fence down out in center field because the wind quit on me.

There was nothing else like it anywhere else in the world at the time.

I have a buddy in San Antonio who flew one off of an LST—that's a little less than two hundred feet.

An LST (Landing Ship/Tank) is a large transport designed to carry heavy equipment such as tanks or trucks. Two LSTs were modified with a 270-foot-long, 16-foot-wide flight deck. The L-4 had a thirty-five-foot wingspread, so that left about ten feet of wing hanging over both sides of the flight deck. It looked like an airplane on a sidewalk. There was less than five feet on either side of the landing gear. Ten L-4s were carried on the LSTs and could be launched but not recovered. They were used in the invasion of Sicily and the landings at Salerno with success.

Prior to that, in the November 1942 invasion of North Africa, three L-4s were flown off of the aircraft carrier USS *Ranger*. That was not a success. They were all shot down, two of them by friendly fire.

I went to England first and flew the channel to Saint Valerie, France. What bothered me about crossing the channel was that I was given a seat-pack parachute and a one-man dinghy underneath my butt. There were eight of us and I was the lead airplane. We were five hundred feet off the water when I got to thinking, *What good does this parachute do me?*

We hit a snow squall in France, right on the coast, and we were just about out of gas so I went into a field. The field looked very nice, but it just happened to have four feet of snow in it. The snow was so deep that the airplane just went *swoosh* and stopped. I had to dig my way out from under the wing. That was my welcome to France.

I looked around and *whoosh, whoosh, whoosh.* Four or five more airplanes came in there. Pretty soon there were ten or fifteen planes and all had followed me. We got a set of oxen from a farmer and took a big railroad log and fixed ourselves a runway. We picked the airplanes up, bodily moved them over to the runway, and took off again.

I was assigned to the 8th Armored Division, 398th Field Artillery Battalion.

During the war when you needed ground support, you had to go way back to where the Air Corps was and tell them your troubles. Well, the Air Corps was way back in England, let's say, with concrete runways.

But with this liaison thing you lived with the troops. And when the ground troops needed support from the air, you were there. When your division is on the ground and moving, you find out what's going on and fly eight or nine hundred feet above the troops or enemy lines and do anything that's needed to help them.

You're hooked up to your radio in the airplane and you have direct radio contact with the fire direction center in your division. The airplane is light, weighs twelve hundred pounds and has no armor. You carry a forty-five. That's all you carry.

It's probably the most devastating weapon the Army ever had in World War II. You can talk about bombers all you want to, but artillery fire is absolutely devastating to troops.

You can call up fire missions for anything. The purpose of the airplane was to search and destroy. We could shoot at anything we wanted at any time, just so that it was in enemy territory. We flew right over enemy troops and knocked out roadblocks, tanks, and everything else. All you did was pick up your mike and call your fire direction center. You could have thirty-six rounds a minute into the target. They were so accurate that you could put a round at twenty-five thousand yards into a crossroad.

The fire we called in was steady. They couldn't get away from it. We were flying eight hundred feet off of the ground—we could see a man's whiskers. All you had to do was direct artillery fire and you could put a shell in his pocket.

I've knocked out tanks. The Tiger tank was heavy and so well armored that we had to use white phosphorus. They would catch on fire and the crew would run off. Most artillery shells bounced off them.

It was constant flying. There was no such thing as not being up. George Patton was one of the advocates of this. Way back at the beginning of the war, he flew his own airplane, which was a Cub. He recognized how perfect the plane was for ground support and communication.

And that's what we did, day after day. We flew from dawn to dark, eight to ten hours a day. There was no way of getting away from the Cub. How can you get away from a plane at eight hundred feet? It was bad news for the German army.

There was a directive issued to the Germans and we got a copy of it. To get a Cub—to get one of these liaison aircraft—the German got a leave. More than for a B-17 or a fighter.

We worried about German fighters more than anything else. A Focke-Wulf could be a speck in the sky one minute, and the next minute he was on you. The L-4 is a fabric airplane and we had no protection. The floor is plywood and we had no guns. Anything will knock one of them down.

When it got to the point that we were creating so much hell with their troops, fighters began getting after us. One of the things we learned was that if you saw a fighter, you rolled it over and got down below tree level. The fighters wouldn't come after you, because they were too fast.

Then they learned that if they dropped their wheels and flaps and just started hosing us on the way down, they could get us. But there were damn few "L" pilots knocked down. Very, very few.

The trouble with flying was that we were mostly away from food. Everybody else in the flying game had a regular mess that they went to. We just sat around under the wings. I've slept many an hour under the wing of an airplane in the snow.

When you got through flying all day, then you'd try looking for your division headquarters to find out what's going on for the next day. That's called a critique. You find out where HQ is and spend half the night finding out what they were going to do so you'd know what was going to happen. You'd have to know where the front lines were and whether there would be a push or not.

I guess the worst shooting I ever did was toward the end of the war. In the Hartz Mountains there was a German regiment going up a mountain pass. I caught them in that pass, adjusted some artillery at the bottom and at the top of the pass, and then worked it up and down. It was bad news. I didn't go in there. I didn't have to go in there. There was no way they could get away. Artillery was one of the most devastating weapons ever developed the way it was used.

Normally, we just used jeep gas or anything else we came across. We'd strain it through a chamois. That was hard on the engines, but we didn't often come across aviation gas, which was what the plane was supposed to use. In the Battle of the Bulge our gasoline froze and would get ice crystals in it. When it gets very cold, the ice crystals will stop up carburetors.

We couldn't get engine temperatures up during the Battle of the Bulge. But we were the only ones flying. The Air Corps was grounded because of bad weather. When Patton was operating, the Cubs were up. He didn't care what kind of weather it was. I've flown in five-hundred-foot ceilings. You're just stuck right underneath the ceiling. At five hundred feet someone could throw a helmet through your prop.

The only time I really got scared of ground fire was once when we were given big binoculars—very powerful. On one of my first missions I was looking around for something to do. I found this German soldier in a tree. He had his rifle laying on a limb shooting right at me. I could see his whiskers, but of course nothing happened. I don't think there were any duck hunters in the German army.

I got some ground fire. When we got holes in the wings or holes in the airplane, we carried a little stick with us, like a kid's balloon stick. You'd stick it in the hole where the bullet went in and pulled it out where it came out. If the stick didn't hit anything you forgot about it.

The airplanes took lots of punishment. I've had lots of holes in the wings and the fuselage. None of them ever hit me. You got used to it, if there was such a thing.

It was against the rules to get down on the ground and go look at anything. In enemy territory you're asking for it, and I knew better. But once I came up on a little valley where my outfit was trying to pass through. They were all armored—all tanks—and were going around the perimeter of this little valley when the Germans ambushed them. They were in the middle of the valley and out came the guns. The Germans had half of our vehicles on fire when I got there.

I called for a fire mission, neutralized the German guns, and of course I went down to look. When I got low, out of the corner of my eye I saw this guy come out of the ground with a machine gun. He stitched me pretty good—twenty-eight holes in the fuselage right in back of me all the way to the tail. I never did go back in there, and I never did go back down anymore to look at anything, either.

I heard that someone had put bazookas on Cubs, so I went down to division and got a sergeant down there who knew something about bazookas to put two on the airplane. It was a little civilian airport and at the end of it was a boxcar spur. I thought, well, that would be a good target to practice on. I wanted the bazookas to cross at one hundred yards. So, of course, I demolished the boxcar. Afterward I found out that it was full of Leica cameras. I'd never looked in it.

I used the bazookas. I found an old boy plowing up a civilian airport with a mule. I suppose he figured we couldn't use it if he plowed it up, so I dove on him with my big old Cub and my two bazookas and turned them loose. I killed the mule and the man ran off.

The next time I used them I saw a German motorcycle dispatch rider going down the road. I dove on him and turned them loose again. A big old hole appeared in the road and he came walking out of it.

There was a Cub pilot, a schoolteacher—he was called Bazooka Charlie. He killed Tiger tanks with the bazooka mounted on the Cub.

I can remember landing at a little strip out of gas. The strip was surrounded by woods, and there was sniper fire all around it. This sergeant came out of the woods with three prisoners. A jeep was put out there to patrol around them, and more and more prisoners were brought in. I was sitting under the wing, hoping I didn't get hurt. The sergeant came over with these three prisoners. He had one of those big M1s.

He said, "Mind if I look at your airplane?"

"No."

We could smell the cordite from the fighting in the woods. Bad news. He looked at the airplane and said, "I wouldn't get in that thing. It looks dangerous."

I got to thinking. "Sergeant, you don't know what dangerous is. You've been fighting in these woods. Everybody's different."

I had great empathy for the GIs on the ground. I'd see them walking down the road and they'd wave at us. They'd come across a roadblock that you'd knocked out, and they knew what you had been doing. If you wanted a meal, all you had to do was stop at an infantry outfit. They'd roll out the red carpet.

I told my mother-in-law about the time I stopped and got some chow and was served on china. I didn't have a mess kit with me. I didn't pay much attention, but the guys were throwing the dishes into the ditch. This was Haviland china and we were at the Haviland factory. So instead of washing their mess kits, the guys were using that Haviland china and then throwing it away. She like to come unglued.

I hit a cable toward the last part of the war and got pretty well messed up physically. It broke me up, mostly the plumbing, and I lost a kidney. I went to Regensburg, Germany, after the crash to a German maternity hospital. As soon as a girl was moved out, one of our wounded was moved in.

Finally, I got orders to come home and I was in this damn hospital. I was more or less ambulatory and wanted to go home, so I went out and stole an airplane. People would come into the hospital and they'd leave their planes there too long, so I went out and stole one and brought it back to the outfit.

I think that it was the best job in the Army. Nobody ever had a box seat like that.

# CHAPTER 15

DAVE MASSEY, duster pilot, San Joaquin Valley

*". . . when you hit the wire, if you're fortunate enough to have
it arc in two, then you can get loose."*

Burnet to Conroe, Texas, August 18, 2000

The far shore comes up and I pull up to pattern altitude for a landing at Burnet, six miles past the lake. The Burnet municipal airport should be a prototype for all airports. It's a little gem. Clean, well maintained, and surrounded by groves of trees, it looks like a Norman Rockwell illustration. The friendly folks at the local flying service greet me with a smile, free coffee, and a courtesy car, which I probably should have used. A picnic grove sits between the hangars. I look around possessively. I'd love to fly out of a place like this, although I have no idea what the town is like.

I refuel and reluctantly climb into the cockpit. Once seated, I really don't want to leave. I lean my head back in the warm sun and take it all in. It's too bad that we can't lead five or six lives, trying different places and different lives each time. I could see spending years at this airport. Pilots of Burnet, you are lucky.

My reverie is destroyed by a twin in a hurry to fuel. He must wonder at the Stearman pilot idly sunning himself at the pumps. Sir, I am smelling the roses.

I fire up, taxi out, and slowly push the throttle forward. To get a better look at the town itself I begin a climb on up to thirty-five hundred feet. If I hadn't made the fuel stop I would still be flying quite low, still among the hills of Texas. I would have come over the town at a thousand feet and dropped back down among the folds of the earth. But I didn't and now I'm climbing.

When you climb a Stearman, you are all but blind to what is in front. There is ten feet of fuselage in front of the windshield, and the big radial engine and bottom wing pretty much blank out the forward field of view. Wise pilots make gradual S-turns during a climb and I generally do. This time I'm not doing enough of it.

Coming up on thirty-five hundred feet, I begin to level off. I roll in some forward trim and throttle back—just in time to see the gray top of a television tower come out of nowhere and glide ominously by, just under the nose. It felt like I could have reached out and touched it. Sphincter muscles crash shut. A cluster of red lights and strobes flicker malevolently at me as I slam the throttle forward and swing the airplane violently up and away, almost standing it on its tail. My mind knows that I have missed the tower, but my reactions don't. My heart is hammering. A television tower at thirty-five hundred feet! I can't believe what I'm seeing. I look at the chart accusingly. But, there it is, plainly marked. That tower is 3,124 feet high. I was probably a couple of hundred feet above it. Maybe. The terrain here is about twelve hundred feet above sea level. That tower, laid out on the ground, is almost a half a mile long. I'm sure bigger ones exist, but I've never seen them. And almost unseen is the web of cables that stretch out in all directions to support the tower. Hit one of those wires and you are history. Fly inside of the web and you are in for some rare excitement. Had I been a little slower climbing out, or leveled out lower . . . I look over every inch of my course line on the chart for more of these monsters but find none. I've had my luck for the day. For a lifetime. And a refresher course in chart reading.

# Capt. Robert Boyett, P-47 pilot
# On the Rhine, 1945

## *"My prop has stopped!"*

One morning we took off and I lost my wingman. I never did find out exactly what happened to him; he joined up on somebody else. I had another young man join up on me; it was his first mission. It was a bad day, hazy and smoky. The visibility in these combat areas was not very good with all the shellfire, smoke, and dirt.

Now, the Germans would take old vehicles, make them look good, and they'd line them up on a road under power lines to make them look like convoys. So this morning we spotted one of these convoys. We had us a convoy hemmed in and we went after it.

The pilots who had survived their first ten missions learned that the Germans did these things, and would go across the vehicles low enough so that if there were power lines, they would go under them. But my wingman had not learned this and he went through one of those power lines. There was a cable—I'd estimate at an inch and a half in diameter—that went in right above his prop hub, and the prop hub screwed it right back into the engine. It tore the top three cylinders off of the twin-row eighteen-cylinder engine. He immediately lost all of his oil.

The cowling was standing up and he was screaming, "My prop has stopped!" But really it wasn't stopped; it was just that the cowling was standing up in his face.

We immediately got him in tow and assured him that his prop was not stopped and he was still flying. We lined him up, called the base, and took him straight back. He flew about forty minutes in that old P-47 without any oil. We told him that when he went in for a landing, he wouldn't have a second chance. When he pulled the throttle back, the engine was going to seize.

He got just one shot at it. We took him in fast. The cable had gone back into the wings and had broken on the main spar on both sides, and he was trailing that big cable out the back. That's how strong the wings were on that airplane.

The end of the runway was at the Rhine River. He came in so fast that he was going to land in the river, so he pulled up and did the best hammerhead stall you ever saw; put his wheels down and landed as pretty as anything you could hope for. Of course the prop was frozen solid.

That engine would do things you couldn't believe. I've seen them with whole cylinders blown off, forty-millimeter hits in the engine and that engine would run until you pulled it back. They were some engines. The twenty-two-hundred-horsepower Pratt & Whitney eighteen-cylinder, twin-row radial.

I thought about that tower in Texas and its wires for a long time— particularly for the rest of that leg. Now I'm a zealot about those little symbols on the chart. They almost permanently cured me of low flying. Almost. The tricky thing is that sometimes towers or wires are put up and it's awhile before they show up on the charts.

Later I had a chat with a former San Joaquin Valley duster pilot, Dave Massey, about wires. Duster pilots deal with them every day. But they're a little different type than the guy wires on television and cell phone towers and are more like the telephone wires that are found on the approach end of many runways.

Wires generally break. Power lines, you've got to remember, have current going through them, so normally when you stretch the wires together they're going to arc in two. There is going to be a flash of current going through and it will pop and burn holes in the airplane, but usually it's a momentary thing. The average size power line is five-eighths of an inch in diameter. A lot of them are smaller, but if you start hitting anything above a half-inch line, you are going to have some major problems. And just the sheer weight of the power line—you don't think about it, because it's a strand of wire—but remember that you might have a quarter of a mile of wire on both sides of where you're at, and there's a tremendous amount of weight there. It's supported every 330 feet by a pole. And so between that span of poles, you've got a lot of weight of wire there. So when you hit it, it's not going to break like a thread. It's like hitting a bridge really.

What happens is that when you hit the wire, if you're fortunate enough to have it arc in two, then you can get loose. If it doesn't arc for some reason, it starts to slow you down immediately. And when it slows you down, you start coming down. It grabs ahold of the airplane in some way, wraps across the front, across the struts, wings or whatever, and it may pull you sideways, so you may have to deal with that also.

I've hit phone wires, which are usually a copper wire without much current, and those seem to be worse than a power line, because they're just like a spider web. It just grabs ahold of you, and it starts slowing you down, and you've got to put in enough force to it to break the wire. Typically what you want to do when you do hit a wire is to go to full power. Prop and throttle forward. That prop out there is your salvation. If the wire doesn't arc in two, hopefully the prop will cut it. Once you hit the wire, it's going to do damage to the airplane—I know guys who have hit wires in the Stearman where it cut the struts in half.

I've hit three sets of wires, and the thing that goes through your mind is, *Oh, shit. I wish I could have that last ten seconds over again, because I'd have done it a little different.*

You try to hit it right on the propeller, right on the crankshaft. That's your best hope of getting through it. And you bring in power. That's when you find out how big your balls are. You know what I'm saying?

Then you get to call PG&E [Pacific Gas and Electric], the repair service . . . naturally they send you a bill for it when they get it all repaired. Every man-hour, every part, every component, all the overtime that there is, and it ain't cheap. So you get to pay for all that too.

Negotiating power lines as an obstacle—it's usually easier to go under them, if there *is* room to go under. It's usually easier and safer to go under, because you haven't had to change the direction of the airplane. Any time you change the direction of the airplane, like pulling up for a power line, you've slowed the airplane down. And when you're heavy, you've got to get the nose back down to get that airspeed back, because your speed is going to continue to decay to the point where you are going to be landing out there in about three seconds.

And then there are the trees . . .

## Lt. Albert B. Nickels, P-47s
## Italy, 1945

*". . . it just rolled over and went in."*

Then there was the one I was on just before the end of the war, my seventy-fourth mission. There were aircraft all over the sky, the Germans were retreating in droves, and we all knew that it was getting close to the end of the war.

I was leading a two-ship formation, I think Ralph Crommet was with me, and we were just up there for targets of opportunity. Rover Joe [a spotter plane] gave us a target at an intersection of a highway where there was a lot of transport. We bombed that and then came around for some strafing runs. There were a bunch of motor vehicles in an olive orchard there and we began working them over.

I was making some long, low passes, and my wingman called to tell me I was getting awfully low. I told him I was aware of it, but that the plane I was flying was real heavy and mushed on pullout something terrible, so I wasn't making any steep runs.

On my fifth run something hit me. I don't know what it was, but the left side of the panel just in front of the cockpit had a hole in it, and it looked like there were flames coming from it. All this happened so fast that I didn't watch too much what I was doing. I suddenly woke up and tried to pull out, but by that time I was in the trees. I wasn't too worried yet because I had seen the Jug come back really beaten up several times. The engine seemed to be running okay, and I had hopes of flying home.

But it was evidently too beat up and when the nose came up the plane rolled over . . . I had no control . . . I tried everything in the world. I even cut throttle, gave it full throttle in those few seconds that elapsed in there, but it just rolled over and went in. I was upside down when I hit, and I don't know how I survived. The good Lord knows, maybe, but I don't.

You can imagine how fast I was going, because when you put the nose of a P-47 down, you're doing three hundred real quick. Anyway I went in, and I never had any idea I would ever come out of it alive when it rolled over on its back and headed for the ground.

After all the noise and confusion of the crash, I tried to assess my physical condition, but I couldn't see! Apparently, the force of the crash caused the blood vessels in my eyes to rupture, and I could see nothing but light and dark. In looking out of the cockpit and back in, I could see the difference, but I couldn't distinguish anything.

I could feel the warmth of a fire and also found that I couldn't unlock the seat belt. I could feel that the canopy was no longer there and knew that if I could just get free from the belt, I might be able to get out of the plane. I was wedged in kind of a real crouched position.

Something from the back had pushed the seat and me forward, so I was bent over without much room to move. I couldn't get my hands between my legs and my chest, so I thought maybe I could take my knife and cut the belt, but my knife had been torn out of its scabbard in the crash.

I thought, then, that I might use my forty-five to shoot the bolt on the side of the seat, but the gun was gone too. It was probably a good thing, because I might have shot myself! I finally reached under my legs and between them to reach the release.

When that happened, I just fell out of the cockpit and hit the ground. The impact was pure agony and I wanted to stay there and get my breath, but the heat was getting pretty bad, so I rolled away.

I couldn't walk, so all movement from then on was rolling. I would roll a bit, and the pain in my chest and back was so intense that I would just have to stop. Then the fire would get hotter and I would roll some more.

I finally got pretty far away and I sensed that I was probably in a row of trees, because there was grass and leaves all around me.

It was probably an hour later that I heard some voices. Before this, I had been trying to see what was around me so that I might be able to hide or something, but though I was gradually regaining some sight, I still couldn't distinguish things enough to tell where I was. I did try and pull some grass and put it over me, but it was a futile effort.

When I heard the voices, I moved and immediately heard a shot. My head lifted off the ground, because the bullet had creased my temple that was laying on the ground, and that caused my head to bounce upward. Blood spurted out and there was another shot.

I felt the blood from the first shot and thought, *Well, I guess I'm dead and just don't know it yet.*

The Germans left; then as time went on, I got a little better and I could see a little more . . . but still just a little more than light and dark.

Sometime later . . . how can you tell time when you can't see your watch . . . I could hear some more German voices. Well, my folks were from Germany and I could speak the language pretty fluently, so I called out to them, asking them to take me to a hospital. One of them came up to me and said they were not able to take care of their own wounded, much less an American! He said they were in full retreat with nothing but the things they were able to carry on their backs. They were going home! He did stay, however, to bandage me a little from my first aid kit on my parachute strap and take everything I had on me that was worth anything.

He turned and walked away about ten feet or so, then turned and shot twice in my direction. He evidently shot over my head on purpose. I guess to make the noise so he could tell his comrades that he had shot me. I was lucky that he was just regular army instead of being an SS trooper, or I would surely have been killed.

From then on I began to think I just might survive. I was beginning to see shadowy forms and could tell it was getting toward evening. The flight had taken place on the twenty-sixth of April and we had taken off just about noon on the mission, so I had been out there for several hours.

While I was lying there, it was amazing . . . I could hear the constant drone of airplanes from every direction. The amount of firepower that was going off was unbelievable. The ground fire shooting at the planes was constant, and I just couldn't imagine our planes being able to fly through all of that without getting shot down.

Just before dark I heard some Italian voices nearby. I learned later that it was an Italian farmer and his son, who had come by expecting to find my body but found me instead. They had a bicycle and they put a board between the seat and the handlebars, lifted me up, and put me on it. My feet kept falling off the board, and with what I found out later to be five broken ribs, a dislocated ankle, a broken arm, and internal injuries, the ride was anything but pleasant. They took me across a plowed field in that condition!

They took me into a farmhouse and up a circular stairway into a small room in the attic and put me into a nice bed. There was a skylight there, and I could tell I was able to see better as time went on. They couldn't speak English and I, no Italian, so it was all hand signs and point-ing. I was able to learn, however, that they would leave me there until it was good and dark and then take me somewhere else.

Then we heard German voices and the Italians left hurriedly to go downstairs. I heard a lot of noise and some screaming, and in about thirty minutes they came back in. Later on one of the people taking care of me told me that the Germans had kicked one of the female family members who was pregnant, because the family would not tell if they had seen or helped the American pilot. I have often wondered if that lady lost her child.

In another thirty minutes or so, they came after me again and put me in a cart and piled straw on top. That's how I went from the farm-house to the nearby town. I don't remember the name of that town, but it was near Modena. The man climbed up front and here we went, down the road. I experienced again the pain of bouncing around with all my injuries, but at least I felt I was getting somewhere. I was getting to see better and better.

They carried me into a church and down into the basement, which they had converted into a makeshift hospital. They laid me onto a hospi-tal bed. By this time I was getting very dehydrated and kept asking for "aqua," "aqua" . . . *water, water!* They gave me wine instead, and that stuff had springs on it, because it would hit bottom and come right back up. In a few minutes the doctor came by and announced that he would take care of me. He was Greek and had been captured by the Germans several years before. He wasn't a "human" doctor; he was a veterinar-ian. I didn't complain, however, and he took good care of me. He told me that the water was contaminated, so wine was better for me. He said he had no equipment but would do his best to keep me comfort-able. It's a wonder I didn't die from dehydration before I finally was able to get some decent water.

One interesting and sad thing, really, was that there was a girl—a nurse, I guess—who arrived shortly after I got there, and who stayed with me all the time I was there. She could speak a few words of English, and she pointed out my hospital "roommates," on either side. They were both German. One was in a coma and the other was out of his head. She said they had others in the hospital, too. I was in there, as well as I remember, for the second day when the veterinarian came run-ning in to tell me that an English major had come to town, quite by mistake, and they were trying to get him to come to the hospital. He did come but said he was lost and not sure that he would be able to get back to his unit and that I might be worse off with him than if I stayed right where I was. He promised to report my presence there if, and when, he got back.

Sure enough, they did come the next day to pick me up in a "meat wagon." They explained that on the way up there they had encountered some partisans, and one of them had been shot up pretty bad, so they would be stopping there on the way back to pick him up.

Meanwhile, the lady who had been taking care of me insisted on accompanying me in the ambulance. She had been with me every second of the time since I had come to the hospital, and really tried to take care of me. There was lots of conversation in Italian, but they could not get her to leave the ambulance. Finally, one of the technicians broke her loose from her hold on me and bodily threw her out of the vehicle. She fell face first to the ground, and they slammed the doors shut and took off. I hated to see that, and I wish she could have gone along. It really did irk me, but there was nothing I could do.

We got out of town and were heading for the place where they were going to pick up the partisan when all of a sudden there was lots of shooting, and some of the bullets went through the ambulance. They got to the point where they were to pick up the wounded man, but he wouldn't get in without his gun, his hand grenades, ammo, and everything with him. They argued and finally got him into the vehicle just as the Jerrys started shooting again.

When we finally got back to friendly territory, we had about fifteen bullet holes in the ambulance. I did find out that there was a dike on both sides of the road and that the Germans probably could only see the top of the vehicle as it sped along the road, and the bullets all went through the top part, missing all of us lower down.

We finally got to the first aid station in about two and one-half hours, and they put me in a back room, where they started taking x-rays. I heard them saying that they probably couldn't do much for me. They thought I wouldn't make it, but I got better.

The next day, they put me on another ambulance and took me into Florence, Italy, and there I got excellent treatment. I guess I was there a week or more and I continued to get better. I still couldn't write, so I got someone there to send a cable to my folks saying that I was alive. I found out later that they got the cable on Mother's Day.

# CHAPTER 16

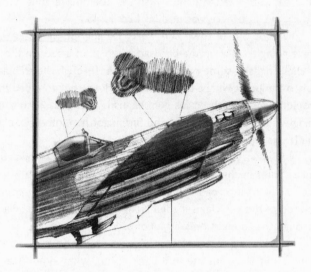

CAPT. JOSEPH C. PIMENTEL, Spitfire pilot, France, 1944

*"You ought to see what happens when you send a tracer
bullet through a hydrogen-filled balloon!"*

Conroe to Hammond, Louisiana, August 20, 2000

Montgomery County Airport in Conroe, Texas, is another idyllic garden airport. Carved out of a grove of tall pines, the two big, diverging runways are separated by acres of lush grass. The airport more resembles a park or a meadow, and I'd love to land on the grass, but I'm afraid of surprises ("Oh, you didn't know about the sprinklers?"). The Stearman was designed to be flown off of sod and is not all that comfortable on a hard surface. On sod, if this aircraft touches down slightly crabbed relative to its direction of flight, it simply skids for a while until the drag of the tail wheel pulls it straight. Sod is very forgiving. On a hard surface, unless the aircraft is perfectly aligned, there is a lot of lurching around and heavy use of the rudder and tail wheel as the pilot seeks to straighten the aircraft out. If the crab angle is too much, the big ground loop will follow shortly.

Some of the Kate, Val, and Zero replicas from the 1970 movie *Tora, Tora, Tora* are based at Montgomery, and one of these hulking Val replicas sits incongruously in the tie-down area among the dainty Cessnas, looking like Jesse Ventura attending a preschool. A stroll through one of the big hangars reveals a few AT-6s and a MiG-15. Tragically a big hangar fire in 1994 consumed many valuable aircraft, including a number of World War II types.

The buildings here are new and well maintained, the line folks friendly and helpful. I leave shaking my head. The airport that I fly out of in Southern California, Whiteman Airport, by comparison more resembles a mining operation/RV storage lot overlaid with a faint bouquet of industrial pollution. It is a depressingly ugly airport with only one merit: convenience to my home.

It's a damp hazy morning and I look at the Stearman in embarrassment. The fabric covering on the fuselage is rippled from the morning humidity. It looks like a really bad fabric job, and maybe it is, although I am told that the looseness is a good thing. It seems that if put on tight, the cotton covering on the fuselage will continue to shrink over time, and when it does, it will bow the stringers. (Stringers are the lengthwise supports that help give the fuselage its shape.) Keeping it loose like this will guarantee that the stringers won't distort. I've seen airplanes where this has happened, and I suppose the loose fabric is the lesser of the two evils. When there is no moisture present, the fuselage fabric is drum taut and beautiful.

I fire up, taxi out, and take my choice of runways. There is no wind and there is no traffic, so it's my call. I pick runway one-four, throttle up, and the Stearman leaps into the air. This airplane loves to be near sea level on cool moist mornings with the thick air. Although the moisture makes the air less dense, the engine thrives on it. It's a poor man's water injection. This is nothing like the Las Cruces takeoff.

The moisture in the air has a penalty, however, and although the sky is without a cloud, visibility is severely limited. I'm still flying east, of course, and looking into the morning sun as I get to altitude, there is no visible horizon. I find myself flying into an impenetrable white haze. I can see down and to the rear, but straight ahead is marginal. I can still navigate, but I see landmarks only when I pass over them. Keeping the wings level without a horizon is very difficult. I'm not in danger of falling out of the sky, but I'm doing a lot of wandering.

If I could see a horizon, the wings would be instinctively held level and I would remain on course. Without the horizon I'm constantly dropping a wing, making a shallow turn, and losing the course line. I should really be on the gauges. For a while I try the old trick of positioning the sun to help hold a heading, but this works only until the sun rises and is blocked by my top wing. Then I have an inspiration.

The sun is now in the eleven-o'clock-high position, and I notice that it leaves bright, hard sunball highlight reflections on the stainless steel flying wires, the kind one instinctively avoids looking at. I reason that if I can stop the highlights from moving up and down the wires, the airplane won't be turning and I'll be able to hold my heading. The highlights are very touchy, instantly responding to any movement of the airplane, but it works beautifully. I can also use the shadows cast on the lower wing by the flying wires, struts, and stays. Hold them in place with the stick and the airplane is not turning. This feels much more effective than chasing the magnetic compass. I amuse myself with my homemade artificial horizons and wonder how many other biplane pilots have ever noticed these things. Probably many, but there aren't many biplane pilots to pass the word along, so these things must be rediscovered. I fly these highlights and shadows all the way to my fuel stop in Opelousas, Louisiana.

I love the names that I'm starting to see on the chart. The Neches, Sabine, Calcasieu, and Atchafalaya Rivers. Opelousas, Saint Landry Parish, Chataignier, and Basile. Gone are the "El-this" and "Santa-that" of the West.

Nearing New Orleans, something very odd happens. As I approach the north shore of Lake Pontchartrain from the land, I change my mind about the destination for the day. I had intended to land at Slidel, which is just east of New Orleans, but I had been hearing traffic from Hammond, a little town about thirty miles north of New Orleans, and thought that it might make a better destination. I'm already slightly past Hammond when I make this decision, and I have to bury my head in the cockpit with a chart to figure out a new course. After perhaps too long a spell of chart reading, I glance out of the cockpit and see nothing but a pale whiteness everywhere. I am solid IFR [Instrument Flight Rules]. No ground, no sky, no right, left, up, or down. I am even too startled to use my highlight and shadow technique. At first I think I have flown into a cloud, but the color isn't quite right. The airplane is not yet making any noises of protest, which is good, so I simply strain to catch a glimpse of something. My white world remains unchanging, so I begin to ease into that traditional maneuver that is the airman's friend, the 180-degree turn. I use the shallowest of banks, not wishing to disturb things too much. My blind flying instruments consist of the basics, a needle, ball, and an airspeed indicator. The needle is an air-powered antique that I wouldn't trust to taxi with, but I sense that we are about to become good friends. Although I am instrument rated, my currency is almost as old as this airplane, and I don't want this to become a refresher flight. As the ship begins to turn, far to my rear I can faintly see the receding shoreline of the lake, and I instantly rack the airplane back around in that direction.

The problem is that I have flown out over the lake, and in my hazy-day horizonless world, the lake, which is quite large, is the same color as the sky. In fact, it is a reflection of the sky, so there is no perceptible up or down. "Spatial disorientation" is the term for this phenomenon, and it can be very spooky. It can be experienced at night over the desert or anyplace where lights on the ground are sparse enough to look like stars in the sky and there is absolutely no other light, such as moonlight or the glow of a city. I've never experienced it in the daytime, however. Later that day, while talking to one of the local duster pilots, I related the phenomenon, and he smiled knowingly and shook his head. It is apparently well known in the area. He pointed to a legend printed on the New Orleans chart, which read: CAUTION: BE PREPARED FOR LOSS OF HORIZONTAL REFERENCE AT LOW ALTITUDE OVER LAKE DURING HAZY CONDITIONS AND AT NIGHT. (I'm going to have to pay a lot more attention to these charts.)

"Yep, there are a fair number of airplanes sitting on the bottom of that lake. You were fortunate to have caught that glimpse of the shore."

But I'm not the first. Navigating in low visibility and near instrument conditions has always been a trial for pilots. This is how one P-47 squadron in Normandy dealt with it.

# Capt. Joseph C. Pimentel, P-47 pilot, France, 1944

## *"When we had instrument conditions, we had nothing but bad news."*

In Normandy, once the invasion beachheads had been secured, we operated out of an airstrip the engineers had dug out of an apple orchard, which was of a sorely limited usable length. The P-47 with a full load of fuel, a couple of five-hundred-pound bombs, and the ammunition for those eight .50-caliber machine guns needed all the runway it could get for takeoff. The airstrip had barely enough.

Some of us had evolved a takeoff procedure to suit. We'd get to the end of the runway, one at a time, pour on takeoff power, full throttle, and lift the tail off while we stood on the brakes. When everything reached a steady state with maximum power, we'd let go of the brakes and get the dear bird staggering off the ground as early as possible and out of that orchard with its load. We would then most often collect into two-plane elements for the combat mission run.

The reason I am going on in detail about this is to describe the manner in which we were obliged to operate out of Normandy, owing to the limitations brought on by temporary airport facilities, proximity of enemy forces, poor weather, and unfavorable terrain. Later we were able to enjoy operating out of fully developed airfields once the Luftwaffe had been kicked out, places such as Le Mans, Chartres, and finally Paris and Rheims. Thanks to our airstrip's apple orchard camouflage plus the presence of a line of low hills, during bad weather or low light conditions the problem of getting home and finding our airstrip could be spooky.

The P-47 was great to fly, either on contact flying or on instruments, assuming that you had well-defined instrument conditions, and plenty of altitude. Unfortunately, those conditions were seldom present during fall and winter months of 1944 in Normandy. When we had instrument conditions, we had nothing but bad news and we had to fly anyway. The worst of it all was coming home in, say, a thunderstorm with freezing conditions outside. We might have an airplane with an engine misfiring, or an airplane with damaged control surfaces, or both. We'd be struggling along and anxious to get home. We'd know that the field was somewhere near but have to be careful when letting down, because we might run into something such as one of those hills.

But just as bad—and maybe worse than that—were the British barrage balloons on their invasion beachheads, code-named Gold and Juno. The Yanks at Omaha and Utah had adopted the practice of pulling their balloons down so that they were always just below the bottom of the overcast, hence visible, unless attacked by enemy aircraft. In the event of an attack, the balloons were allowed to run up into the clouds. The British *always* ran their balloons up to the limit of their cables' length, which was about five hundred feet, and if the balloons disappeared into the soup, so much the better, no matter who may be flying up there.

Of course this practice was very discouraging to the Luftwaffe, but it was also a pain in the neck to us. We had figured out a procedure for letting down in foul weather, over the channel waters, to a level at which we could at least see the surface. We could then locate the Cherbourg Peninsula and follow the coastline clear around if necessary, until we found a certain little inlet, which led directly inland to our airstrip. We could find our way under the soup at four hundred feet, going three hundred miles per hour, see that cove, drive in, and find home.

But you had to get around the balloons first. We finally lost an airplane to one of those goddamn Limey balloon cables. The kid fortunately didn't get killed. The kid was lucky. He only cut off a three- or four-foot piece of the wing and managed to land the P-47, gear up, at T-1. It was just a pile of junk, of course. T-1 was a dirt strip just above Omaha Beach. It was the first airstrip bulldozed as a consequence of the invasion effort for emergency and wounded evacuation purposes. That airstrip was already well littered with wrecked aircraft of many types when our second lieutenant made his crash landing.

I happened to be the only one in the outfit who spoke any French, much less British English, so I was elected as spokesman to somehow go and get those balloons pulled down. I was told to take a jeep and drive over to the Caen estuary, where most of the British balloons were situated. Caen was the name of a critically designated French town that the British had yet to capture. The Caen estuary was absolutely lined with Limey balloons, and it was a really poisonous place to try to get past under bad weather conditions.

I was ordered to go over there and negotiate an adoption by the British of a procedure with their balloons, similar to that being followed by the Americans; that is, to hold the balloons down beneath the overcast unless attacked by enemy air, at which time of course run them up into the clouds. It made so much more sense.

I finally found myself talking to a beefy red-faced Limey artillery officer in charge of their balloons. This man clearly despised aviators, particularly American ones. Of course he didn't enhance my views of the British either. The upshot of my trip was altogether negative. The British view was to stay with their existing methods, and the worse the weather, the better. I had to come home with my tail between my legs, having failed miserably.

Then, not long after my effort, one day an RAF Spitfire appeared in our airspace. It had been shot up rather badly and had taken a slug or two in the engine coolant system. And the pilot did not know where he was. His Merlin engine overheated and finally quit running, so he had to land somewhere or bail out. He chose the former; he had spotted our airstrip. We were all off on a mission, so there were no airplanes visible on the ground, and that British pilot thought it might well be a German field. He landed on our strip, wheels up, and let the Spitfire scoot clear off of the end of our runway and into the dirt and trees. He jumped out of that airplane and ran off into the orchard beyond, disappearing without a trace. He just left his airplane and ran. We never did find that pilot; he might still be in those nearby hills. [He laughs.]

Well, you can imagine what a bunch of GI mechanics will do with an untended flying machine suddenly delivered onto their doorstep, gear up or not. We were still going off and doing our missions, but it wasn't long at all before our line chief had that Spitfire back up on its feet again, with a restored Merlin engine installed, bullet holes patched, and the prop ticking over.

The mechanics had painted all of the markings off of the Spit, and my C.O., a major named Mitt Evans, said, "That's *my* airplane. Nobody else gets to touch it."

He did fly the Spit. Well, it wasn't long before I beat Mitt Evans in a five-card draw poker game and won half-interest ownership in that Mark IX Spitfire. It had four twenty-millimeter cannons in the wings, similar to the armament that the German fighters used, and he and I had a lot of fun learning how to shoot with that lovely, lively, Limey fighter! That's the way it worked out for Major Mitt and me. We were good friends, except when we played poker.

I now had half interest in the Spit, so I went out like he had been doing on target-of-opportunity sweeps, just shooting at any swastika that showed up. I soon learned to love that marvelous English machine—so much different from the P-47.

Then one day I was coming home from one of those sweeps in the Spit, just rocking along with my head in the clouds right below the soup. That way, if you got jumped, you could pull right up into the cloud deck and disappear. It happened that I was just over the maximum reach of those British balloon cables, and suddenly there the balloons were, all stuck at the top of their cables, right in front of my airplane! I said to myself, *"Oh shit!" Look at this!"* and I ducked back up into the soup. I did a 180, went back about five miles, then let down again. [He laughs.] Here is this British Spitfire, no markings on it, heading toward their nest of balloons. I armed the guns. It was then that I learned, to my vast delight, that the British inflated their balloons with hydrogen rather than helium such as ours used. You ought to see what happens when you send a tracer bullet through a hydrogen-filled balloon! They blossom! What a reward!

The Englishmen sent out armed patrols all over the Normandy peninsula trying to find out who the hell had done that, because they knew that it wasn't the Germans and they knew that they were missing a Spitfire. They actually knew damn good and well who did it, but they couldn't prove it unless they found the airplane.

So we had to get rid of that Spitfire. We heard all kinds of warnings from our own higher echelons. I'm pretty sure that everybody upstairs knew what had gone on, but nobody pushed it or tried to prove it.

Anyway, we did get rid of that Spitfire, but we didn't destroy it. We landed it at a Canadian airstrip. Mitt and I did that one day. I flew a C-64 Noorduyn Norseman and Mitt flew the Spit. He landed it, parking it far out at the end of the runway. I landed the C-64 behind Mitt, picked him up, and we left the scene. We had no more trouble with those barrage balloons, by the way.

On the ground in Hammond I begin to tie the airplane down. Trying to get a feeling for the local weather patterns, I ask the lineman if it rained much around these parts. I was beginning to pick up the lingo.

"Hasn't rained in three months" he replies. "We're having a drought here."

So, to my later chagrin, I resist the temptation to put the Stearman in the nice snug hangar just a few feet away.

The car rental agencies are closed (it's Sunday), but I catch a ride to town, check in to a motel, and go to the restaurant next door for lunch. After about an hour and a half, I step outside to be greeted by an angry black sky, laced with lightning. The next half hour is spent on frantic phone calls to the airport and various cab companies as I watch the storm build in intensity. The rain is nearly horizontal, and I can hear the beat of hail. I get back to the airport to find the Stearman serenely sitting on its wheels, a light sprinkling on its wings. It had hardly rained there at all, but the thundershower had blown down trees all over town. The Stearman immediately went into the hangar.

Southern hospitality is not an exaggeration. Within twenty-four hours of landing at Hammond, I had been offered free hangar space and a ride to town, been introduced to a Mustang pilot for an interview, and been invited to spend an afternoon at one of the nicest airports I have ever seen. (They just kept getting better.) Covington Vincent airfield is about fifteen miles east of Hammond, well off the beaten path and carved out of a Louisiana pine forest. It is a grass strip, thirty-seven hundred feet long, and about as countrified as an airport can be. It is cooperatively owned among ten pilots, who take turns mowing the strip, clearing the brush that constantly threatens to take over the runway, and generally doing whatever it takes to keep the airport safe. There are a half a dozen hangars and shelters spotted on the property as well as a large general maintenance shed, an air-conditioned pilot's lounge, and an official airport dog. It is the quintessential country airport. There has never been a theft of any kind and only one accident—a doctor who landed long, stood on the brakes, and plowed into the trees at one end. He survived; the plane did not. In the telling of the tale, the man's occupation was deemed to be important. Doctors, for some reason, get more than their share of abuse in aviation and are notorious for flying equipment that is beyond their ability to manage.

The Stearman over the Santa Clara River, fifteen miles from the Pacific Ocean and Mira Loma Flight Academy (Oxnard, California), where it all started for this airplane in 1941. Although delivered in the traditional Army Air corps blue and yellow paint, by the war's end it had been painted all silver as shown, probably after one of its major repairs. Photo courtesy of Robert M. Brown

On the ground at Mira Loma (Oxnard) it sits on the same ramp and in front of the same military hangar it occupied during the war. Its days at this field have been eventful and have included a taxi accident, a ground loop which took its wings off, a bird strike (actually many birds), and a partial engine failure on take off. In spite of all of this Arthur Fiedler, who has nine Germans and at least one Stearman kill to his credit, is about to go for his first Stearman ride since primary flight training 58 years ago.
Author's collection

*Air Cadet*
*James I. Longan, 1942*
U.S. Army photo

| MODEL PT-13B | | | | | | SERIAL NUMBER 41-806 | | | | |
|---|---|---|---|---|---|---|---|---|---|---|
| c-13244 COST **$7,129** | | DATE RECEIVED 3-10-41 | | | | MANUFACTURER Stearman Division | | | | |
| DATE DROPPED | | | | | | REASON | | | | |

| DATE | | AGE | FLYING TIME | | | | | | TRANSFERRED | | | REMARKS |
|---|---|---|---|---|---|---|---|---|---|---|---|---|
| F.Y. | C MO. | | THIS MONTH HOURS | T | SINCE LAST DEPOT WORK HOURS | T | SINCE FIRST COMMISSIONED HOURS | T | TO | DATE SHIPPED RECD | AUTHORITY | |
| 1 | 3 | | 3 | | | | | | Santa Maria, Calif. | 3/13/41 | | Wrecked 1/5/42 |
| 1 | 3 | | 33 | 5 | | | | | | | | Oxnard Airport, |
| 1 | 3 | 1 | 36 | 5 | 36 | 5 | 36 | 5 | Oxnard | 3-18-41 8-41-916 | | Kelly E Kimes A/C |
| 1 | 4 | | 85 | 1 | | | | | | | | Taxiing Accident |
| 1 | 4 | 2 | 85 | 1 | 121 | 6 | 121 | 6 | | | | Rep. J.H. |
| 1 | 5 | | 118 | 2 | | | | | | | | |
| 1 | 5 | 3 | 118 | 2 | 239 | 8 | 239 | 8 | | | | Wrecked 5-13-42. |
| 1 | 6 | | 91 | 3 | | | | | | | | Oxnard, Calif. |
| 1 | 6 | 4 | 91 | 3 | 331 | 1 | 331 | 1 | | | | A/C, James I. Lon |
| 2 | 7 | | 88 | 2 | | | | | | | | gan. Ground loop |
| 2 | 7 | 5 | 88 | 2 | 419 | 3 | 419 | 3 | | | | ed upon landing. |
| 2 | 8 | | 78 | 0 | | | | | | | | Rep. AF |
| 2 | 8 | 6 | 78 | 0 | 497 | 3 | 497 | 3 | | | | |
| 2 | 9 | | 82 | 5 | | | | | | | | |
| 2 | 9 | 7 | 82 | 5 | 579 | 8 | 579 | 8 | | | | |
| 2 | 10 | | 64 | 2 | | | | | | | | |
| 2 | 10 | 8 | 64 | 2 | 644 | 0 | 644 | 0 | | | | |
| 2 | 11 | | 49 | 7 | | | | | | | | |
| 2 | 11 | 9 | 49 | 7 | 693 | 7 | 693 | 7 | | | | |
| 2 | 12 | | 87 | 2 | | | | | | | | |
| 2 | 12 | 10 | 87 | 2 | 780 | 9 | 780 | 9 | Glendale Cal.Aero Trng.Corp. | 1-14-42 | | |
| 2 | 1 | | 34 | 7 | | | | | | | | |
| 2 | 1 | 11 | 34 | 7 | 815 | 6 | 815 | 6 | Oxnard, Cal. | 1-24-42 | | |
| 2 | 2 | | 93 | 4 | | | | | | | | |
| 2 | 3 | 12 | 934 | | 1406 9090 | | 9090 | | | | | |
| 2 | 3 | 13 | 1406 63 | | 9153 | | 9153 | | | | | |
| 2 | 3 | | 151 | 0 | | | | | | | | |
| 2 | 4 | 14 | 151 | 0 | 1066 | 3 | 1066 | 3 | | | | |

*The aircraft records for Stearman 41-806. The notations for Kelly Kimes's and Jim Longan's crashes are in the right-hand column. In the upper left-hand corner is the price of the aircraft, from Boeing; $7,129 without the engine. With the engine, prop, and various options it came to $12,291.*

Greg Horrell and his MiG-17 project. The former F-16 crew chief is helping to breath new life into this beautiful old fighter. The other side of the aircraft is covered with Cyrillic messages from Russian Air Force generals who visit the area to confirm U.S. compliance with the SALT treaty. They came to visit when they heard that there was a MiG-17 near-by. Greg's hospitality knew no bounds. I responded by flying away with his hangar key!
Author's collection

The American Airpower Heritage Museum in Midland, Texas. I couldn't have found a nicer hangar for the week I spent there. The Stearman is being sheltered by an RAF Shackleton bomber and a Curtis C-46 Comando transport.
Author's collection

*Cavite Naval Base, Phillipine Islands, 1944. The bombs are just begining to fall on the newest landlords, the Imperial Japanese Navy, as the B-24s from the 5th Bombardment Group, including the* Red Headed Woman *pay it a visit. The area is densely built up with shops, jetties and hangars.*
U.S. Army photo

*The result: total destruction. The only thing left standing is a pair of hangars and a sea-plane (without its wings) parked on the apron in the outlined area.*
U.S. Army photo

*Ordered to take out the seaplane and its hangars on the next mission, they did just that from 12,500 feet. The large urban area to the extreme right received very little damage.*
U.S. Army photo

*Bill Blair, co-pilot on the B-24,* Red Headed Woman. *The rest of the crew is pictured on the cover of this book.*
Photo courtesy of Bill Blair

Bennettsville, South Carolina. A much decorated Frank Rogers flew Wildcats, then the Hellcats of VF-16 off of the U.S.S. Lexington in the South Pacific and accounted for many Japanese aircraft. He came back to South Carolina and bought himself a Stearman for $851.00 from a fleet of war-wearies at Palmer Field where it had been stationed. He flew it for four years, then sold it in 1950 to a duster outfit for a dollar less than he paid for it. Here's his bird, back to visit him fifty-one years later —a mile away from the now-closed Palmer Field.
Author's collection

Marianna, Florida — forty minutes after I landed and twenty minutes after a violent storm roared through. I had only one tiedown secured as the storm hit and almost lost the airplane as the winds tried to blow it into the fuel truck. Four hours later, a hail storm hit and the winds ripped the cockpit cover but caused no other damage. There were no hangars available here and no time to fly it out.
Author's collection

Hawthorne, in Orangeburg, South Carolina, lent a further international flavor to Stearman 41-806. The airplane trained American, Royal Air Force, and Free French pilots. The site is now a retirement village without a trace of its former use. Four of the eight bases that the aircraft was stationed at are gone. Hawthorn was run by Bevo Howard, a six time World Aerobatic Champion. Author's collection

*A graduating class at Hawthorne. One instructor at this base, frustrated by the language problem, carried a rolled up newspaper and instructed from the rear seat. If the student made a mistake he was swatted with the paper. Could that be my airplane in the background?* U.S. Army photo

*Joe Pimentel,
Thunderbolt, Spitfire, and
L-4 pilot, barrage balloon buster
(probably one of the first since
Frank Luke), Black Forest tree
trimmer, and, of late, cattle
rancher.*
Photo courtesy of Joseph C. Pimentel

*Captain Pimentel on his way to work in 1944.*    Photo courtesy of Joseph C. Pimentel

*Air Cadet Everett Farnham with all of about sixty flying hours. "We would . . . turn the Stearman over and do a 'split S' down into the pattern." After primary training his next flight in a Stearman would be done sixty years later while sitting on a bag of laundry in the bucket seat of 41-806 (I didn't have a seat cushion). It didn't faze him a bit. These guys were tough.*
Photo courtesy of Everett Farnham

*Lake Okeechobee, Florida, is off of the left wingtip. It is dawn, August 28, 2001, and I am heading south towards Clewiston, Florida. The Atlantic Ocean is another eighty miles further. There is nothing quite as impressive as a sunrise through the wings of an old biplane.* Author's collection

*Everett Farnham and his P-38. He had 240 hours and no multi-engine training when he arrived in North Africa (Berteoux, Tunisia) and was told to go check out in a war-weary P-38 or be assigned to P-39s on coastal patrol. The P-39 tour was not considered a combat assignment and the aircraft were little more than moving targets for the Germans so the choice was clear. At first more wary of the P-38 than of the German aircraft hunting him, he grew to appreciate the virtues of the aircraft. He flew it 750 hours and came to consider it the "Cadillac" of fighters.*
Photo courtesy of Everett Farnham

*Air Cadet Joe Pimentel at Rankin Field in Tulare, California, in front of his Stearman. Before his training was done he had managed a bail out from an AT-6 at Luke Field when the instructor let a five turn spin go flat. Almost sixty years later at a Rankin and Sequoia Field reunion he was up once again in a Stearman as a handful of these aircraft and Vultees showed up to hop the "old, bold" pilots of World War II. He still flies a cub off of his ranch.*
Photo coutesy of Joseph C. Pimentel

*Sights like this were common in local airport boneyards during the '60s and '70s as the Stearman and other World War II aircraft were left out to rot. Most of the boneyards are gone and what is left of these aircraft have been or are being painstakingly restored. An entire cottage industry has grown up around the Stearman aircraft and, amazingly, most parts are readily available.*
Author's collection

2 Dec.    COL    LTR    CHALL      POINT         MAG

⑪                                          N    E    COURSE    MILES    TIME

01 – 07                                A  Lake Varano    315-°    168

07 – 13      RG    B    H      B  Badia         332°     385

13 – 19      RR    P    I      C  IP Chiusa     282°     16

        98  Roosevelt I  EXCEED.  D  Target      225°     15

BOMBER  376  Roosevelt II    " II

FIGHTER  Stapley    HEADTOP    E  M. Biovo River   138°    95

F TO F  Cowtail              F  Lake Varano   152°    290

CHANNEL   B                  G  Base          135-°    168

TAKEOFF  0820                                          1137

ON COURSE  0850              Foggia           202°     30
RENDEZVOUS  0940

TARGET TIME

Escort 36 B-24's to bomb M/Y at Bolzano, Italy.
We were attacked by about 35 109's & 190's. Houtz &
Judd each got a 109.

Dec. 2, 1943

*These are "flimsies," or notes taken at mission briefings. Courses to target, mileage, call signs, frequencies, and rendezvous times are all included. They made a tasty snack if capture was imminent. Everett Farnham kept all of his flimsies, one for each of his 54 P-38 missions in Italy, Germany, and Yugoslavia. What a journal!* Courtesy of Everett Farnham

*At 1,500 feet over South Carolina on the way to Chattanooga. Although the flight was done during August and September and in the south, a good leather jacket is "de rigueur." You never knew when a climb to 8,500 feet or higher would become necessary to get over clouds and it is ALWAYS cold at those altitudes. Here I am, an unsuspecting innocent, about one hour away from some very nasty weather and scud running.* Author's collection

*The Chattanooga terminal, looking for all the world like Monticello, is just over the wing. The ground crew at the Jet Center here couldn't believe that the aircraft was built by Boeing. The airport and city were nice and friendly as was the next stop on the trip, Savannah, Tennessee. How often does an airport manager offer to make you breakfast?* Author's collection

This Sherman tank is the gate guard next to the runway at Connie Edwards ranch. It watches over a wonderful collection of World War II and other exotic aircraft including a clutch of German/Spanish Messerschmitt 109s and HA-1112s. Author's collection

Visible behind the Stearman is one of the two Catalina flying boats kept inside this very large hangar. There were at least four or five other vintage Grumman amphibian types here on this Texas airstrip. Author's collection

Connie Edwards himself: a charming, knowledge-able and hospitable Texan. His comment on the Stearman was, "It's a beauty but you must have the sorest ass in the world." Author's collection

# CHAPTER 17

LT. (j.g.) HARVEY LIVELY, USN, USS *Fanshaw Bay,*
fifty miles east of Samar Island, 1944
*"They want you to go out and bomb the Jap fleet."*

Hammond to Bay Minette, Alabama, August 25, 2000

I arrive at Hammond airport at 7:00 A.M., and the Louisiana humidity is way up. The fuselage fabric is rippled again this morning from the moisture, even though the airplane is in a hangar. I'm well and truly in the South now. Embarrassed, even though absolutely no one is around, I quickly roll the Stearman outside into the sunlight, which soon heats, dries, and tautens the fabric.

I feel like saying, "Okay, world, now you may look at my idiot child airplane. She dribbles her oil a bit and her fabric is rippled, but in the sun she shapes right up." I'm fastidious about the airplane, and it bothers me to see it like that. Unfortunately, there is nothing that I can do about it short of recovering the fuselage. The wings don't share the problem, because the fabric is stitched securely every inch and a half to each wing rib. The wing is a work of art. On opening the wing inspection panels, one is greeted by a hidden spiderweb of lacing that holds the cotton fabric in place. Some fabric airplanes are cursed by wing fabric that balloons upward between the ribs while in flight. Not these. These wings are perfect. You win some, you lose some.

I load up my gear, do my preflight, run up, and am soon in the air talking to Gulfport Approach, where I request flight following. I'm about to enter an area that is thick with military air bases, particularly Navy, and I don't want to become impaled on the nose of a Navy TV-2. NAS (Naval Air Station) Whiting is dead ahead, and NAS Saufley and NAS Pensacola are nearby. This is where Hellcat, Corsair, Dauntless, and Avenger pilots came from fifty-six years ago. This is where Lt. Harvey Lively was trained to toss five-hundred-pound armor-piercing bombs at Japanese cruisers.

## Lt. (j.g.) Harvey Lively, USN, USS *Fanshaw Bay,* fifty miles east of Samar Island, 1944

### *". . . four shells splash right along side of us."*

It was in the second battle of the Philippine Sea that we really ran into a lot of trouble.

We had been eating and operating for some time without the above-average meals that we were accustomed to. I was not scheduled to fly that day and had gone to the wardroom for breakfast. There was no one else there that morning.

A sailor came in and said, "Mr. Lively, come on up. They want you to go out and bomb the Jap fleet."

I thought that it was just a sick joke and said, "All right, I'll be up after a while."

So I finished my coffee and wandered up onto the catwalk and saw four shells splash right alongside of us. I figured out without too much of a problem that this was for real. You could see the whole horizon lit up by gunfire.

Their appearance was a complete surprise. Nobody was expecting this. I mean absolutely no warning whatsoever. Unbelievable.

Though unbelievable, it was indeed for real. What Lieutenant Lively was seeing was a 0658 wake-up call from Adm. Takeo Kurita as four battleships, including the monstrous *Yamato,* with her 18.1-inch guns, eight cruisers, and twelve destroyers of the Imperial Japanese Navy, came churning through the San Bernardino Straits, intent on mayhem. Their range was seventeen miles and they were closing at twenty-four knots. Their immediate targets were the fragile seventeen-knot escort or "jeep" carriers of *Taffy 3,* the northernmost group of Task Force 77.4. Left essentially undefended by Adm. William F. "Bull" Halsey's pursuit of a Japanese decoy force designed to draw American forces to the north, for the six jeep carriers and their screen of three destroyers and four destroyer escorts there could be only one conclusion to this lopsided battle—annihilation. The wolf was among the sheep.

But *Taffy 3,* under the command of Adm. Clifton "Ziggy" Sprague, in the face of hopeless odds, quickly launched all aircraft, opened fire with the five-inch guns of the carriers, and as the Japanese ships closed, ordered gunfire and torpedo attacks by the thin-skinned destroyers and destroyer escorts. Each jeep carrier had a composite group of sixteen FM-2 Wildcat fighters and twelve TBM Avenger bombers, and soon the Japanese were buried under a rain of aircraft attacks, which were quickly fortified by the aircraft of *Taffy 2* and *Taffy 1,* equal-sized groups to the south.

I went to the ready room. This is where we had our flight gear, and I was assigned the last plane on the deck. It had a full load of .50-caliber ammunition, eight rockets, which are the maximum, and four five-hundred-pound bombs.

When we launched, we had to have enough wind down the deck, and we had turned back toward the Japanese fleet to get that wind. But by the time they got to me, they had already launched the others and had started turning back out of the wind. I just barely made it off by sheer luck, maybe a little bit of skill, and got myself airborne.

It was about five-tenths overcast, we were in a rain squall, which really helped us along, and I joined up on some other planes. There were two ahead of me. The first one started in on an attack and I lost him in the cloud cover. The next one started in and they hit him, and he did a half spin but recovered. His bombs were near misses.

It became readily apparent that this was no time for procrastination, so I pushed the mixture control to "rich," the throttle to "full power," and started my run. I fired my .50-caliber guns to disperse the antiaircraft fire, which was rather intense. Then I fired my rockets and dropped my bombs.

The Avenger that Lively was flying employed a glide-bombing technique that used a 45- to 60-degree glide as opposed to the old dive-bombing angles of its predecessor, the Douglas Dauntless, which could dive at 75 to 90 degrees.

By the time that I had fired my guns and rockets, I was getting really close to what I'd consider to be the optimum for dropping my bombs, and I pickled them off, one by one, and felt three distinct jolts.

I didn't feel a jolt from the first one that I dropped, because it landed in the water off of the stern and the water cushioned the explosion. The primary damage that did was to knock the steering out, which left the cruiser going around in a circle. I didn't get the bump from it that I did from the others. I felt the impact from the second, third, and fourth bombs and was credited with three direct hits on a *Mogami*-class cruiser. I'm sure one of our pilots put a torpedo into the disabled cruiser not too long after that.

After I pulled out of the bombing run, I ducked down to within a few feet of the water and fired my guns at the forward ships of the enemy formation. My gunner was also firing his .50-calibers at any ships within his range. Had these ships fired at us, they would have also been firing on their own ships. We quickly departed the area only to find that we were unable to find a carrier to land on. The cruiser was still very much afloat and going around in a large circle at about four knots. It kept peppering us, so I dumped it back down on the water and went on out and found another carrier to land on.

That carrier the USS *Marcus Island,* a sister ship to the *Fanshaw Bay.* We were promptly loaded with a torpedo and launched to search for targets of opportunity. We had no escort or any other company. We were *solo mio.* We found an enemy cruiser, obviously damaged but still alive and ominous. While circling to evaluate the situation, four fighters from another group joined up with us. I gave the signal to attack, and we had started our run-in when suddenly we found ourselves alone. The fighters had left us. Fortunately, we were still out of range of the cruiser's firepower.

After circling for a while and evaluating the situation, I dropped the torpedo in the open sea, headed in the direction of the disabled cruiser, but there was no prize for a near miss and we went home. It had been a long day, six and one-half hours against the enemy.

After making contact with our group, we were directed to proceed to and land at Tacloban in the Philippines. The airstrip at Tacloban was composed of Marston matting [a prefabricated interlocking metal contruction material], which had very recently been laid by the U.S. Army Corps of Engineers. My landing was a good one, and I had parked and secured my plane when shortly a Curtiss SB2C Helldiver came in to land. This aircraft ground looped and burst into flames. I turned away and said a short prayer, and when I looked again there was the pilot, walking away, unscathed. There were a lot of occurrences like this that were unexplainable at the time, and I always believe that I had a "co-pilot" riding on my shoulder.

There were six jeep carriers and they sank two of us, the *Gambier Bay* and the *Kitkun Bay*. I was on the *Fanshaw Bay*.

They hit us, but one mistake that they made was to use armor-piercing rounds, which went right on through the ship, causing very little damage. They thought that we were Halsey's fleet and they would have needed armor-piercing rounds because he had cruisers, battleships, and fleet carriers. If they had used high-explosive rounds, they would have sunk us. They hit the ship five or six times, but the rounds just went right on through. They had us. They could have sunk every one of us. But something made them peel off at the critical time, and thank God that they did.

That "something" was undoubtedly the fury of the American air and naval response. In their heroic attack, the destroyers USS *Hoel, Heerman* and *Johnston,* supported by the destroyer escorts USS *Dennis, Butler, Raymond,* and *Roberts,* closed to point-blank range and were buried under massive salvos from the Japanese. Three of the escorts, the *Hoel, Johnston,* and *Roberts,* went to the bottom, but not before blowing the bow off of the cruiser *Kumano* and convincing Admiral Kurita that he was facing a far more powerful force.

Confused and intimidated by the hornet's nest of air, torpedo, and gunnery attacks that he had stirred up, Kurita ordered a general withdrawal. His golden opportunity for a massive Japanese victory in the Battle of Leyte Gulf was gone, and with it three of his cruisers.

I land for fuel at a little airport in Bay Minette, Alabama. From the air, Bay Minette looks like a lovely little town—almost an "Our Town" with a wandering railroad track through its center. It is inviting and I'm tempted to spend some time there. The airport is a quiet place with a single runway and no taxiway. The earth falls away steeply on both sides of the runway, which appears to run along the ridge of some hills—not a good place for an off-runway excursion. Where the earth is scraped bare, it's a bright terra-cotta red. This is a new sight for me, but in this region I see that it is quite common. A beautiful stand of pines surrounds the field on all sides.

I decide against staying and refuel hurriedly. The weather folks have an advisory for afternoon thundershowers in the Marianna area, and I would prefer to be on the ground during that event.

In my haste to depart Bay Minette I manage a sloppy wandering take-off, getting perilously close to the runway edges with each rudder correction. Perhaps the drop-off psyched me a bit. The airplane demands that its pilot pay attention, not an unreasonable thing. You can't drive this aircraft off of the ground; it must be flown.

As I climb out, I pace a freight train peacefully chugging its way through the woods, and since I'm climbing, our speeds almost match. I'm disappointed when the tracks veer off to the northeast. I would have liked the company.

## Lt. Channing Sargent, USNR
## Japan, 1945

### ". . . He pretty well blew himself up."

On one of our more interesting runs, I think we had twelve planes that time, we were supposed to go in on an airfield, but it was socked in and we couldn't hit it. We went to our secondary and it was socked in also. So we were coming across the mainland of Japan and really looking for a "target of opportunity," I guess you'd call it, and not really looking very hard when all of a sudden we heard this gibberish that I couldn't understand over the radio and the fellow that was leading did a split S, flat on his back and he was gone, straight down. We were all sitting around there for a second or two wondering what was going on.

This guy had spotted a train in broad daylight—a double header, chugging across the flats down there—and he had gone after the train.

Now this pilot had been an RAF jockey in Hurricanes and I think he had shot up everything in the world—tanks, flak towers, airplanes, and ships—but he had never hit a train and he was going to get this one. He was gone. We decided that it was a pretty good idea, so we went too.

We set up a traffic pattern—just a nice racetrack pattern on that train—and just had a ball. The main engine went off like a firecracker, it just blew rivets and sheet metal all over the place, but the second one we never could get to blow.

The second guy in dumped two rockets on the tracks in front of it and curled those up so that it was dead in the water. Didn't even have a moving target, and that was our thrill for the day.

One of the fellows on that run went in and had some beautiful gun camera film. He fired off two five-inch rockets. You could see them fire off through the gun camera, and all of a sudden the film went blank. He had not pulled up after he let go of the rockets, and the rockets got there just about the same time he did. He pretty well blew himself up.

But the F6F [Grumman F6F Hellcat] was a pretty tough airplane. He cleaned one cylinder completely off that engine. He got back to the ship, landed aboard, and they counted over two hundred holes in this airplane from debris, rocks, and junk that had come up from the blast. He had about two quarts of oil left in his engine.

Now we were two hundred miles offshore and he had flown this thing back to the ship—the ugliest mess you had ever seen in your life. They just pushed it over the side. Totally unsalvageable. Every leading edge in that airplane was full of holes. That was an interesting run. Kind of fun, but I don't think it was fun for him.

Most of the time things were pretty routine—you got shot at, you shot back. Sometimes you got hit, most times you didn't. We had some kamikaze attacks on the ship occasionally. On the cruise before, on the *Wasp*, they had taken probably a five-hundred-pounder. The guy had popped out of the overcast, dropped his five-hundred-pounder, and then ducked right back into it. How he got that close, I don't know to this day. It went through the ready room and down through the hangar deck. Punched through the armor plate of the hangar deck, went about three levels below that, and wiped out a whole bunch of people.

I don't know if you remember those nylon flight suits, those green nylons? There were some of those hanging on the ready room wall. We kept all of our flight gear in the ready room. The flash, even though it was that far below deck, melted most of those flight suits. Just left the zippers. That made believers out of a bunch of folks. They didn't want to wear those cockeyed things when things were hot. They didn't burn like cloth and would melt into the skin. They were a mess.

## Lt. James Van Voorhees, P-61 Black Widow pilot
## Germany, 1945

*". . . you could still see those tracks, because they shine."*

We went to a small base in England, about a hundred miles north of London, for about six weeks, but we didn't have our airplanes yet. It was a night fighter base for the British, and they had the Mosquitoes. They would take us up to show us how they were doing things, and we would just go along as a passenger in the Mosquito, which was a great experience, because it was a fantastic little airplane. It would do things that the P-61 never thought of doing, but it would also do some that you didn't want it to do. It would burn at the drop of a hat, because it was all plywood. And they lost a lot of them that way.

We finally got our P-61s over there about the time that the Germans were moving out of France and into Germany. They sent us to a field about sixty miles north of Lyon. I could never figure out why we were there, because in order to get to Germany we had to fly clear around Switzerland. The Swiss wouldn't let us overfly, because they were neutral. By the time we got there with our fuel burn, we were lucky if we put in an hour and a half over Germany, and they had nothing flying to speak of except their training planes and the jets. The jets wouldn't go up at night, but occasionally we saw some taking off as we were coming back early in the morning.

We'd go into Germany and my radar observer would say, "I can see a train on the track about fourteen miles ahead." And so I'd pull back the throttle about ten percent and drop about five degrees of flaps. Pretty soon he'd say, "About three miles and you should have a visual." Even if you had just a starlit night, you could still see those tracks, because they shine. Well, the minute the tracks don't shine anymore, you know that the train is over the top of them, and we'd start firing the twenty-millimeter cannons down the roadbed. You'd see the tracers bouncing off, and when they didn't bounce off anymore you knew that you'd hit the steam engine. At that time you'd push the throttles forward and get out of there, because they had antiaircraft on a lot of the trains. You'd always fly into them instead of coming behind them. The day fighters always came in from the side.

We'd also fly down the highways and seek truck convoys. We'd just start firing down the highway, and since most of the highways were elevated, the trucks would drive off and turn over. Basically what we were doing was stopping their transportation.

# CHAPTER 18

AIR CADET ARTHUR FIEDLER, Marianna, Florida

*"They wanted no part of being a fighter pilot."*

Bay Minette to Marianna, Florida, August 25, 2000

About twenty miles outside of Marianna I tune in the AWOS, or Airport Weather Observation Service. This is a nice little device that broadcasts the current weather at an airport in one of those flat metallic synthesized voices that you hear on computers. The weather at Marianna is reasonable except for one item. The voice says, "Caution, thunderstorms in the area."

Where in the area, voice? Ten miles or fifty? To the north, to the south, or to the east? Or to the west between Marianna and me? Voice gives no clue.

I have visions of groups of thunderstorms, loitering like predatory wolves, just out of sight, waiting to hear of the passage of this innocent

California pilot, then pouncing. I approach the area warily, but the weather is beautiful as the airport appears over the nose.

From the air, Marianna Municipal Airport looks like it once was impressive. There are at least six runways pointed in every conceivable direction, although only two of them are active. Most are overgrown and weed-choked, including one of the two actives. There are taxiways everywhere, also inactive. An advanced training base during the war, this was where fighter pilots were taught their craft. This was fighter pilot finishing school. Once, hundreds of AT-6 trainers lined these ramps and prepared their student pilots for P-51s and P-47s. An air cadet who made it this far was almost home free.

## Air Cadet Arthur Fiedler
## Marianna, Florida, 1943

### ". . . hot pilot stuff."

Marianna was another "little ol'" southern town meriting some attention only because of the war and the school that had been established at the local airport. Our quarters were quite nice with two cadets per room and usually six cadets to a building.

We flew the AT-6 Texan, which was not a difficult transition to make, as we used the same airspeeds as we had in the BT-13. This was an all-metal, low-wing monoplane with a 650-horsepower engine, enclosed cockpit, tandem seating, retractable landing gear, and provisions for mounting a .30-caliber machine gun in the cowling. Although not pertinent to our training, the aircraft could also mount a .30-caliber machine gun in the rear cockpit and thus could be used for aerial gunnery training also. It was relatively easy to fly, and I remember I was checked out on my first flight of some two hours' duration.

About this period in our training we were all the hottest pilots going—or so we thought. There was one instance in which I almost got into real trouble. Why I did this I don't know, but I suppose it was to impress my instructor. In the T-6, the landing gear could not retract if the weight of the airplane was on it. As a result, one could start the takeoff roll, keep the stick well forward to keep pressure on the gear, hit the power button, and pull up the landing gear handle while still on the takeoff roll. As soon as you left the ground, the weight came off the landing gear, which immediately retracted. It was an impressive sight to a bystander who knew anything about flying. It was hot pilot stuff.

Of all the times to do this, I chose to do it with my instructor in the backseat. It was executed perfectly, but then came the "explosion" from the back cockpit. He reamed me up one side and down the other for fifteen minutes, all the time threatening to wash me out—and of course he was right. If the airplane had hit a slight bump in the runway, the weight would have come off the landing gear momentarily and, whoosh, the gear would have retracted. If I did not have flying speed at this time, the result would be one airplane bellied in because of a stupid stunt. After that I was a little more selective in what I did with my instructor aboard.

In this phase we had a lot of individual combat, supposedly only with our instructor but in reality just about any time we ran across another airplane. I took pride in the fact that no one ever got on my tail. My friend Tom Evans and I engaged in this activity many hours during our stay at Marianna, and sometimes got down to ground level with our wings just about scraping the earth. We rationalized that it was good practice, and if we could not hack it in training, it would be better to find out now rather than when we were in combat. In retrospect, I question such a philosophy, but when you are nineteen years old, many immature decisions appear perfectly normal.

One day we were told that P-51s would put on a demonstration for us, and at 1400 hours we were all assembled on the flight line when four of the sleekest-looking birds I ever saw came roaring across the ramp ten feet above the ground doing at least 425 miles per hour. Wow, it was impressive to say the least! Then for several minutes they executed some simple formation aerobatics. As a final act they dove to ground level in trail to perform a barrel roll right off the deck. The leader leveled off at ten feet, waited a few seconds, and started his roll. The four did the barrel roll simultaneously, which meant they should have all been in level flight, and when the leader pulled his nose up to roll, all four should have been in position to do the same. However, the number four man was still in a slight dive, and so when they all started the roll, his nose was pointed slightly down rather than up. That was fatal.

There were as many versions of what happened as there were observers. Some insisted he went in upside down, others that he had hit a wingtip, others that he had dished out, and so forth. The one indisputable fact is that he crashed and was killed. A tremendous cloud of dirt was raised as he hit the area between the taxiway and ramp. Suddenly above the cloud, a fully open parachute appeared perhaps one hundred feet in the air. For a split second everyone thought that he had bailed out and they cheered, but the truth was that his body was torn apart, and in some manner the ripcord snagged on something as the parachute was thrown into the air and deployed. We were all shocked to learn that these pilots had just returned from a combat tour in the South Pacific. To have one survive combat and then lose his life in this manner seemed like a gross injustice.

For most of us, the incident did not change our minds about wanting to be fighter pilots, but just increased our caution about doing low-level acrobatics. However, there were several pilots who immediately submitted requests to be transferred to multiengine training. They wanted no part of being a fighter pilot.

A few days later, Evans and I were called into the commandant's office and told that we were to fly a special mission back to our basic flying school at Macon. Early in 1943, the B-17s raiding Europe had reported very, very light losses. As a result, many of the students in basic were requesting assignment to multiengine flying school in the hope they would be assigned to B-17s. Very few requested single-engine flying schools. The commandant told us we would fly to Macon and put on a little show for the students in our AT-6s, and then land to circulate among the stages. We were supposed to extol the virtues of being a fighter pilot and tell everyone how much fun it was to fly the AT-6. That afternoon our instructor took Evans and me up and we ran through some of the maneuvers we would do. I was amazed that he had the confidence to allow us to fly in such close formation with him—and close it was. I am sure that we had no more than four or five feet between our wingtips and his elevators, and our props were right beside his wingtips.

Early the next morning we took off and flew to Cochran Field, which halted all operations while we did about fifteen minutes of loops, buzzes, and other maneuvers in formation. At times I was afraid we might chew up the instructor's wing, we were so close. This of course required a lot of throttle jockeying, which put the props in and out of low pitch and in turn created a tremendous din on the ground. I was told later that this impressed the students more than anything else we did. We concluded by making a perfect three-ship formation landing.

Reflecting on this, I can only conclude that our instructor must have been as crazy as we were to do this. We spent the afternoon in each of the stages talking to students and trying to persuade them how great it was to be a fighter pilot, but the majority of them were convinced that bomber pilots had the best chance to survive the war. Little did they know what the future held for bomber pilots without fighter escort.

Flying was definitely a fantastic experience to many of us at this stage, and we all knew that barring something unusual, we would be graduating shortly as second lieutenant pilots. Most of us ordered uniforms from Sol Frank in San Antonio, Texas, as had the classes before us. He was the most famous provider of uniforms for newly graduated second lieutenants in the Air Force.

Our last phase before graduation was gunnery at Eglin Field. Here we were introduced to the AT-6 with a .30-caliber machine gun on the left cowling. We learned the tactics of air-to-air gunnery as well as air-to-ground gunnery. I did well and was awarded the Expert Machine Gunners award.

One incident I recall with much satisfaction. I was in the first flight assigned to the ground gunnery range on a morning when the air was perfectly calm. Later flights, especially afternoon ones, had to contend with summer turbulence, which bounced the airplane all around. Under these circumstances it was difficult to line up the sight with the target and even more of a problem to keep it there while firing. All firing had to be done between two lines on the ground or it was a fouled run. As I recall, we had to start firing at approximately three hundred yards from the target and quit firing at one hundred yards. Those distances may not be exact but they are close. On this particular flight, the conditions were absolutely perfect. There was not one bit of turbulence and I shot a record score. Of the one hundred rounds I fired, all except one hit the target. I insisted that the one round must have gone through another hole in the target, but they would not agree, saying 99 percent was enough for anyone.

The twenty-eighth of July 1943 dawned clear, bright, and hot. That afternoon about 1:00 P.M., four days before I became twenty years old, I received my wings and shiny gold bars and by an act of Congress was made an officer and gentleman. It seemed at that time that all my dreams as a child had finally come true, although it was difficult to believe it had really happened. I could not even contemplate what adventures were in store for me, but at that time I was so imbued with pride and patriotism, I was ready for anything.

I touch down on Marianna, a lonely Stearman in the middle of six runways and a huge, empty ramp where Arthur Fiedler and hundreds of stunned cadets watched the P-51 crash almost sixty years ago. Many of the old buildings still stand, and it looks every inch a military airfield. I taxi to the administration building, shut down, and wander inside.

"Would you have a hangar that I could use for the night?" I ask, thinking about the thunderstorms. Heads nod in the negative.

"Sorry, no hangars here."

"How about a shelter?" I ask. I had seen a shelter with about a dozen airplanes in it as I landed.

"All full up." I glanced outside, and sure enough, there was no room at the inn.

"How about those concrete structures along the ramp?" I had seen what looked like military hangars from the air.

"They're condemned. The roofs are falling in."

"Nothing, huh?"

"Nothing."

The size of this field belied its lack of facilities. The T-6s of fifty years ago were tough, heavy airplanes that were simply left outside, unprotected on the ramp. They were unfazed by thunderstorms.

"Okay, well I do need some gas, so let's get started with that," I suggest.

When I walk outside the first thing I notice is that one of the "thunderstorms in the area" has apparently heard of my arrival and is on its way to greet me. The sky to the east looks black, but the storm is still quite a way off, so with no particular sense of urgency I begin tying the Stearman down. I get one wing tied down securely when the fuel truck pulls up. I abandon my tie-down efforts on the other wing and stand up on the front cockpit edge as the lineman leisurely takes his ladder off, attaches the static ground line, and uncoils the fuel hose. I can smell the rain in the air, but surely we have plenty of time. He hands the nozzle up to me and I began fueling. Glancing back eastward, I can see that the storm is heading for us at a good clip, a bit faster than I thought. It is now at the edge of the field, about two miles away, but even as I consider that piece of news, rain begins to fall, enough so that I have to cease the fueling operation before I get water in the tank. I cap the tank, hand the lineman the hose, and just as I step off of the wing, the full fury of the storm hits. It must have been crossing the ground at every bit of sixty miles per hour. I have completely misjudged events.

Almost before I can react, the wind hits us and the airplane begins to lift. The storm is coming from the rear quarter and it slams the rudder hard over. The lock on the tail wheel releases from the pressure and the tail now begins to swing. The one wing that is tied down isn't going anywhere, but the rest of the airplane is free to pivot into the fuel truck, which is parked in front of it. I lunge for the grab handle on the side of the fuselage, dig my heels in, and hang on. The Stearman really wants to become airborne again, and I don't seem to be much of an impediment. The rain is now a deluge and almost horizontal with lightning exploding all around us. Seconds before, I had been standing on the fuselage like a lightning rod pouring avgas into the wing tank.

I shout for the lineman to move the fuel truck. I know I can't hold the airplane. He begins slowly coiling up the static discharge line.

"Move the fuel truck. I can't hold this." I shout again. He begins folding and stowing the ladder in slow motion. The airplane is now dragging me as it swings toward the fuel truck. The lineman is oblivious.

"Move the goddamn fuel truck, NOW!" I shout, all pretense of civility gone. I guess we aren't going to be buddies after this, but I've finally gotten his attention and he sees the peril. He jumps for the truck and drives it out of the way, fuel hose and nozzle bouncing behind on the pavement, just as the airplane, dragging me with it, arcs into the space just vacated by the truck. I let go, race for the unused tie-down and run the tie rope through the eyebolt on the wing, tying the world's fastest knot in the process. I run for the tail wheel and get a rope on it. The wind lifts the tail, and I'm in a tug of war with the elements. It's like bulldogging a steer. I get the tail wheel cinched and jump for the cockpit to secure the gust lock. The ailerons have been steadily banging a tattoo since this started. The wing walk is slippery and I fall heavily, narrowly missing punching a hole in the wing fabric. I slam the gust lock on and snap the cockpit cover into place. Disgusted with myself, I run for the terminal. Looking back, the airplane, cocked at an angle, has all but disappeared under sheets of wind-driven rain. We had walked out to fuel the airplane in calm sunlight two minutes ago, and I had come very close to losing the Stearman.

Now I have to apologize to the lineman for my little slipup. I feel really bad and apologize repeatedly. He accepts the apology with good grace, and we stand inside and watch the exposed airplane strain at the ropes under the onslaught of wind and water.

"Does it ever hail during these thunderstorms?" I ask, not really wanting to know.

"Not often," is the heartening reply.

After about a half an hour, things quiet down and I am able to go back out and repark my wandering airplane. I had put so many knots in those ropes that they look like a rosary of Gordian knots. The airplane isn't going anywhere tonight.

"Is this about it for the day?" I ask, motioning to the sky.

"Yeah, that should be it," he replies. We go back to the fueling operation, and that done, I head for town and a motel to lick my wounds.

At about 7:00 P.M., after making a few phone calls, I start thinking about heading out for dinner. I had seen a cafe about a half mile down the road, so I grab a good book and open the door. The sky, which has turned ugly again, has been waiting for me and explodes into a major pyrotechnics display almost as if on cue. This new arrival is apparently "Son of Storm," and it contains hail. The noise is deafening as it pounds on the cars in the parking lot. What must it be doing to the airplane?

My heart is heavy as I call the airport. Yes, it is raining; no, it isn't hailing; and, yes, the airplane is okay, so far. This is a repeat of Hammond, Louisiana.

I had seen a jet charter operation from the road as I got my ride into town and noticed that they had a very large hangar with nothing in it. I made a desperation call to them and got "Wally." Would they shelter my airplane? They are my last hope.

"No, we haven't any room," says Wally.

"But your hangar is empty."

"Well, we have a Lear Jet coming in."

"Your hangar is easily big enough for a Lear Jet and a Stearman."

"No, it isn't. We don't have any room."

"Thank you." I hope that they slammed the hangar door on Wally's Lear Jet.

There is really nothing I can do at this point. I can't fly it out. There is no hangar or shelter. There is no quick way to get back to the airport, and even if I manage that, there is nothing I can do if it starts hailing except watch it tear up the fabric. I am checkmated. I begin thinking about how I will disassemble the surely damaged airplane in the morning and ship it home.

# CHAPTER 19

CAPT. NORMAN COHEN, B24s over Italy

*"You mean you can't land and take off?"*
*"Never have," was his reply.*

Marianna to Sebring, Florida, August 26, 2000

The morning skies are clear and innocent, as if disowning the mischief of last night's storm. I catch a ride to the Marianna airport and am amazed and relieved to see the Stearman still on its wheels. There are trees and power lines down all around the airport, and clearly damage has been done to the countryside. The airplanes parked on both sides have been blown sideways, and are at angles due to some sloppy tie-downs, but the Stearman sits stubbornly straight, just as I left it. It's sobering to think that the survival of the aircraft depends on my ability to tie a knot, a craft that in spite of an eternity in the Boy Scouts, I've never really mastered. Shoelaces still sometimes defy me. Deficient in expertise, I excel in enthusiasm, tying multiple crude granny knots in tie-downs wherever I find a loose end, on the theory that quantity can triumph over quality.

The airplane seems frail to me with its fabric cover, but these airplanes soldiered on as trainers and dusters for years, never hangared and left to the elements. Damage from the rain and wind seems to be limited to a torn cockpit cover, but it had seen better days anyway. Some rain got into the cockpit, but not a lot, and I count my blessings and start wiping. The fabric is in perfect shape. Either there was no hail here or it just bounced off. I check the airplane over very carefully and, finding no damage of consequence, fire up.

Taxiing out to runway two-six is like a trip across a Kansas wheat field. The little-used taxiways and huge ramp are covered with tall grass growing out of the concrete expansion joints in neat little strips, crisscrossing the acres of concrete and almost obscuring the taxiways. There are no longer enough airplanes to keep the grass down, and it's clear that Marianna is losing its war with nature. Even the runway is almost unrecognizable, and I have to lean over the side and look down into the weeds to find the runway numbers. I want to make sure that I'm taking off on a runway, and not a taxiway or a service road. I half expect to see Dean Jagger standing at the end of the duty runway as he did in the opening of *Twelve O'Clock High*.

And they were right about the old military hangars. The roofs are falling in. The whole airfield has an air of genteel decay. The war is won. The government is done with this airfield, and it is going back to nature.

I key the mike to advise of my takeoff and discover that there's hidden damage somewhere in the radio. I can't transmit and suspect that water has found its way into a place where it shouldn't be. Well, Bernoulli makes airplanes fly, not Marconi, so I advance the throttle on the theory that the breeze will soon dry things out, which proves to be sound thinking. My radio wakes up while crossing over Tallahassee.

As I head south into Florida, I'm really watching the weather as the remnants of Hurricane Debbie are supposedly coming north. After first threatening Florida, the hurricane has veered southwest into the Gulf of Mexico but left some activity still going on in southern Florida. The weather was clear when I left Marianna, but I soon start seeing a scattered to broken cloud base at around two thousand feet. To the south there appears more of the same, but thicker. I get an update on the weather, but so far there is nothing ugly along my route of flight.

What I am seeing with my untrained California eye is a typical, beautiful Florida summer day with scattered clouds forming in the morning, which gradually thicken and rise to four thousand feet by the early afternoon. Then there's usually a graduation ceremony around 3:00 P.M., when the "achievers" of this cloud show become cumulonimbus monsters and spawn thundershowers in the late afternoon. These are local and are easily avoided. Everybody who flies down here knows the drill, and I am beginning to figure it out. Being a student of relatively unchanging Southern California weather patterns, I just need to be retrained.

The growing cloud formations with their valleys, pinnacles, and overhangs begin to get my attention and are a great temptation to fly through. Open cockpit flight into clouds is a fascinating sensation. First there is the threat of collision as you close on an apparently impenetrable gray wall at ninety miles per hour. But there is no impact, just a soft bump as the aircraft enters the cloud, followed by the sting of water vapor on the face. The open cockpit gives an intense sensory experience that is lost in a cabin aircraft, where the clouds are more like a movie on the plastic windshield.

Too soon my first destination, Cross City, Florida, is over the nose. This isn't exactly an international hub, but it comes highly recommended by connoisseurs of the airport hamburger from as far away as Louisiana. It's just your average airport in northern Florida, but one with a nice little restaurant on the field and friendly people. It's a Saturday morning and the radio traffic is very heavy today, as aviators from far and wide converge on this little airport in their hundred-thousand-dollar machines for their hundred-dollar hamburger. The hamburger doesn't cost the hundred dollars, but by the time the fuel, insurance, and hangars are factored in, it probably comes very close. It's an aviation tradition and I, of course, participate in the ritual.

The Stearman always attracts attention at these places. It's like casually showing up at a high school class reunion with Madonna on your arm.

"My date? Oh, her. That's just Madonna."

I try to be modest, cool, and give it my best "aw, shucks" imitation, but it's especially difficult when the inevitable question is asked.

"Where are you out of?"

"Southern California."

Mouths that have been busily chewing stop. Drinks that were being raised pause. The room goes silent.

Whatever follows depends on the speaker's frame of reference. Experienced Stearman or duster pilots usually reply along the lines of: "Jeeeesus. What year did you leave?" Or, "Who'd you piss off to get that job?" You gotta love 'em.

But then there is always the less cynical, the guy who has scraped together his last nickel to learn to fly, or if he is incredibly fortunate and determined, has managed to buy a thirty-year-old Cessna or Piper and who would cheerfully strangle his elderly grandmother for a chance to fly around the country in an old biplane. These guys get a faraway look in their eye and just keep circling the airplane, taking it all in.

The coffee shop conversations are light and fun, the burgers good, and soon I am on my way out of Cross City heading south. My destination for the day is Lakeland or Arcadia or Sebring or, "I don't know, just whenever I decide to set back down."

I see Arcadia, Florida, on the chart. Now there's a possibility. I know a fellow who learned to fly there. Norm Cohen. He should be with me right now. We could go in there and he could shoot the landing. It's only been fifty-seven years. I flew with him earlier this spring. It was a bit of a conspiracy.

## San Fernando Valley
## June 26, 1999

*". . . I ain't telling them I dropped bombs there."*

It was his birthday and his wife and another couple had mischievously taken him out to the airport that sunny Sunday morning. They innocently stopped off near the Stearman hangar to visit a "friend"—all prearranged, of course. Seeing the old biplane was predictably irresistible to Norm; he wandered over in his Sunday casual sandals and shorts and politely asked if he could look it over. I invited him in.

He examined the Stearman carefully for a long time while I worked on it, and then in the course of small talk he finally revealed, "I flew these in primary in Arcadia, Florida, in 1943."

I was waiting for something along those lines. "Well, good," I replied, "then you shouldn't have any trouble flying it today."

I reached into a locker, pulled out a flight suit, and tossed it to him. Holding the flight suit, the look of confusion that crossed his face was wonderful. His protests were waved aside as his wife and friends reappeared to explain the birthday plot and that, yes indeed, he was going flying today in the same kind of airplane that he flew fifty-seven years ago. As the realization of what he was about to do came over him, a huge grin chased away the surprise and he was as excited as a kid at Christmas.

Norm Cohen is a big guy. In the classic World War II photograph, posing with his crew in front of their B-24J at its Foggia, Italy, airfield he dwarfs the other crew members. Pilots his size were frequently assigned to the bombers, and he made the cut. He is nineteen years old in the photo, a second lieutenant, an aircraft commander in charge of nine men, ten thousand pounds of bombs, and a brand-new $250,000 four-engine Liberator bomber built by Ford Motor Company at its plant in Willow Run, Michigan.

Today—sitting in the Stearman front cockpit, with his size undiminished by age—his head rises well above the windshield. The Stearman, indifferent to its load, rumbles down the runway and takes to the air without a protest. The grin hasn't abated.

"It's your airplane, Norm," I said, as we leveled off at altitude and slid through a pass in the San Gabriel Mountains. He didn't have to be asked twice, nodded, and soon was comfortable with the Stearman.

"How long has it been since you've flown?" I asked.

Over the crackle of the intercom he explained that he had parked his B-24J at Bryan Field, Texas, in 1945 and hadn't touched an airplane since. It had been almost fifty-five years since he had controlled an aircraft, and yet he was holding course and altitude as if he were back in his B-24. The Air Corps had trained this man well.

Norm Cohen had credit for fifty missions flown out of Foggia for his employer, the 15th Air Force. He had visited Czechoslovakia, Germany, Austria, Rumania, and Italy with his bomber, all within a hundred-day period and all in his nineteenth summer. None in the crew received a scratch, although the airplane frequently returned damaged.

"We're going to vacation in Vienna in a few months," he said, smiling impishly, "but I ain't telling them I dropped bombs there."

He wasn't always a really good B-24 pilot though. Fresh out of advanced flight training, he was assigned as a copilot but drew an aircraft commander who wouldn't let him fly the airplane.

"I told him—and we bunked together for several months—you're making a big mistake not letting me handle the plane. There may come a time when I need to." Together they flew across the Atlantic to Marrakech and on into Italy in this sorry state.

When they got to Italy, the operations officer said, "How are you guys at formation flying?"

Norm replied truthfully, "I've never flown formation. I was only the copilot, and the aircraft commander wouldn't let me touch the controls. All I did is flip toggle switches."

"You mean you can't land and take off?"

"Never have," was his reply.

He never flew with that pilot again.

Intense training followed. "They'd get me up at six in the morning and I flew until it got too dark to fly, doing takeoffs and landings and close-in formation for about two and a half weeks, daily. There was no time off."

He got his transition training in a combat theater. Within weeks he was an aircraft commander. Not bad for a kid who was court-martialed in primary.

Nobody gets court-martialed in primary and still graduates pilot training, yet Norm managed it.

He laughs, "I had finished my primary training in the Stearman and I was finished at Arcadia, but they hadn't transferred us out yet. We used to go out over the Gulf, not far out, just a few miles and we'd be chasing each other around. And I got caught. And I got court-martialed. It cost me twenty-five dollars a month for three months, and I was restricted to the base for sixty days." Somehow the words "washed out" were never uttered by the court.

"I went to basic and now we were in the Vultee BT-13s. They never mentioned the court-martial. They just left us alone. Remember, we were on an honor system. They never even asked.

So we finished our basic training and they said 'By the way, has anyone in this class been court-martialed for breaking flying regulations?' I believe it was the 96th Article of War—coming within five hundred feet of another aircraft in flight. It's pretty hard not to do when you're doing what we were doing."

"So did you fess up?" I asked.

"Yeah, sure. And the training officer said, 'Did you leave the base?' I said, 'No sir. I stayed on the base.'"

He had wisely obeyed the restriction. They had given him enough rope—and he had proved honorable. Had he left the base he would have been through.

"Ordinarily what I did was a washout."

But that was the end of it. He had made it out of primary and basic flight training in spite of the court-martial.

He smiles ruefully. "If you've got fifty or sixty hours, you are a hot shot."

Fifty missions, two Air Medals, and a Distinguished Flying Cross later, he finally learned to fly the B-24 properly when he went to B-24 instructor school in Georgia. He got his green card (instrument rating) and they taught him to fly the airplane in ways that he never knew possible, such as how to keep it in the air on one engine. He learned emergency procedures that he had no idea existed when he was in combat. He was ready to take on Japan. But it was August 15, 1945. The crusade was over.

Norm Cohen was discharged at the convenience of the government in 1945. He was twenty. Don't forget, your old employer must take you back!

Over eighteen thousand B-24s were built during the war. When the war ended, almost all of the surviving aircraft were scrapped. Of the handful left today only three are airworthy.

Foggia is a prosperous agricultural town where the runways now hear the whine of turbines. The mighty roar of the Liberator and its Pratt & Whitneys is a faded echo.

Arcadia, Florida, where he learned to tail chase and had his character tested, is now a sleepy little municipal airport catering to Pipers and Cessnas.

But fifty-five years later, Norm Cohen can still fly an Army Air Corps plane.

# CHAPTER 20

CAPT. ARTHUR FIEDLER, Ploesti, Rumania, 1944

*". . . I now found myself sliding into formation with this new 109."*

S ebring to Pompano Beach, Florida, August 28, 2000

It's 6:00 A.M. on Hendricks Field, a former B-17 training base. They don't call it Hendricks anymore—they call it Sebring now and run car races on its taxiways and one of its runways. But the pattern and width of those runways are a giveaway to the bomber origins of the field.

There is a brand-new, gorgeous terminal finished in a fashionable burnt orange, and a pricey luxury hotel built to overlook the runway so that it is possible to watch the races from one's balcony. Man is so clever.

At this hour it's exquisitely quiet on the field, without a breath of a wind and a temperature that I can't even feel. It's like being in a womb. I truly hate to violate the stillness with the whine of the Bendix starter, but I have places to go.

I rumble down the wide runway, lift off, but keep it low and am quickly over Lake Istokpaga waking up the water birds. Sorry guys.

Today I have brought my camera into the cockpit to shoot what I can. It's not a decision taken lightly, because it's a big, old-fashioned iron Canon and there's no place in the cockpit for it. For such a big airplane, there are very few places to stow things. There is really no place for my cup of coffee, for instance, which I consider a major ergonomic omission. I have a tough time flying without my morning coffee. The map case is for maps and that's about it, although it is possible to jam in a Styrofoam coffee cup. Whether the coffee stays in the cup is another matter.

The airplane has no floor that is reachable. Drop the camera and it will probably punch a hole in the cotton floor before rolling back to the tail wheel. If that isn't enough, there is a maze of control cables, bell cranks, torque tubes, pedals, and control sticks that it can get hung up on. Get the camera stuck in any of those things and it will become an exciting flight.

But I've brought it anyway. It will be my project for the day, since taking a picture while flying alone is always problematic. It can be done, but it is ugly.

If the air is smooth, it's sometimes possible to simply trim the airplane for straight and level flight, then let go of everything and take whatever pictures are desired. Hopefully the aircraft will continue to sail on serenely in the direction that it was pointed. But this Stearman has never responded very well to trimming. On the ground I've checked and adjusted rigging, experimented with trim tabs, and warped its wings with strut adjustments, but inevitably the airplane wanders off in some arbitrary direction like a dog sniffing out a lawn.

An alternative is to hold the stick with the knees. This is a Rube Goldberg autopilot that works just about as well as letting go completely. Usually in the time that it takes to adjust the camera's f-stop, focus, and click off a few frames, the plane is in a graveyard spiral determined to punch a hole in the ground. Of course I am blind and not looking for other airplanes once my eye goes on that viewfinder. Each shot is a variation of this routine. Sometimes, when I pull the camera from my eye, I simply can't recognize the terrain. That's because the cornfield that was on the left before I did that twenty-second bracket is now behind me to the right. A nice small digital camera would help things immeasurably, but I use what I have. When I'm done I lash the camera to the frame of the airplane, glad the ordeal is over, and luxuriate in my new ability to see what I'm doing as I fly.

There was a model of the Stearman that was fitted with a Fairchild aerial camera in the backseat. It was a reconnaissance aircraft and featured a .30-caliber machine gun on the lower right wing. Why, I have no idea. A few of these were used by the Philippine Army Air Corps before the war, but when the Japanese showed up with their Zeros and Nates, most were immediately destroyed.

However, one Stearman did manage to fly a very famous mission to photograph Japanese artillery emplacements that were menacing Corregidor in the darkest days of that campaign. Escorted by five P-40s, this reconnaissance Stearman managed to overfly the Japanese positions and do its work. On its return it was intercepted by six Japanese fighters who were kept busy by the P-40 escort. The pilot and crewman of the Stearman of course had the option of bailing out since they were nothing but a target for the Nates, but they chose to stay and try to make the field. Brave men. Two of the Japanese fighters were able to just get at the wildly diving Stearman as it landed at Bataan Field, shooting a few holes in it as it rolled out, but hurting no one. That Stearman photo mission was successful and the Japanese went home very unhappy.

Bailing out of a perfectly good airplane rather than being a target was occasionally done, although considered poor form. Lt. Arthur Fiedler watched it happen during his second kill in the Mediterranean. It perhaps could have been called an "intimidation" rather than a kill.

## Capt. Arthur Fiedler, Ploesti, Rumania, 1944

*"I was astonished to see the enemy pilot jettison his canopy and bail out."*

It was on the twenty-eighth of June 1944 during a fighter sweep near Ploesti, Rumania. Responding to a radio report of Me-109s at thirty thousand feet, the squadron began a high-speed climb through layered clouds to reach the bogies. I had difficulty releasing my left drop tank and so ended up lagging behind the squadron in the climb. At about twenty-seven thousand feet, climbing through a clear area, I glanced left and spotted two aircraft, but was in the next layer of clouds before I could check them out. Stopping my climb, I eased back down through the clouds and observed the aircraft some five hundred yards away. Each had radiators under both wings—Me-109s.

I decided I would attack the leader and then take on the wingman; however, as I approached to within two hundred yards, the wingman went into a right skid, which immediately told me he was trying to ID me.

I took a lead on him, opened fire, and was rewarded with hits along the length of his aircraft. He now snapped inverted and did a split-S, at which point, with the adrenaline flowing, I completely forgot about the leader and dove after the wingman. At approximately thirteen thousand feet, the 109 pulled out of his twisting, rolling dive, and I opened fire again with instantaneous results. Smoke began pouring from his aircraft, the left wing dropped, followed by his nose, and shortly we were in a vertical dive with his aircraft trailing a large plume of black smoke.

Due to the varied terrain we flew over, it was impossible to always know the altitude of the ground below. Accordingly, one did not want to make the mistake of continuing the dive too long at five hundred miles per hour and go in with an enemy aircraft he had just shot down. So at an estimated five thousand feet, I began a pullout, watching to be sure the 109 crashed and did not attempt a low altitude escape.

The Me-109 continued straight down to impact, and since I had received credit for a "probable" a few days earlier, I decided to confirm this victory with pictures of the wreckage. Descending to about fifteen hundred feet, I turned off my machine guns, pointed my aircraft nose at the crash site, and recorded it on my gun camera film.

I then began a climb to altitude but was astounded to see another Me-109 cross my path heading northeast. I instantly turned my gun switch on, racked into a left bank, pulled a lead, and opened fire. There were about ten to twelve flashes on the Me-109's fuselage before all four of my machine guns jammed, due to the g's I pulled. Because of my slower airspeed as I started my climb out, I now found myself sliding into formation with this new 109. Now the adrenaline really began flowing as I tried to figure out what to do. We were heading toward Russia, and I was afraid to turn away, as this would give the 109 an opportunity to get a good shot at me before I could get out of range. At the same time, it was most unhealthy flying formation with an enemy plane should any friendly fighters spot us. I doubt they would take the time to identify the "wingman" as a P-51 before they opened fire and shot us down.

After a short time, I decided to draw my .45 automatic from my shoulder holster, fire in the direction of the 109, and hope this would cause him to turn away. I could then immediately turn the other way and head full speed for home. As I raised my right hand to pull down the zipper of my A-2 jacket, I was astonished to see the enemy pilot jettison his canopy and bail out. Completely bewildered, I turned around and took a picture of him in his parachute to preserve this bit of evidence also.

Why he bailed out, I don't know. Perhaps when I raised my hand to the zipper on my jacket, he thought I was gesturing for him to bail out. Or perhaps one of my initial shots had wounded him, and he decided to bail out at this time. But during the period we sat in formation, we were both looking at each other and I saw no indication he was wounded. My attention was riveted on his face, and when I got back to base, I could describe the rust color of his helmet and his oxygen mask, which appeared to be about the same color as ours. But hard to believe, I do not recall seeing the German cross or a number on the aircraft, which was only about forty feet from me. That must be what tunnel vision is. These were my first two victories, and for a short while I was called Svengali; however, since I failed to hypnotize any other pilots, causing them to bail out, this was a short-lived thing.

Lake Okeechobee glides by on my left. The sun is just coming up in the east and the lake reads as a molten pool. The wing is catching the same reflection, and the light coming through the struts and wires glints off of each wing rib and paints a picture made in heaven. I unstrap the camera and record it. It becomes the desktop image for my computer. Each time I fire up my soulless Mac, I'm at fifteen hundred feet over Lake Okeechobee.

Soon my immediate destination, Clewiston, is on the nose. I can see it from a long way off as a dun-colored stripe against a universe of intense green sugar cane fields. It's a fairly small strip and there are two large airplanes in the pattern. From a distance they look all out of scale to the runway and I'm puzzled, but as I get close I recognize the distinctive shape of a pair of Douglas C-47s shooting touch and gos. Now that is unusual. Here is an airplane that is almost a relic and is rapidly disappearing. It is, in fact, almost a contemporary of the Stearman, and somebody is still training to earn a living in it. The great-grandfathers of these pilots might have flown those airplanes sixty years ago. Later, on the ground, I watch them for a while and notice that with each aircraft, as power is brought in for a touch and go, one or both engines will fart or stumble before coming up to full power. Yep, just like a lot of Stearmans. Must be a genetic mechanical feature of the 1930s.

With these two old C-47 veterans in attendance, I am honor bound to grease the Stearman on the runway today and I really focus. With perhaps two thousand uneventful landings in this airplane behind me one would think that would be easy, but consistency in the Stearman has always eluded me. Glinty-eyed, jaw set, I hunch over and concentrate. My airspeed coming down final is a perfect seventy miles per hour. I'm over the fence at sixty-five as I gently rudder it straight from the crab that I had set up to see past the nose. I keep pulling the stick back, back, and . . . chirp! There, the tail wheel touches just as the stick hits the stop. The mains squawk happily just a heartbeat after the tail wheel and we are down. Perfect! No, not perfect. We're angling off the runway! Feed in opposite rudder—no, no, that's way too much. Now we're going off the other way. Opposite rudder. Damn, now I'm one cycle out of phase with what the airplane is doing.

"Easy. Easy." I'm talking to my airplane, admonishing it like a living thing as I work to straighten it out. And it does straighten out, and the weaving probably wasn't even noticeable to anyone watching, although the rudder snapping back and forth sure would be. But when the pilot does everything just right in this airplane, plops it down perfectly, and lets it roll just a few feet straight down the runway, he knows right away that he's done a good piece of work. He has a big smile, and maybe even walks a little more confidently when he gets out. Everybody wants to believe they are the absolute best in their chosen areas, and in this airplane a good landing is always a confirmation of one's abilities. And a dose of luck.

Of course when that same pilot has evolved to that exalted plateau where he is convinced that he can fly the crate that the airplane came in, it will totally humiliate him. Maybe he will even break something if he is particularly ham-handed. It's a process that is very much a reflection of life.

The Stearman should know better than to try to get away from me like that. It's been here before and it knows this runway. The aircraft military records from Maxwell AFB say that 41–806 was assigned to the 5th BFTS, Clewiston, Florida, in February of 1945. The war had less than seven months to go. Why it was sent there from its new home at San Angelo, Texas, after its very short stay, and why it was sent at all from its California home of almost four years is one of those mysteries known only to the Air Corps. As I am finding out, California to Florida is a very long trip for an airplane that was designed to do an hour or two in the pattern and then come down.

On the ground, my first surprise comes when I find out what the 5th BFTS stands for. Clewiston was the Number 5 British Flying Training School. I knew that the United States had trained British pilots in this country, but I didn't know where. Now I have found at least one place. But it was the "when" that interested me. In this case it seems that the 5th BFTS had opened its doors for business in September of 1941, three months before the United States was at war with Germany and Japan. It no doubt highly irritated the Germans and the Japanese to know that a neutral United States was training British pilots, but it couldn't have come soon enough. The Lend-Lease Act of March 1941 had made it possible.

Just to keep things technically correct, these schools were owned and operated by civilian contractors. In the case of Clewiston, the firm of Riddle-McKay owned and operated the field as well as two others in the immediate area, Carlstrom and Dorr Fields. At these fields, British pilots trained alongside American cadets and the Americans earned RAF wings as well as U.S. Air Corps wings on graduation.

The accident rate at Clewiston was exceptionally high, with nineteen British cadets being killed in accidents in its four years of operation. Many of these accidents were at night, where the blackness of the surrounding Lake Okeechobee and the Everglades no doubt contributed to the potential for the spatial disorientation similar to what I had experienced over Lake Pontchartrain.

There is very little of the original field left. It has become a skydiving center, and no one I spoke to knew very much of its history. Two of its three runways are gone, plowed under to grow a few more acres of sugar cane. Only one building out of the dozens constructed remains. It's used by the skydiving business. There is a sweet little museum on a side street in the town of Clewiston with a ten-foot section set aside for the 1,325 pilots who trained there. The curator is very knowledgeable and is the keeper of the flame.

Reunions, although there have been some, are difficult here for the simple reason that many of the pilots who trained at the 5th BFTS live in England.

The twenty-three British airmen who died in training at Carlstrom and Clewiston Fields rest in Oak Ridge Cemetery in Arcadia, Florida, in a plot of ground that has been deeded to the British government and is considered to be British soil. British and American flags fly over it.

Sadly, knowledge of Clewiston's place in history seems to be fading away, with little more left of its physical presence than an old building, a display counter in a storefront museum and one old Stearman to attest to its role in the lives of thousands of young men.

Pompano Beach now lies just over the nose, and the Atlantic Ocean beyond that. Clewiston is sixty miles behind me and sixty years back in time. I swing out across the beach and over the water. I'm "feet wet" in Navy parlance and thirty-nine hundred miles from where the Stearman began this journey for the second time.

The Pompano Beach tower gives me a right base entry with an instruction to report the lighthouse. That's a reporting point I've never used before. I fly up the beach, with condos on my right and the Atlantic on the left, and sure enough a lighthouse soon comes into view. I can see the Pompano airport and its big blimp hangar, another leftover from the war. I pull the belt tight, but the landing in Pompano is a greaser. I feel good. It's been ocean to ocean and we haven't broken anything.

# CHAPTER 21

CAPT. WILLIAM M. THOMPSON, C-47s, D-Day

*". . . a beautiful, clear night and an almost full moon."*

Pompano Beach to Savannah, Georgia, September 2, 2000

The humidity lies heavily on the otherwise exquisite, flamingo pink and baby blue morning sky as I roll the Stearman out of the hangar at Pompano Beach. I work up a very big sweat with the very little effort of pushing the airplane sixty feet, but I know that very soon a ninety-mile-per-hour breeze will be cooling me. The humidity has a musky scent to it that makes one very aware of its presence. It's a nice change from my native California, which I believe has a giant air freshener hanging from a mirror somewhere in the Sierras.

I've just spent four great days here enjoying Miami and sitting on an Intercoastal Waterway hotel balcony, catching up on my journal and watching the parade of ships down below. The "Intercoastal" is a river/channel/lagoon that parallels the Florida eastern seashore for much of its length and extends north past Florida as well. In Pompano Beach, it's a nicely manicured channel, about two hundred feet wide, lined with marinas, restaurants, homes, and resort hotels. I had lucked into a decent off-season rate on an efficiency apartment on the waterway, so knowing a good deal when I saw one, I set down roots and gave up aviating for a bit. It also helped that it was raining a lot and would have been difficult to go anywhere if I wanted to.

The boat culture in the marina below me is fascinating, and the boat protocol of the big cruisers—each bristling with two or three decks, flying bridges, and a phalanx of radar, radio, and loran antennas—is particularly so.

The Intercoastal, as it goes through Pompano Beach anyway, is spanned at regular intervals with bridges that are relatively modest, low-slung affairs. These carry a great number of the locals to and from their work each day, but because of the size of the boats that use the waterway these bridges must, by necessity, be drawbridges.

When one of the cruisers, out for its casual morning cappuccino run up or down the Intercoastal, arrives at a bridge, he must stop or be dismasted by the low overhead. The bridge tender, seeing the cruiser sulkily waiting and sometimes using its horn as a reminder, must stop all of the auto traffic, no doubt already late for work, and raise the bridge to let the cruiser pass. The street traffic almost immediately backs up at least a full block during this process.

I wonder what thoughts go through the minds of these commuters as the cruiser—with *Wretched Excess* painted on her transom, graced with a local nymph getting her tan on the flying bridge, and driven by a Jimmy Buffet look-alike—imperiously sails past the backed-up traffic. I know what mine would be: *How can I get one of those?* But I doubt if the commuters would share my enthusiasm. They're probably thinking far darker thoughts.

The smaller powerboats that launched from the marina on fishing expeditions were also high on my interest list. Two people on board, six fishing rods plugged into various sockets along the sides, and equipped with fish finders. The fish don't stand a chance. Why not just use grenades?

And finally, there are the cigarette boats. These are missile-like watercraft with hulls forty to sixty feet long, carrying two to four people at near subsonic speeds across the water. Isn't man's ingenuity wonderful? I loved it all and was sorry to leave Pompano Beach, particularly its neat little bistro, Mulligan's, but that is a story for another time.

Departing northbound out of the Pompano airport, I talk to Palm Beach Approach, but a malfunctioning transponder makes it problematic to go through their airspace. A transponder electronically enhances my radar image so that I may easily be identified and tracked. My guess is that the Stearman is a bit of a stealth aircraft with its slow speed and mostly wood-and-fabric structure. In one of my earlier lives I was a radar operator and remember that our scopes would eliminate painting anything slower than sixty miles per hour, a speed that I'm fully capable of in a head wind. I swing to the west to go around the Palm Beach airspace and discover some very interesting terrain called the Loxahatchee National Wildlife Refuge. It appears at first glance to be lush green fields stretching to the western horizon, but closer inspection reveals that there is water under that green and it is well and truly a swamp. Two days previously I had seen a *National Geographic* special on the alligators in this area with a special emphasis on their attacks on humans. Not a place for an engine failure. Palm Beach is defined on its western edge by what amounts to a long straight seawall that seems to draw the line as to what belongs to man and what belongs to the 'gators. Lacking survival gear, I fly on man's side.

Flying north up the east coast of Florida is as easy as it looks. Keep the blue on your right, the green on your left, and the cars underneath. I can't miss and soon my first fuel stop, Titusville, edges into sight. Titusville is another pretty little ex-military airport with the distinctive triangular runway system, but with a terrible name. The airport is called Space Coast Regional in the publications that deal with such matters. To me the name sounds like three different types of geography each awkwardly trying to modify the other. I guess that it is an accurate name, but one totally without the charm that the airport really has.

As I slide down final, I see in the run-up area a Douglas C-47 transport in D-Day invasion stripes getting ready for the Sunday morning hamburger run. The Valiant Air Command, a northern version of the Commemorative Air Force (this is northern Florida), has a museum at this airport, owns the C-47, and it's nearing lunchtime. I'll bet the boys are on board getting ready to head out for Cross City and its great weekend breakfasts. I'd love to look at the museum, but I'm pressed for time this morning. There are thundershowers predicted along my route of flight today, and I'm racing them to Savannah. As the weather briefer phrased it, "VFR [Visual Flight Rules] flight is not recommended."

If that C-47 was in England fifty-six years ago on June 6, 1944, as its paint job suggests, it had far better flying weather than I was headed for but a far more dangerous flight ahead of it.

## Capt. William M. Thompson, USAAF
## 85th Troop Carrier Squadron, C-47s, D-Day

### ". . . a beautiful, clear night and an almost full moon."

Now it was Monday, June 5, 1944. We received one final briefing and were told that we could expect heavy losses. Engine start-up was at 2235 hours, taxi and takeoff at 2300 hours with a full load of 101st Airborne infantrymen (23 men). This takeoff time placed us flying over the English Channel at midnight.

It was a beautiful, clear night and an almost full moon. We also had been briefed that Allied bombers and fighters had bombed out a corridor across Cherbourg Peninsula, through which we would fly. All German gun batteries had been knocked out and therefore we had nothing to worry about.

We passed between the islands of Guernsey and Jersey, making landfall on the western side of the Normandy Peninsula. We were to fly through that corridor to our designated drop zone on the east coast of Normandy, but as we approached the land, we entered a low deck of clouds at approximately twelve hundred feet altitude and were on instruments as a flight of three C-47s and left flight element of the squadron V of Vs.

I executed our instrument procedures for circumstances such as these by turning left forty-five degrees for one minute, then resuming the original heading of the formation, thus providing separation from the rest of the flights.

This placed me out of the bombed-out corridor and up near the

German stronghold near the city of Cherbourg. I started letting down to try to break out of the clouds. I finally broke out at five hundred feet above the ground, and when I did there were ground searchlights on my flight of aircraft with a string of tracer bullets coming across my windshield, which I assumed to be .50-caliber machine guns.

They certainly had our altitude, and the tracers were making a perfect cross right in front of my windshield. Apparently they were leading us too much, because they were accustomed to shooting at faster aircraft. This only lasted a minute or so, even though it seemed much longer. I thought they really had us.

We were wearing flak vests, and out of the corner of my eye I caught my copilot's head retracting down into the flak vest momentarily. I thought of a turtle pulling his head back into his shell when being threatened.

I saw water and the eastern coastline coming up. Realizing that I had to be north of our designated drop zone, I started making a right turn toward the south to get our paratroopers nearer the zone. During our mission briefing it had been impressed on us, DO NOT DROP YOUR PARATROOPERS INTO THE WATER! When I made my right turn I placed my right wing man in the position of looking across my aircraft and seeing the water.

Not knowing what I was doing—and of course we were not allowed to talk on the radio for the duration of the mission—he started jumping his troopers. Quickly realizing that my three aircraft loads of paratroopers and equipment were organized to function as a unit, I signaled to drop all three aircraft loads, hoping that they could form up on the ground together, knowing full well that I had dropped them two to three miles north of the designated drop zone.

I'll never know how my decision affected the war effort or how it may have affected several lives.

Later, after the Germans had surrendered, when flying some American POWs out of Germany, one of them was one of the men I had dropped on D-Day. Of course history tells us now that we scattered troops all up and down the Cherbourg Peninsula.

After dropping our troops that night, I stuck the nose down and dove for the deck to get out over the water and head for home base. I detected a vibration in the aircraft and hollered, "I think we have been hit." The crew chief looked at all of the instruments very carefully and said, "Sir, everything is running okay." Then I realized that we had released parapacks from the belly of the aircraft at the same time that we had dropped our troops, leaving eight-foot shroud lines slapping against the belly of the aircraft, thus the vibration.

So we made it back that night and landed at home base at approximately 0300 hours in good shape. I learned later that fifteen hundred C-47s had participated in this initial invasion, parachuting in eighteen thousand airborne troops, and approximately ten thousand were flown in by CG-4A gliders.

The flight to Savannah, four hundred-plus miles, should only require one fuel stop today, but after a lot of angst I decide on what seems like an almost unnecessary extra stop. If the weather is wet when I get to Savannah, I want enough fuel to be able to run and hide. As events unfold, it turns out to be a good plan.

As I am leaving Titusville and its PR-firm airport name I look to the east and see a thrilling sight—the Cape. Cape Canaveral. I've seen it for thirty years on television, and the events that have had their beginnings there—Mercury, Gemini, Apollo, the space shuttle, and *Challenger*—have seared images into my memory and that of most Americans. It sits off my right wing, a dramatic surprise that brings a shock of recognition. And in the middle of Merritt Island sits a gantry, probably getting ready to launch another shuttle. I'm moved by the sight. It's like turning a corner in New York and unexpectedly seeing the Statue of Liberty. By chance, when I first notice the gantry, it is framed in the struts and flying wires of this old bird, and I know that I'm looking at sixty-five years of history in one glance. I know that some of the pilots who flew those first Mercury missions, John Glenn for one, learned to fly in a Stearman. Yet I know that many of the men and women who fly those missions today have probably never even heard of the airplane.

I keep moving north, and soon Jacksonville slides by and the character of the land begins to change. For the next fifty miles I find myself moving over convoluted inlets and islands of the Georgia coast. No hard-edged Florida beach here. There is a battle going on between the sea and the land, and each has made inroads into the other. Some of the inlets are good size stretches of open water. Not a wise passage without survival gear, but it is incredibly beautiful and I stay the course down low among the birds. The engine is sounding solid. Besides, the airplane knows the route.

I make my second and last fuel stop in Brunswick, Georgia. As I pass over the town I can smell the pulp mills, a not altogether unpleasant smell but one that the townsfolk are probably sick of. Landing in Hammond, Louisiana, I had smelled a fragrant, soaplike aroma as I got low over the area. Clewiston, Florida, smelled like a fire, which was not at all unreasonable since they burn off sugar cane fields after harvest. I can't account for the soap though.

At Brunswick a Gulfstream jet holds while I'm in the pattern. He tells me he just wants to see the Stearman land. I try to put it down right in front of him and we exchange pleasantries. I'm sure that he would love to fly my airplane as much as I would love to fly his.

After fueling, as I leave Brunswick I look back at the airfield and notice a very curious layout. It has a single long east-west runway and a taxiway that wanders south to a huge circular concrete ramp unlike any I have seen before. I have since discovered that this ramp was once lined with blimp hangars that housed very efficient little 250-foot blimps, which could patrol for up to twenty hours at a time. They were designed to ruin the day for the World War II German U-boats and were quite successful at it. German submarines, which had it all their own way early in the war, suddenly found life very dangerous along the Atlantic and Gulf coasts. The blimp hangars at Brunswick, costly to maintain and without any particular usefulness after the war, were all torn down, but their ramp remains and is now used as a driving course for federal agents. I had noticed a blimp hangar while at Pompano Beach and assume that it was part of a chain. The Germans built close to eleven hundred U-boats during the war, and almost a thousand of them went to the bottom, many, no doubt, because of the blimps of Brunswick and those along the coast.

I change frequencies and pick up wind and landing information for Savannah, which is now only fifty miles away. It warns of ugly weather for the area and recommends a check with Flight Watch, which I do.

"No sweat, it's big but it's out in the Atlantic." Then almost casually he adds, "Oh, and by the way, Stearman, there is an area of precipitation heading for Savannah that should reach the airport just about the time you will. Good luck." I lay on another hundred rpm and hunker down in the cockpit, fondly hoping the Stearman will go faster.

But the Stearman takes its own good time and the dark skies of Savannah crawl into view. I'm vectored by Savannah Approach to a long final for runway nine, but as I get close I notice something odd about the run-way—it's hard to see, and what little I can see looks very wet. There is a cell sitting over the field.

"Savannah tower, Stearman seven-two-one. Is it raining at your field?" I inquire.

"That is affirmative, seven-two-one. It's raining hard."

*Thanks for the timely warning,* I think to myself.

"Savannah tower, seven-two-one is going to break off the approach, head west, hold, and wait for the cell to pass."

And so I wander off, like a whipped dog, the loser of the race with the thunderstorm and set up a little holding pattern above a couple of lakes.

Soon I'm joined in this activity by an American Airlines DC-9 and a pair of 737s who share my sentiments about thunderstorms. I orbit for about an hour while the weather sorts itself out. Had I not made that extra fuel stop, orbiting would not have been an option and I would have proba-bly provided afternoon entertainment for the folks in the tower. Landing during a thunderstorm is not an impossible task but one that carries with it certain possibilities. Gusts, wind shears, and water on the runway are all potential excitement builders. All I want to do after four hundred miles of open cockpit flying is to peacefully wrap myself around a hot cup of coffee.

Finally one of the 737s goes for it, lands with no trouble, and the rain and the risk melt away. We all emerge from our discretionary absences and are cleared to land, each in turn, on runway nine. The wind, of course, by now has shifted to one-eight-zero at twelve knots. On a DC-9 that makes very little difference. On a gusty afternoon with a slippery runway after a storm has passed, however, that crosswind can make a huge differ-ence to me. There is a runway one-eight here. That would land me into the wind. Why the hell don't they just clear me to land on it?

"Savannah tower, Stearman seven-two-one would like runway one-eight." I'm full of righteous indignation.

"Roger, Stearman seven-two-one, make a right base for one-eight. Cleared to land," they reply amiably.

But my friend in the tower does not have my best interests at heart, or is remarkably parsimonious with help, good sense, and information.

So I touch down on one-eight in a shower of spray that pulls the airplane first left, then right, then straight. I splash my way to the general aviation ramp and negotiate one of the last hangar spaces on the field. It costs almost as much as my motel but is worth it. I tuck the airplane away safe, dry, out of the wind, and feel very good about my judgment, luck, and timing. Some days the bear eats you—some days you eat the bear. The coffee was especially good as I sat safely inside over an early dinner and watched the atmosphere explode into every conceivable thunderstorm phenomenon.

It rained for four days.

I came to Savannah to see the Mighty Eighth Air Force Heritage Museum, so the rain was good. There is nothing like being in a museum on a rainy day, and the rain was appropriate to the somber mood of the displays. This is a recently built institution devoted to the air war in Europe, and I wanted to look at the oral histories in their library. From bases in England the Eighth Air Force had sent B-17s, B-24s, and their fighter escorts against the Germans and took tremendous casualties in an effort to destroy Germany from the air. At one point, no more than one out of three aircrews could count on completing their tours. This museum, as well as other World War II tributes are long overdue. The men who fought that war, the ones who are left are nearing eighty. This was a quiet generation that accomplished great things and didn't ask for much afterward.

The museum is beautifully done with touching photo essays and videos throughout. As I read the oral history transcripts, I am amazed at what the men went through. Many of these personal stories have been written recently as a legacy to their children and grandchildren. These men know that they don't have forever. Most incidents are probably painfully recalled. Some are compilations of letters by desperate mothers and fathers as they tried to find out what happened to their MIA sons. Others are tributes by survivors of ten-man aircrews or squadrons to buddies who didn't make the bailout bell or couldn't get out of their burning Mustang. This was a remarkable generation that was called upon to stop what was clearly the blackest of evils. They did what it took to end it and then got on with life. I was an infant during that war, and these men were always immense heroes to me as I grew up. They are even bigger after my visit to the "Mighty Eighth."

## Lt. Basil Lyle Shafer, USAAF
## Nuremberg, September 10, 1944

### *"So I was falling free . . ."*

Most of the crew had about twenty-five missions when we were shot down. That happened over Nuremberg on September 10, 1944, on a Sunday morning about 10:00. We had gone in to bomb a factory and got hit very hard with antiaircraft fire. The plane exploded after a few seconds.

There were nine people on the crew that particular day. We were flying deputy lead and were the plane flying off the wing of the lead plane. If the lead plane got shot down, we were supposed to take over. So we had a bombardier and a navigator. By this time, because the Luftwaffe had been pretty well grounded, we took off a waist gunner. So instead of having a ten-man crew, we had nine. And instead of having a bombardier on every crew, gunners—usually waist gunners—were trained as a "toggleer." He'd simply toggle the bombs off of the lead plane that had a bombardier. Each plane usually carried a navigator, because if the plane got separated and had to get back, he was needed. But you didn't need a bombardier.

So the crews had been skinned down by that time. We were flying with nine. Six of the men were killed; three of us got out—the tail gunner, the navigator, and me.

It was common practice to fly without wearing a parachute in the B-17. My particular experience was a hair-raising situation for me and probably one of the most dramatic things that has ever happened to me during my lifetime. It was something I really wouldn't talk about to people after the war. I just didn't think that they would believe what I was going to say.

The plane exploded. I looked around and the only thing behind me was the back of my seat. The reason I survived the explosion—we were going over the target at the time we were hit, flying straight and level— was that I had put my arm up along the edge of the window and was leaning down to get my flak helmet, which was down under my seat, under my feet. That was when we got hit.

My right arm was shattered. If I'd been sitting up, I'd have been hit in the head or chest. We always wore a flak vest. We'd put on our flying suit, then our parachute harness, which had two snap rings on the front and the chest pack just snapped into this harness. On top of the harness, we wore the flak vest. We put a flak helmet on over our other helmet, so as the flak came up, we had at least some protection.

So I was trying to get my flak helmet when we were hit. The plane started tumbling; it was full of smoke and fire. One guy came flying over me and went up against the ceiling. We were really tumbling quite violently, and of course I thought I was going to be killed.

Then it occurred to me that I could, maybe, grab my parachute and see if I could salvage something of this. When the pressure was right, I released my seat belt and tumbled out of the seat. I grabbed my chute by the handle as I fell free from the airplane and just ripped the intercom and oxygen connection loose as I fell.

So I was falling free. The plane and I had separated and we were falling at different speeds. I had the parachute pack in my hand and was trying to put it on, but I couldn't get it hooked. Then I realized that I still had my flak vest on.

It's a very simple device to get rid of. There is a little red cord on one side, and when you pull it the vest releases. I pulled the cord and the back floated away. But the front stayed there and I couldn't quite figure that out. Then I realized that I was falling on my stomach. So I pulled off the front of the flak vest. I pulled it aside and it just floated off. I hooked my chute on one hook. I never did see the ground, but I knew that I had only a couple of minutes to do all of this. It was a long time in one sense of the word.

So I hooked one snap and thought, "Well, gee, I don't want to break a leg; I've got time so I'll hook up the other snap." Then I pulled the ripcord. I was skyscraper high when the thing opened up. I swung three or four times and hit the ground, right in town, in Nuremberg. Actually the Nuremberg suburb of Schweinau. I almost landed on a flak battery in an open lot. I was still on my back when a sailor and an air raid warden were right on top of me.

They asked me if I had a gun. I said, "No." We never carried guns on missions. We wore them around the base but were told to leave them at home. It was a good idea, because if you had a gun the Germans were liable to kill you. Anyway, I was captured and stayed at this place until about five o'clock in the evening. I stayed right there where I was captured . . . sitting on a bench.

# CHAPTER 22

*"Those that weren't sold were bulldozed into a pile alongside the runway at Hamilton and burned."*

Savannah to Orangeburg then Bennettsville, South Carolina, September 8, 2000

Day four of the deluge dawns in Savannah. For the last two weeks there has been a stagnant area of low pressure over the southeast. I say that like I'm a meteorologist and know what it means. I don't. This is what the weather briefers tell me, and I grunt knowledgeably into the phone. I suppose that at some time in my training the concept of stagnant low pressure was crystal clear, but the old premise applies—use it or lose it. The only thing that it means to me is that there have been very low ceilings and thunderstorms every day, with epic peals of thunder and lightning that don't seem to affect anyone but me. I launch two feet off of the ground when they go off. When you are from Southern California and not that used to thunderstorms and that kind of noise, they get your attention. I just thank the gods that I'm not flying each day.

But this morning I'm up at 5:30 checking weather. It's six hundred feet overcast, one-half mile visibility with rain, and I go back to sleep. I check it again at 7:30. It's eight hundred feet overcast with rain. I get some breakfast. At 9:30 it's eight hundred feet broken, four thousand feet overcast with rain. Hmmm, for me flight is still not legal from this airport but is moving in that direction. At 11:00 it's twelve hundred feet overcast with a spectacular three miles' visibility, and I'm at Savannah airport paying bills and loading up. It's time to go.

Clearance delivery asks me for my heading and altitude. I give them a heading, but for altitude I tell them that I will be "clear of clouds." I'll be "scud running," and they understand. Scud running is an ancient and honorable activity among pilots that consists of dodging clouds and cells, sometimes quite low to the ground. Over the airport there is a twelve-hundred-foot ceiling, but I can rest assured that wherever I go the odds of the ceiling getting lower than that are good. And no doubt there will be patches where the clouds go right down to the ground. These are places where I must carefully pick my way around. It's a bit like working one's way through a moving maze.

There are many factors that must be considered in doing this. First there can be no obstructions along the route. Particularly towers. I've had quite enough of towers. Rising terrain is also bad. Hills and mountains have a way of rising right into overcast. Escape routes are good. Where are the areas of improving weather that I can escape to, and what is "Plan B"?

Some pilots just won't do it. Some do it routinely. It has to do with skill and confidence levels, how badly you want to get somewhere, perceived safety, and I guess ultimately, one's psychological makeup. It's a bit like investing in the market, except that in the market the downside is limited to losing only your money. It's a challenge just like many things in life.

So I take off to the north for Orangeburg and pick my way through the scud as best I can. Most of the time I'm well under a thousand feet, and the ground beneath me under the low overcast and rain has an ominous character. It's sparsely inhabited, dense, dark woodland with sinister serpentine rivers occasionally showing themselves through the foliage. I can see malevolent winged monkeys flitting through the trees, thoughtfully watching my progress. The voice of the wicked witch—"I'll get you, my little pretty"—can be faintly heard above the rumble of the engine. If this plane were to go down in these woods, I would be found in a tree in the year 2057, my bones long since picked clean.

The same woods, in sunlight, as I go north and the weather eases, take on a totally different character and become benign and friendly, with cute little Hansel and Gretel farms dotted here and there. Happy, merry workers toil in the fields, pitching hay into quaint oxcarts. They stop and wave. How charming. The sky turns blue, the clouds are puffy white and sparse. It's amazing what a little sunlight will do for one's perception of life.

The military records say that Stearman 41–806 was assigned to Orangeburg, South Carolina, in December of 1944. It was assigned to the 4954 Base Training Unit, which was the military counterpart of the civilian flying school operated by Bevo Howard, a noted aerobatic pilot. This school had been in operation since October 4, 1941, and trained both American and Free French pilots. Now I truly had an international airplane— American pilots in California, British pilots in Florida, and French pilots in South Carolina. Very exotic. We were serious about winning that war.

There were two fields in the Orangeburg operation: the main field, where the cadets were housed, and the municipal field, four miles away, which was used for landing practice. There were probably other auxiliaries as well. The military field, with its two large hangars and complex of administration and cadet barracks is gone. A couple of foundations and pieces of the ramp are the only things that remain. A very nice, rambling Methodist senior citizens' complex now exists on the property. I visited it and in one of the communal rooms found a showcase with a few shelves dedicated to the activities of the old air base. Dozens of smiling young cadets gathered around silver biplanes look out from photographs into a room populated with silver-haired elderly women who perhaps dated these men fifty-five years ago. A yellowed English/French dictionary, with an emphasis on aviation terms rests on one of the shelves. Airplane . . . avion! Fuselage . . . fuselage! One of the instructors, I'm told, insisted that his French students sit in the front of the airplane, contrary to the accepted practice of students flying from the rear, so he could swat them with a newspaper when they made a mistake. Because of the language problem, this instructor felt he had no other way of expressing his displeasure.

Aerial photos of the base show a busy military field at the height of war. Stubby little live oak seedlings, planted by the cadets, line the approach road to the base. Their efforts have yielded a stunning winding road, now canopied by sixty-year-old trees that lead to the senior citizen complex. Along the highway that parallels the field is a sign that reads: *"HAWTHORNE SCHOOL OF AERONAUTICS. From 1941 to 1945, 5,924 American and French pilots were trained here, totaling almost 330,000 flight hours. Site is 1 mile N.W."*

I land the Stearman at the Orangeburg municipal field four miles to the north. It knows that it has been there before. As I clumsily wrestle with a gusty crosswind, the airplane simply takes over and does a perfect wheel landing. I am just along for the ride.

In March of 1945, 41–806 is sent up to Palmer Field, one hundred miles north, in Bennettsville, South Carolina, where it begins instructing at its eighth and final base. The war in Europe is almost over and has just another month to go. The fighting in the Pacific will last until August, and the military has been winding down flight training since 1944.

Palmer Field, like Orangeburg, is mostly gone now. You can see what is left of it from the Bennettsville municipal field two miles away. Two large hangars remain as storage sheds among some newer industrial buildings. The field—and it was just that, a sod field, no cement or asphalt runway here—now grows beans. All of the cadet barracks and the administration buildings are gone. Photos of the field and its now-forgotten students grace the walls of the very small Bennettsville municipal terminal, which was used as an auxiliary field. The Stearman remembered its days here also and once more, softly touched down on the runway.

It kept on taking students up and down, safely, until that fifteenth day of August in 1945 when the war ended. On that day, all across the country, the training came to a stop, the planes were parked, the switches went to OFF, and the military had to face the problem of what to do with its one hundred thousand airplanes. Actually they were thinking about that well before the war ended and in 1944 set up the Reconstruction Finance Corporation to dispose of the soon-to-be-huge military surplus. Palmer Field now became a surplus disposal site, and all of its Stearmans went up for sale. Vets had first choice, but anybody with a few hundred dollars could walk the ramp, pick out the best one, and fly it away. The airplanes needed a few things done to them before the old Civil Aeronautics Board would license them, and those who bought one soon got a friendly letter from the manufacturer, Boeing, that said in part: *"We have received informa-tion from the Defense Plant Corporation that you have purchased a Boe-ing 'Kaydet' airplane. Although you did not purchase your airplane directly from our company, we wish to extend every effort to help you realize the utmost from it. . . . Accordingly we are forwarding a copy of the first service bulletin which we have issued pertaining to the Kaydet."* The first recall letter!

There followed a list of mechanical items that had to be accomplished on each model of the Stearman. Some of these items were not inconse-quential. The old Civil Aeronautics Board required, for example, that the aluminum firewall be removed and replaced with a stainless steel firewall. This required removal of the cowlings, engine, and motor mount, and that was a lot of time and money for the unsuspecting purchaser. But it was done, and today every Stearman flying has a stainless steel firewall.

Stearmans were sold from fields all over the country. Those that couldn't be sold were soon destroyed. At Hamilton Field, north of San Francisco, they were lined up nose to tail on the runway and put up for sale. I have the handbook from one of these aircraft. There is a notation inside the front cover, which says: *Stearman PT-17 $450.00—with spare engine.* Those that weren't sold were bulldozed into a pile alongside the runway at Hamilton and burned.

At Palmer Field, after sitting through the winter, 41–806 got lucky and found a home. In February of 1946, twenty-six-year-old Navy vet Frank Rogers wandered in one day, picked it out of the line as the best of what was there, and paid $851.90 for it. That was a lot of money for a Stearman back then, so no doubt the modifications had already been done to it. He probably used some of his discharge money to pay for it.

Frank was not a novice in aviation matters. After graduating from Clemson University, he had joined the Navy and learned to fly in Atlanta in the N3N, a Navy-built biplane similar to the Stearman. His abilities and the convenience of the government put him on the road to fighters, and after some interim steps in Vultees and Texans, Frank was soon flying Hellcats for Fighting Sixteen (VF-16 squadron) off of the carrier *Lex-ington.*

In 1944 he found himself in the Battle of the Philippine Sea and the Battle of Leyte Gulf and acquitted himself very well. His Distinguished Service Cross citation states that he shot down two Japanese aircraft and participated in the destruction of ten more. The first Battle of the Philippine Sea became known as the "Great Marianas Turkey Shoot" and was a pivotal battle in the war. Over three hundred Japanese aircraft were destroyed on that day, and some Japanese pilots were so panicked they were seen to ditch perfectly good aircraft in the sea rather than risk being shot down and killed in them. Three Japanese carriers went to the bottom and it effectively destroyed the Japanese navy as a threat.

A highly decorated Frank Rogers left the Navy in 1945, moved back home to Darlington, South Carolina, and the family farm. But he bought himself the Stearman, because he was still an aviator and loved to fly.

He kept and flew it for three years. Marriage and children soon loomed on the horizon, so in July of 1949, 41–806 was sold for $850.00, $1.90 less than he had paid for it. Like most things from our past, the memories of the silver airplane grew dim.

Frank Rogers had just turned eighty years old and was still living in Darlington when he got a puzzling call. Had he owned an airplane fifty years ago? Yes, he had.

"Was it a Stearman?"

"Yes, it was."

"Was its number N-five-five-seven-two-one?" Well, he couldn't rightly remember the "N" number.

"Mr. Rogers, were you born on August 2, 1920?" (They put birth dates on aircraft registrations applications back then.)

"Why, yes."

"Well, Mr. Rogers, I believe I own the airplane that you bought over fifty years ago from Palmer Field, in Bennettsville. It looks pretty much the way that it looked the day that you bought it, and I am in the area. I would be pleased and honored if you would like to see it again after all these years."

It was uncertain who was more excited, Frank or his charming wife, Jesse, but a date was made and kept. As I rumbled over the Bennettsville municipal airport and the old Palmer Field at pattern altitude, I could see two lone figures waiting on the apron. Frank would never get to see his Hellcat again. It didn't exist anymore. But he would be able to mount up his old Stearman one more time. Emotions ran high at the little Bennettsville airport that afternoon as I touched down and taxied in. We spent time over, under, and in the Stearman. We took pictures and talked about Frank

Rogers's war. We looked at yellowed citations for bravery and photos of a slim boyish twenty-four-year-old fighter pilot receiving his decorations. I wish I could say that Frank mesmerized me with detailed accounts of those times and battles, but I can't. For Frank, too much time has gone by and they are all misty, imprecise memories.

Others have talked about those days though.

## Lt. Walter Bruce Longino
## On board the USS *Bunker Hill*, 1944

### *Of kills, ditchings, rescues and quitting.*

*Of kills . . .*

Again we set out after a bogie. As it happened I was flying an F6F-5 and the other three in my division were flying F6F-3s. The "dash-five" was a little bit faster. We were supposed to be up at about eighteen thousand feet and were vectored to the northeast. The Jap was going east and we were closing on him.

I used my speed to gain altitude, so I was actually at about 19,500 with the others spread out below me. We were told to look sharp, that the enemy had turned toward us.

Here I was, fifteen hundred feet above everyone else, so I was looking down. I don't know why, but I glanced up and there he was, just whistling along. He didn't see me, and I yelled "Tally-ho up!" I yanked back on the stick and got my nose up and just ahead of him.

I just touched the guns and my aircraft immediately spun out. I recovered down around fifteen thousand feet and was looking around to see what was happening when the Japanese aircraft passed me going straight down with John Topliff in behind him. I must have killed the pilot and gotten the starboard engine. I fired only thirty-two rounds.

The plane had rolled over and gone straight down. Topliff saw the Jap when I yelled tally-ho and had rolled in behind him. He was ready to shoot when the Jap's starboard engine blew up. I figured later that he must have been up around twenty-three thousand feet. I think it was a Dinah.

We'd been over Clark Field and were coming back from that strike when one of the bomber pilots that we were escorting came up on the radio and wanted to know, "What the hell is wrong with you fighters? Don't you see those planes taking off?"

We looked down. There was a dirt field down there, and there were streaks of dust where aircraft were taking off. Two divisions of us went down and I got one plane. I know I got him but did not get credit for him. I don't believe any of the combat was at over two hundred feet. Everything was right down on the ground. I never saw a shot fired at us. I think what happened is that we caught a bunch of students, but when we got back it was reported that there were all kinds of airplanes. Maybe I just didn't see them all, but I didn't see any airplane even retract its landing gear.

I saw a number of funny things happen. The guns in one of my wings weren't firing right, so I kicked the charger. We had buttons we punched to recharge the guns, but instead of kicking my left wing re-charger I kicked my right wing on to "safety." An aircraft was landing and I was shooting at it with only one gun. The runway was going one way, we were going crosswise to it, and I was getting him with the one gun as he landed. As soon as the plane slowed down enough, he jumped out, ran across the wing, jumped into the grass, and ran into the woods. The plane flipped over and burned.

I was shooting at another one that was landing, but I think the pilot may already have been dead. He flew in between two trees and wiped off both wings. In a matter of a very few minutes, we had fires burning all over the place and nobody else was in the air.

Not one of the eight planes that went down got a hole in it. I know I never saw an enemy gun fired but there were all kinds of claims that came out of that action.

*Of ditchings . . .*

The day of the Saipan landings, June 15, 1944, we went to do photo reconnaissance of Guam. We made one photo pass, and I was hit in the top half of my rudder. McClusky was hit in the left wingtip. There was a lifeguard submarine offshore and we rendezvoused with it. McClusky wanted to know if I wanted to go back for another pass.

I didn't want to, but I didn't want to say so. I don't think any of the others wanted to go back either, but nobody said so, so we went back for another run.

We climbed up over the center of the island, where there were some ragged clouds, and pushed on over through them. I was number three in the formation, but somehow, when we came out I was leading the works.

Orote airstrip on the Orote peninsula was our target, and I didn't think anyone was shooting at me, but the flak was breaking in back of me so heavily that the other three aircraft pulled out. I would have pulled out, but I never saw the others and I didn't think the flak gunners saw me.

The next thing I knew my whole field of vision was full of fire. I continued my dive right down to the water, to about fifty feet. I was about to tell Brownscombe that I'd been hit and have him look me over when I heard him say, "You'd better get that thing in the water."

By then I could see that I was being shot at from behind. I could see shots hitting the water all around me.

The submarine was right there, so I turned toward it. Brownscombe called the sub—the call sign was Silver Slipper—and asked that it be turned into the wind. I just went straight to the submarine, put a wingtip on the conning tower, straightened up, and was going to land when Brownscombe said, "Turn forty-five degrees to your right," so I turned forty-five degrees and landed.

When I hit, water came in and I thought I had gone underwater. I released my safety belt, but I had hit and skipped and I was fine. I hit the second time with my hands on the windshield and I was over the side and gone. I took about five or six strokes, turned around, and could see the tail going down. I could see the submarine coming a couple of yards away at most. A submarine appears to be pretty low, but when you're in the water it seems to be pretty high.

I pulled a dye marker and started swimming toward the sub. I looked back and saw I'd swum out of the dye marker, so I pulled another one and waited in it. The sub came around, and by then the skipper had lost sight of me under the bow, so he was backing full, trying to stop it. There was a sailor up on the bow and he dropped me a rope, which I grabbed hold of. I wasn't going to let that go by, but the sub started towing me underwater. The sailor had enough sense to let go of his end, and I popped up about amidships with the sub stopped.

They dropped me another rope. I was going to climb up that thing, but I couldn't bend my elbows I was so weak. A couple of sailors dropped down and hoisted me up. There wasn't a scratch on me.

I had been in the water twelve minutes.

Then I couldn't get off that submarine—the Stingray. The captain was Sam Loomis, and I was the fifth and last pilot to be picked up. One of them, Brantly, had been picked up a couple of days earlier. The submarine had to go in and tow him out on the periscope. It was one of the most spectacular rescues of the war.

Bruce Longino's brother was a bomber pilot.

*Of rescues . . .*
My brother was in the 13th Air Force and was flying B-24s in the same area where I was.

I had just gotten back to the ship in mid-July after I'd been shot down when I got a cable from my dad, telling me that Randolph had been shot down over Yap and was missing in action.

I sent a letter to the commanding officer of his squadron and told him that I was a Navy pilot in the same area and would like to learn more of the circumstances of my brother's shoot-down so I could better estimate his chances of survival.

In the meantime, he'd been picked up by a submarine. He was leading the squadron into Yap and was jumped by fighters and shot down on the way out. The submarine was on the surface, saw the flight go over, saw the column of smoke go up, and figured it was more smoke than a fighter would put out. The fighters were theirs. The bombers were ours.

So the sub took a bearing on the smoke, and three and one-half hours later it found my brother floating around.

He told the people aboard the sub that he was the pilot, the last one out, and that his right wing was down. So they drew an arc on a chart, followed the line back, and found seven more men. The last one was found after they'd been searching for two and one-half days. They found him in the wake of the submarine. He'd thrown his life jacket away and was trying to catch the sub. He was the tail gunner and weighed about 130 pounds.

Our family had been notified that my brother had been shot down, but were never notified that he'd been picked up until he wrote to them. He was on the sub for seven days. When he got back he learned that he'd been made commanding officer of his squadron. The first letter that crossed his desk was my letter asking about him.

*. . . and quitting.*
We'd been having operation after operation after operation. They'd tell us that after the next series we were going to be relieved. About this

time the average period at sea was about four months. We'd been out since January and this was in October.

We were finally notified that the torpedo and dive-bombers were going to be relieved and that the fighters, plus as many extra fighters as could be rounded up, would be put on board and that we would be a fighter carrier completely. Everybody went home but us.

We held a meeting and sent word to [Admiral "Bull"] Halsey, "Fighting Eight quits." We were going to refuse to fly.

Halsey knew we'd been there a long time but hadn't realized it had gotten that bad. Nonetheless he needed a minimum of twelve volunteers to act as division leaders and relieve everybody else.

So we held a meeting. There were speeches by the captain of the ship and by our C.O., the air group commander. They called for volunteers and there was one volunteer. Word was sent out that there was one volunteer from Fighting Eight. The next message was to relieve us all. So we left Leyte Gulf.

We were about fifteen hours from the gulf when word was received that the Jap fleet had come out. It was the Second Battle of the Philippines. I think we were the nearest large carrier to it.

We fully expected to be turned around and ordered into battle. We were the most experienced bunch out there then. At the time every man in Fighting Eight had been ordered before a disposition board composed of a flight surgeon and others. Every man who was mentally and physically capable was to be retained on board.

We went before the board and the board grounded the entire squadron, with the exception of three people who were relief pilots and had just arrived.

Halsey was told there was only one volunteer and that the whole squadron had been grounded. That was when he said, "Well, send 'em home."

We were put ashore at some island . . . to await transportation.

For Lt. Bruce Longino, USN, the war was over.

# CHAPTER 23

CAPT. JOSEPH C. PIMENTEL, Thunderbolt pilot, France, 1944
*". . . we'd fill the place with .50-caliber slugs."*

Bennettsville to Chattanooga, Tennessee, September 9, 2000

The next morning, the airport manager's wife picks me up in Bennettsville and drops me at the airport. We chat for a while and she tells me a little of her life at the small airport. Her husband runs the ag spray business out of the airport, and they both manage and maintain the small, immaculately kept, municipal airport and terminal. It's the American dream. Own your own business and have a good time doing it. He does the flying, she does the book work and helps load the aircraft with chemicals. I ask her if she is concerned about handling the chemicals, and she replies that most of them are pretty safe these days and if the right protective gear is worn there should not be a problem. But you can tell that she isn't thrilled about that aspect of it.

Although they are still called dusters, very little actual dusting is done today. Chemicals are now sprayed as a liquid. In the bad old days one of the most dangerous payloads for a duster or ag aircraft was sulfur dust. Sulfur acts as a fungicide to control mildew.

The problem with sulfur is that it's highly explosive (remember the sulfur on the heads of kitchen matches?). When the airplane is flying in a fine mist of sulfur powder, it is an explosion waiting to happen, and many duster pilots have lost their lives as their airplanes exploded in flight. Fortunately, "aerial application," as it's now called, is a much safer activity these days, although a visit to any duster strip will frequently reveal the wreckage of an ag aircraft sitting on a flatbed.

Dave Massey, my "duster" connection in the San Joaquin Valley, told me of the hazards of dusting with sulfur.

> Sulfur dust is probably the worst. Sulfur is flammable. Add to that the component of static electricity, because the airplane creates static electricity as it flies through the air. Where the dust comes out of the airplane there is air coming out of there as well. You've got static right there with the dust. We bond the airplane to make all the different components one unit. A bonding strip electrically ties components together so that you have continuity between everything and you don't have static electricity trying to jump from one component to the other.
>
> Normally what happens when you have an in-flight fire is that it starts in the spreader. Or it will start behind the airplane because the hot exhaust is kicking out little red-hot carbon cinders. You don't see them unless you fly at night. Well, those hot carbon cinders go back there and will get into the aerated sulfur, and the burn rate of suspended sulfur in the air is faster than that airplane is going, so it is going to catch you. It can start back there and it races forward . . . and will actually go up in the spreader and up into the hopper. The only way to really get it shut down is to close the hopper. But what can happen is that if the sulfur in the spreader catches on fire, it can actually burn that rubber seal to the point where it starts leaking sulfur and feeds itself. Then you can't shut it off.
>
> The fumes associated with burning sulfur will take your breath away. One minute you're breathing fresh air and the next minute you're breathing sulfur fumes. You're outta air. And it's that quick.
>
> So to prevent fires we run a long stack on the exhaust pipe and it directs the exhaust out and up so that it kicks those little cinders up and away.

41–806 was both a duster and a sprayer for twenty-five years. It worked the fields of Louisiana, Mississippi, Missouri, Kansas, and Oklahoma before it became just too inefficient to be commercially competitive. Almost always, when these airplanes were converted to dusters, extensive modifications were made to the aircraft to install the bigger engines, hoppers, rollover structures, and spray equipment. When they are reconverted back to standard category, all of the modifications have to be removed as the airplane is restored to stock. 41–806 shows little or no sign of these old modifications. The repairs were either done well or the modifications were not extensive.

I wish the airport manager's wife well, thank her for the ride in from town, and smile at the hospitality that I have experienced at these small airports in rural America. She was as excited as the rest of us at the reunion of Frank Rogers and his old airplane and was very knowledgeable about the history of the field.

The day before, she had shown us photos of Palmer Field in its heyday. The activity was intense as fresh-faced young pilots grouped around their instructors and mugged for the camera. The big hangars are full of silver Stearmans in various stages of maintenance. Class 43C stands proudly in front of their aircraft, their futures uncertain as the war rages on.

As much as I'd love to see one, there are no pictures dated around mid-1945 that might include 41–806. Not that there is any way I could possibly tell, since the Army rarely put aircraft serial numbers on the tails of Stearman trainers. Actually this is a good thing. I have a photo taken at Oxnard, California, in 1941 while 41–806 was there. Pilots and instructors are grouped around a Stearman in the foreground, while another one is coming over the fence for landing. Either one could be 41–806. I have another taken of the flight line at Santa Maria, California, in 1943. All of the aircraft are lined up on the ramp. Which one is 41–806? It's fun to speculate.

I crank up the Stearman, depart to the northwest, and circle over the old Palmer Field. I'm tempted to do a low pass by the industrial buildings, but this will no doubt upset someone, so I circle the complex and take pictures of what is left. I slowly roll out of my circle and, no doubt for the last time for this airplane, reluctantly head away from Palmer Field, South Carolina, just as it did on February 27, 1946, almost fifty-five years ago. My new heading is west, part of my goal achieved. In the last couple of years, and particularly this last five weeks, I've revisited every field that this airplane was ever stationed at and talked to many of the men that flew it and planes like it. I've learned much about what it was like for them. But I still have another four thousand miles of sitting in this cockpit, so there will be plenty of time to digest this material and many more pilots to talk to.

On my new heading I almost immediately cross the Great Pee Dee River, a muddy brown stream that wanders north to south through the Carolinas to the sea. Although I don't know the origins of the name, it somehow perfectly fits this picturesque little river, and I wouldn't mind sitting on its banks with a fishing pole and a good book right about now. The sun is out this morning and it is a beautiful day to start the trip back. The countryside is lovely, as is all of the southeast, and I stay low to enjoy it.

The morning flight rolls on uneventfully, and soon I fly off of the chart at Spartanburg and before I can get reestablished on my new chart almost cruise through a piece of the Charlotte airspace. I quickly nudge the airplane a little to the south, and while I'm at it set up for a landing at Pickens County Airport for fuel.

While there I check the radar for news from the west. I'm hoping to make Chattanooga today, but it's not looking good. The sky is dark in that direction, and the radar is showing a lot of moisture. The next hundred and fifty miles are across the Great Smoky Mountains, and with a name like that I'm not quite sure what to expect. I have been thinking about this part of the flight all the way across, just as eastern pilots must give a lot of thought to crossing the Rockies or the Sierras. The lineman isn't helpful. "Yeah, it looks like we have some bad stuff headed this way." He drags out the word, "baaaad."

I can see the headline: *CALIFORNIA PILOT IGNORES LINEMAN'S ADVICE. PLANE CRASHES. Lineman says, "I told him it was baaaad."*

I thank him, stock up on candy bar emergency rations and head into the ominous sky. Deciding to go under the lowering cloud deck, I soon have my hands full dodging hills for the first fifty miles. It looks like this flight is not going to come to a good end. There are a number of towers directly along my route, and my eyes are like saucers looking for them. The terrain is grim and unfriendly beneath the broken cloud layer, and I wonder if this is *Deliverance* country. Tiring of this business, I decide to climb up through a hole and take a look around. It's gorgeous. The character of the flight changes immediately. The sun is out, there is a temperature inversion, and it's dry and warm, with cloud tops at sixty-five hundred feet. I'm in a moving outdoor balcony on the world. There are just enough holes to navigate by, so Chattanooga here I come!

It turns into a travelogue flight across the Smokies. The sun is low, putting the clouds in relief and giving them a golden glow. I get lucky and the holes in the cloud layer always seem to be right over the landmark that I am looking for. I know exactly where I am, and the sunlight streaming through these holes is throwing shafts of light into the woods and across the fields. I cross the line out of Georgia into Tennessee. This time I know exactly where the state line is, and I flick the stick, inducing a little thump as I cross. I pass over the Big Frog Wilderness Area, and looking down I envy the frogs. It's beautiful country here in these Smokies, and I could live here in a heartbeat. I just need one or two of those extra lives.

I give Chattanooga Approach a call and discover that my transponder is once again dead. They assure me that they can handle me as a primary target (not electronically enhanced), and after some course changes to establish identity, I'm cleared to land. They even throw in a bearing to the airport for good measure. It's Sunday, it's slow, and they want someone to chat with and so do I. Naturally, the transponder then decides to come back on. They tell me that they have my transponder return and now we are in business. An uncharitable air traffic controller would think that the pilot had forgotten to turn it on, but they say nothing. It started getting intermittent down in Florida, so this isn't the first time. I'll deal with it when I get home. Intermittent problems are the worst.

I find a nice hole in the broken layer, pull power, and spiral down through it. Chattanooga glows like the Emerald City of Oz in the distance, illuminated by a shaft of sunlight. It's been a good flight.

## Lt. Sam Ed Brown USAAF
## Italy, 1944

### ". . . Stick it!"

> . . . the trouble was finding the darn field. When we were within three or four hundred miles of Italy, there were very powerful homing

stations in Italy and in Southern Europe. Ours was called Big Fence. If you wanted the quickest route home, from wherever you were you'd call, "Hello, Big Fence, this is April 66. I need a homer."

Big Fence would come back and say, "Give me a long count."

So you'd count from one to ten and back down to one. Then Big Fence would say, "Steer a heading of 189 and call us back in ten minutes."

So we didn't have any trouble with navigation. We had Big Fence, the map, the Adriatic, the Mediterranean, and the Alps. And all this enabled us to not get lost.

Once or twice we were given vectors by Big Fence, and we knew it was a German intercept station. When you're given a heading of 335 degrees and you know damn well that it would take you up into southern Germany or Austria, it was usually common to say, "Stick it," and ignore the instructions until you got closer to Italy, where you could verify your route.

The Germans tried everything to fool us. We passed German fighters in the air with our exact marking—checkerboard tail and a red nose and big combat numbers on them. A time or two, we suspected a captured B-17 or a captured P-51 or P-47 was flown up around our formations. We'd watch them real close for anything suspicious. It's pretty hard to shoot one of those down unless you're absolutely sure.

But the Germans weren't the only ones that were known to use subterfuge.

## Capt. Joseph C. Pimentel, Thunderbolt pilot, France, 1944

### *". . . Quesada and Donovan had evolved this scheme of employing . . . 'aerial assassins.'"*

In the spring of 1944, when I was ordered to England, they sent me to Ascot, which is where the 9th Air Force had its headquarters. That is where I first encountered General Elwood "Pete" Quesada. I didn't call him "Pete" of course, since I was just a snot-nosed captain, but I liked working for him, and we underlings all referred to him as "Pete" amongst ourselves. Quesada was, in his own way, kind of an Air Force equivalent of George Patton, but in a younger version. By that I mean

Quesada was a real hardnose, a fighting man, ready to take on the 9th Air Force's tactical role.

Quesada was an enthusiastic supporter of Patton's warfare methods. He would take risks and go, as Patton always did. When the two got together, they made a helluva team.

Anyway, I was delighted to find myself working for Quesada, in the program that he, along with William Donovan of the OSS [Office of Strategic Services, which preceded the CIA] had originated. In anticipation of the D-Day invasion of Normandy, they had worked out a scheme by which tactical use could be made, in support of our invasion forces, of intelligence information that they were getting from the French Maquis (underground guerrillas).

They were a bunch of really savage Frenchies over there, who never did give up, no matter what Hitler did to their country—the likes of such as the taking of Paris, Compiegne, Rheims, and so many other of their fond homeland locations. Those Maquis guys and gals took it upon themselves, at great personal risk, to feed espionage information to Great Britain. And when we, the U.S. forces, began pushing onto those Normandy invasion beaches, the Maquis really became very active in our support.

Quesada and Donovan had evolved this scheme of employing (and, I guess I'd have to apply this term to myself) "aerial assassins." They would know for example, from Maquis input, the whereabouts of a planned collection of Nazi "brass hats," meeting to have a tactical or strategic conference. Or they would know of an enemy bigwig's travel plans, or intended movement by rail or truck convoy of large masses of troops. That would signal an attack by us, directed at these particular Nazi events. If it was a conference, we would know in most cases who was to be there, on what day and hour, in which village and which house, on the second or third floor, in a conference room having windows facing east, and so forth. And that's where we'd fill the place with .50-caliber slugs.

We'd paint our P-47s in the markings of, say, the 50th Group or the 356th, making them appear to belong to those groups, then we'd go in there and send those Nazi brass hats to wherever their Valhalla was and then go home. You may know what happened to Rommel, for example, on one of those Normandy roadways. One of our guys shot him up as he was coming back to duty after being ordered by Hitler to put a stop to the poor showing by the other Wehrmacht generals opposing the Allied invasion forces on Normandy.

Of course there were times when we didn't have any special current information. When that occurred, we would go out on typical 9th Air Force air-to-ground combat missions in support of the 1st and 3rd Army spearheads.

We had access to every combat type a given occasion might call for. We got checked out, or were already skilled in a great variety of alternate aircraft along with the P-47, such as the P-51s, B-26s, C-47s, C-46s, A-26s, and B-25s. Occasionally, for example, we'd use British types, such as a Mosquito or Typhoon with appropriate markings. Whatever was necessary to get the job done, we would so do. Any alternative would be contrary to purpose. The pilot's protocol was not to ask questions. You just went out and did what you were sent to do. We would almost always be single or possibly two airplanes. Very seldom would we operate as a flight or a squadron, although sometimes it was essential that we did look like an operational squadron for the sake of appearances. Such events were coordinated by Quesada.

Quesada and Donovan, and of course others at that echelon, had developed this idea and hoped to see how long we could effectively get away with it. It worked successfully for quite awhile. Our system certainly helped allow the Allied forces to establish successful exploitation of the invasion beachheads all the way to Paris and beyond.

I come within an ace of lining up on the wrong runway at Chattanooga but catch my error in time and nonchalantly rack the biplane tightly around, apparently before anyone in the tower notices. Continuing like it was all planned that way, I slip down final to runway two-zero, putting it down well in front of all of the jet skid marks on the seventy-four-hundred-foot runway. I taxi to Krystal Air North, a corporate jet center, because I'm in the mood for some TLC. Used to the bigger jets, a whole crew of linemen come out to see what manner of flying machine this is. They bring chocks that my wheels get lost in, and the airplane looks like a little kid in big shoes. I fuel up, but they are puzzled.

"What kind of an airplane is this anyway?"

I tell them that it is a Boeing, and that really confuses them. They look at me like I'm putting them on, which I am. Almost on cue a 737 taxis by and they glance at it and then back at the Stearman. Both are Boeings. They can't quite make the leap.

# CHAPTER 24

CAPT. JOSEPH C. PIMENTEL, L-4 pilot, over the English Channel, 1944

*"One of the two of them was smart enough to lower his gear and flaps, to slow down."*

Chattanooga to Pine Bluff, Arkansas, September 10, 2000

"Savannah traffic, Stearman seven-two-one, quarter-mile final, Savannah," I say to no one in particular on the radio while landing at the Savannah, Hardin County, Tennessee, airport. I knew that the skies were empty, and the airport looked empty too.

"Hey, Stearman, are y'all going to sit down and have a cup of coffee with me this morning?" came a woman's Tennessee-lilted voice over the radio that startled me out of my prelanding focus.

The manager of the airport had just come to work and I was her first fuel customer of the day. And so began my "friendly Sunday." A day of welcome and hospitality offered by just about everybody I ran into on this fine day.

The flight leg today is to be Chattanooga, Tennessee, to Pine Bluff, Arkansas, with a stop at Savannah, Tennessee, for fuel. It starts out in a somewhat surreal manner at the Chattanooga airport as I do my preflight in the shadow of the passenger terminal, which bears an amazing similarity to Jefferson's Monticello as depicted on the nickel. Park some MD-80s in front of Jefferson's home and you've got the visual. But I suppose a terminal has to look like something and this one actually looks very solid and reassuring. Flanked around its periphery, like piglets around a sow, are a number of turboprop cargo haulers and commuter jets loading up for their flights to the various airline hubs.

Parked over against the fence, aloof from the crude early morning commercial activity, sits a pretty little yellow J3 Cub. Whenever I see one of these airplanes I always wonder about its history, specifically whether it ever was a military Cub—an L-4. There were a lot made (well over six thousand) and a few came back from Europe. And if it is a military Cub, I wonder if it has any evidence of being in the water. Like perhaps the English Channel . . .

## Capt. Joseph C. Pimentel, L-4 fighter pilot

### "All this foofraw no doubt was designed to give us time to soil our drawers . . ."

This was late July 1944, and American troops had already secured ownership of the Omaha and Utah beachheads in the Normandy invasion. I was flying with a 9th Air Force P-47 Thunderbolt outfit, and occasionally we would get rest tours from combat, which meant taking a ride in a Charlie 47 from Normandy back to England for some R&R. There wasn't much rest in France at the time, so once in a while we'd get back to Limeyland for a day or two.

There is an airfield on the south side of London called Biggin Hill. It was quite famous during the Battle of Britain when the Spitfire and Hurricane boys were stopping the Luftwaffe. At this time, however, Biggin Hill had been designated as a VIP transport terminal, and was also where combat rest-tour flights arrived from the continent, for London visitations.

On this particular occasion, I had come to Biggin Hill with a bunch of fighter pilots all charged up to go out and raise hell in London, chasing girls and drinking too much scotch whiskey. This incident took place while we were on our way back to France. We were there at Biggin Hill waiting to be hauled back to the combat zone across the channel. A bunch of us were sitting in the sun on the flight line, close by airplane revetments for shelter in the event of V-1 flying bomb attacks and such.

The British called their PA system a Tannoy, and the Tannoy would come on with sirens and bells whenever an incoming buzz bomb was about to hit. Otherwise the Tannoy was just a public address system. So, we sat there, nursing our hangovers and waiting to be summoned for our ride back to combat. Finally the announcement we were waiting for came over the Tannoy: "All Allied fighter pilots please report to the operations desk at once!" So we tore over to ops, thinking this meant that we could climb on board a transport and go back to fight the war.

Instead of herding us out to the C-47 or the like, however, they put us on a bus and we went tearing down the tarmac to a half-dozen Piper Cubs. They were called L-4s in those days. The direction given us was to ferry these things across the channel to the invasion beaches. These L-4s were meant as artillery spotters for the Army. The Cubs were all stuffed with recreational gear and each had a temporary extra fuel tank installed. In this case, the front seat was loaded full with this gear, things like tennis racquets, record players, volleyballs, checkerboards, and so forth. We fighter pilots were expected to accommodate ourselves to these strange little airplanes.

As it happened, I was the ranking officer at the time, being a captain while the rest of the pilots were either first or second lieutenants. Out of the six L-4s that we were to ferry across the channel, one had a radio. That was the L-4 that was assigned to me, because I was the senior officer. The purpose of this communications link, we were told, was to allow me to talk to what they called "high cover." A navigational corridor had been established, crossing the English Channel, between a promontory along the English south coast called Selsey Bill and a point close to Utah Beach where our forces were in occupation. The British and the Canadians were farther to the north, and they serviced themselves. The U.S. had it's own independent corridor. You were cleared to use the corridor if you were an unarmed airplane to be sheltered and protected by the high cover. Somebody was to be up there, flying around in squadron strength in either Mustangs, Spitfires, or Hurricanes. We were flying the Cubs at about five thousand feet and they were up at about twenty thousand feet patrolling. All we were supposed to do was stay in our corridor and get across the channel as swiftly as a sixty-five-horsepower engine would take us.

That is where we were headed for when, in a state of great disgust, we departed Biggin Hill in those six Cubs. It had been taken for granted that we could all manage to fly the L-4s. The viewpoint was that if we could fly fighters, we could fly anything, and stepping down to a low horsepower only meant a decrease in the talent required. Whether or not we knew how to fly them, or cared to, nobody asked or wondered. Biggin Hill was utterly British of course, so a certain amount of ethnic antagonism prevailed. Even though we Yanks had nothing but the most extreme admiration for the RAF boys who had protected London, this didn't take away from some of their stuffiness. We had attitudes.

All this contributed to the idea that in departing Biggin Hill and its definitely British atmosphere, we wanted to leave a favorable impression. So, we took those six Piper Cubs out to the end of the runway, taxiing in formation, swung out en masse, and thundered with all of our sixty-five horsepower each, down the runway in formation, lifted off and headed southward to find Selsey Bill. Now, I must confess that we didn't stay in formation very long. Pretty soon we were just a general gaggle of airplanes up there, struggling against head winds, crosswinds, hangovers, and all the rest of it.

Having found Selsey Bill at last, we entered the corridor and set out to cross the channel. All we wanted to do was to get out of these cramped, overloaded, and terribly small airplanes. You can perhaps appreciate the level of alcoholic remorse that was building in each of us. Some tedious interval later, under bleary conditions and around mid-channel and roughly five thousand feet above the sea and with absolutely no orderly arrangement of flight, airplanes all over the place, we flew onward. Certain ones among us couldn't quite keep up with the others, so there was always a tail-end-Charlie, and as senior officer present and the only one with any kind of a radio, I would have to throttle down or up in order to try to keep track of all of them, to make sure that everybody was still with us.

In the midst of all this, two Luftwaffe lads in yellow-nosed Focke-Wulf 190s spotted us. I don't know if they were aware that there was such a thing as high cover, and we'll never know, but they were soon to find out. In any event we had two Luftwaffe hotshots who could divide six by two and conclude that it equaled three air-to-air victories each, as they looked over this gaggle of miserable airplanes down there.

Because they were so confident—and admittedly I'm assigning personalities to the Luftwaffe now—that they had us in the bag, they didn't bother to shoot on their first pass-through. They just tried to scare us to death. After a long steep dive in a real tight formation, they zapped right through the middle of us at about five hundred miles per hour, and then pulled up in a great sweeping climb. All this foofaraw no doubt was designed to give us time to soil our drawers and appreciate the dreadful situation we were in.

But I have to remind you that these six Piper Cubs were being flown by fighter pilots who had an entirely different reaction to the one the Germans had expected to create. What followed next was a consequence of what would inevitably happen with fighter pilots, because the game is always to "check six," and that is to keep anything off of your tail, because you can't see very well in that direction. So, "check six" is a survival tactic, and the reason that I have to mention it is that after those two bogies went through and pulled away off in the distance, in that great sweeping climb, *all* of the Piper Cubs quit worrying about corridors or getting from England to France, and all turned their noses in the direction of those two 190s, watching them like birds watching an eagle or a hawk. Watching them! In the meantime I issued an alert to the high cover via the radio. As I recall, their call sign was "Longbow" and we were "Crackerjack."

I said, "Mayday, mayday, mayday, Longbow this is Crackerjack. Mayday, two bogies." I got a response from the Limeys up there in their Spitfires, but I don't think that the Germans could hear any of this. Usually they did, but for one reason or another I don't think these two heard our message.

While I was exchanging conversation with the Englishmen up above, the two 190s came back at us and this time they started to shoot. You should go back to where we were a little bit ago, with the six fighter pilots swinging these sixty-five-horsepower airplanes around watching the two bogies. Then imagine the vision that appeared the instant those two Luftwaffe hotshots started to shoot. They had four twenty-millimeter cannons in each aircraft, and you could see the gunfire as it lit up the leading edge of their wings.

The instant that they started to shoot and the tracer came our way, all six of the Piper Cubs went into some kind of violent maneuver: hammerhead stalls, spins, sideslips, falling leaves, half-rolls, and a few contortions beyond description. As soon as those bogies went through us this second time—and incidentally they hadn't hit anybody yet—the aerobatics immediately ceased. All the Cubs started watching the Germans again, following them with our noses. We were now long out of the corridor, but nobody cared. And we'd lost a thousand feet of altitude with these maneuvers.

The Germans made one more pass without hitting anything, but then we got into trouble. After those three unproductive passes, they quit flying formation and split up. One went this way and one went that way so that they could pick us off one by one, each in his own time.

Well, if you've ever tried to shoot at a free-floating untethered balloon, you had better be aware which way the wind is blowing, because unless you know, you won't know how to lead your target. No matter how simple it may seem, to shoot something that is completely defenseless, the fact is that it is goddamn hard to hit a balloon when it is not anchored to something. You're never sure which way it's traveling. The balloon is doing whatever it pleases, and there is no way to measure it from something that goes four hundred miles per hour. The smarter of the two 190s thought he'd figured all of that out, and he put down his landing gear and flaps, cut back on his throttle, and he was really going to give us trouble.

And that's when the high cover jumped them. [ Joe laughs mischievously.]

That landing gear snapped up and those flaps disappeared, and both of those Focke-Wulf 190s made a vertical dive for the surface of the English Channel. The last we saw of them was their exit as a whole herd of Spitfires came thundering down, leaving a trail of exhaust smoke and chasing them out of sight.

The Krauts didn't succeed in shooting anybody, but they didn't have to, because we all ran out of fuel just before reaching Utah Beach, where we were supposed to go. To our great and final indignity, they picked us out of the water and into barges. But we didn't lose any airplanes and we didn't lose any pilots. All we lost was our pride and a number of phonograph records that got broken.

I beat the jets and turboprops to the runway with my ragbag and am soon headed westward over a sleepy Sunday downtown Chattanooga, dodging some early morning thunderstorms. The Tennessee River snakes by underneath and I cross it three times without changing course.

The farther west I go, the less rain there is, and soon the Smokies smooth themselves out and the tailwind doesn't hurt a bit either. Life is good as I roll the wheels onto the Savannah runway and head for the coffee invitation, which soon turns into a complete breakfast hosted by the hospitable airport manager.

Some airports are just wonderful places with friendly people, interesting airplanes, grass, trees, and charm. Others are cold, strictly commercial types of enterprises, where no one will give you the time of day without first having possession of your credit card. Savannah, Georgia, strikes me as an example of the latter and Savannah, Tennessee, of the former. In Savannah, Georgia, I spent a small fortune on a hangar for the Stearman and an equally small fortune for a car. Take it or leave it. Actually I considered myself lucky to be in that hangar at all in view of the violent nature of the thunderstorms that beat on that city for a week. But the people I dealt with there were indifferent and full of the tourist city syndrome.

The sweet lady in Savannah, Tennessee, Montille Warren, makes me feel welcome, offers coffee and snacks, the use of a car to go into town if I wish to get a good breakfast, and in general makes Savannah a place that you would want to explore or come back to. As I wolf down some breakfast cereal, which she produces from one of the kitchen cupboards in the terminal, she proudly shows me photographs of the summer clinics that she helped run for the Civil Air Patrol, where kids from all over the region are exposed to aviation for the first time and many youngsters actually learn to fly.

While we are talking, a gentleman in a twin Beech lands for fuel. He is on an Angel Flight. This is a program where private citizens offer their aircraft and their time for medical emergency flights. These can be simple flights such as conveying a refrigerated organ from one hospital to another for an organ transplant, or they can involve bringing a needy patient to another city for treatment. He is a corporate pilot and this is what he is doing on his Sunday off.

These are wonderful people, quietly doing good things in Middle America and they are a pleasure to meet. When you travel, there is a certain loneliness that goes with the activity. Meeting people like this washes it all away.

I reluctantly leave Savannah behind and strike out for Pine Bluff, Arkansas, and my tailwind now becomes a head wind. Pine Bluff, like Gila Bend, lies at the edge of my range or at least at the edge of what I consider to be my personal comfort range. This is a very conservative number and will actually leave me at my destination with quite a bit of fuel, but I like it like that. I would be inconsolable if I ever ran this beautiful airplane out of gas and wrecked it. The FAA would be inconsolable too.

Thirty-five miles out of Pine Bluff I'm redoing my math and picking out landing spots in case my calculations are wrong. I shoot a quick landing at DeWitt, but their gas pumps are locked and the airport is eerily empty. I sit in the cockpit and debate my options. Reworking my math yet one more time I elect to go for it. Twenty miles out from the Arkansas River, my destination, I start to see traces of old riverbed left by this meandering stream. These can be seen as color changes in the earth or as isolated loops of the river now optimistically referred to as lakes. The village of Swan Lake comes up with its namesake lake a mile away and then four miles later, the river itself. I'm home free.

I cross the river and see Grider Field just to the southeast of Pine Bluff. There are two runways and a row of large hangars. This is ex-military. Grider was a primary training field during the war and instructed students in the Fairchild PT-19. The Fairchild was a handsome, modern-looking airplane, and one could count himself lucky if he took primary on a field equipped with Fairchilds. They were easy to fly and land and had no real vices. They had a wide landing gear and one had to work very hard to ground loop a Fairchild. Not many survived to the present because of their all-wood construction, which tended to rot if left to the elements and their engines, which had no commercial application. Fairchild built a little over eight thousand of these elegant little craft, and possibly one hundred are flying today. There is a nice little display in the terminal with pictures of the field as it was during the war. Sadly, there are no PT-19s left on this field.

I land, tie down, and fuel up. As usual, I have plenty of fuel in reserve and needn't have worried. It has turned into a beautiful day today and the sky is a cobalt blue without a cloud anywhere. There are huge open hangars all along the ramp, but I don't give them a second thought. It can't rain today. I get a ride into town, find lodgings, and take a walk to get some dinner. After possibly some of the worst food I've ever had in my life (pasta in Pine Bluff—I should have known better), I step outside of the restaurant.

The sky is no longer so pleasant and in fact more resembles shades of a really bad bruise with greens and blacks and indigos. I guess I'll never quite get over how fast Midwest weather can change. This looks like a replay of my experiences at Marianna, Florida, and Hammond, Louisiana. I stand under the portico of the motel and watch the show begin with a terrific lightning display. Soon the heavens open and a small crowd gathers to watch the fireworks. I turn to a fellow watcher and ask for the general direction of the airport. He points toward the darkest part of the sky and casually mentions that there are also tornado warnings out. I start to excuse myself to go and find a car when he volunteers, "I have a truck. I'll take you out to the airport."

And so Good Samaritan number three has made his appearance and we head out in the downpour. Arriving at the field, I see that World War III is in progress. The Stearman is getting pummeled. The sky is black as pitch, the rain is horizontal, lightning is in all quadrants, and all of the hangars except one are closed and locked. I peer into the only hangar open and find it full. There are two men working in the back, and I ask them if they know of an open hangar.

"Sure, we can get you into the city hangar if I can jimmy the door." He runs to his car and heads for what must be the city hangar. I wish him well in his life of crime.

The other fellow (these are Good Samaritans numbers four and five) motions me into his car and we chase after the hangar burglar, arriving just in time to see the huge doors begin to swing wide. He has been successful. We swing back to my airplane and I fire up, taxi across the ramp at a goodly rate, cut the engine, and roll right into this sanctuary of the city of Pine Bluff. This whole thing has taken less than five minutes and required the cooperation of four perfect strangers. I'm beside myself with gratitude.

We drive back into town, where I find that my original benefactor is the husband of the motel owner and was waiting around to watch the Cowboys game on the big screen in the motel restaurant. I pop for a couple of pizzas, and we all sit down for a pleasant evening of football, with the rain beating on the windows. Life is good and people are good.

But I have one more thing to do this evening . . .

# CHAPTER 25

LT. EVERETT FARNHAM, Italy, 1943

*"He must have been the most surprised German in all of Italy
when he saw forty-eight of these P-38s coming."*

At Pine Bluff, September 10, 2000

I am within an easy day's flying of James Longan, one of the cadets
who flew 41–806 in 1942 at Mira Loma Flight School in Oxnard, California. Jim had the misfortune to ground loop the beast, and this washed him
out of flight training and into bombardier school. He was the first person
I had contacted on this journey, and his recollections had a lot to do with
the whole venture. We talked for quite awhile in that conversation of five
years ago, and I kept in touch with him through the years. I told him of
my intention to fly the airplane across the country and why, and asked
him if he would like a ride in it if I came through his little town. He was
enthusiastic. He sent me his old cadet book from Mira Loma, and I sent
him pictures of the base and cadet barracks as they look today and a picture of 41–806 flying the same hills over which he flew.

Just before I left California, I gave him a call to tell him I would be stopping by for his flight in a couple of months. He sounded a bit tired and said that he didn't know about the ride, but that he would like to come out to see the airplane.

And so I'm calling him tonight, because Jim will be my next stop after Pine Bluff. It's been five years since the first phone call.

"Jim, I'm just down the road and I'll be landing around noon tomorrow." His response is silence.

"Jim, do you want to come to the airport tomorrow and see your old Stearman?" There is a long pause and I know what the answer will be.

"Jim," he says to me, "if it were any other Stearman or any other military airplane, I would come out there in a minute, but that airplane represents a very bad experience in my life. The more I've thought about it, the more I've come to the conclusion that I just don't want to relive or be reminded of that moment. I'm very sorry. I know that I've done a one-eighty on you, but that is the way I feel."

My heart is heavy. Not from his change of mind, but from the distress that I must have caused him. I should have seen it coming. I was so pleased to have found someone who was on record to have absolutely flown 41–806 that I hadn't really considered the circumstances—that maybe the man just wouldn't want to think about a bad thing that happened to him almost sixty years ago. Time does heal most wounds, but I had thoughtlessly opened this one. I could imagine his excitement at being accepted as an air cadet and sharing it with family and friends, then his graduation from preflight in Santa Ana and the sense of accomplishment that must have brought.

Next, it was Mira Loma, the "Country Club of the Air" and the challenge of the mighty Stearman. Then the crash and it is all over in the seconds it takes to lose control of an airplane. You are unsuitable as a pilot as far as the military is concerned. They only have time for fast learners and instinctive pilots. You are removed from the barracks before you can even say your good-byes and corrupt the other cadets. You are sent to another place and told that you are going into another line of work. Actually Jim Longan was lucky. He became a bombardier. The lucky ones remained as flight crew: navigators, gunners, and engineers. The unlucky ones went into the infantry. It happened to a lot of young men, and they had to think about it for the rest of their lives. This was their big opportunity, and for whatever reason, they didn't meet the challenge. For some, no doubt it became a pattern for life, while for others it simply became something to learn from. Most of us have these moments and we think about them for a long time.

I'm sure Jim was the wiser for his failure—if it can be called that. I regret not being sensitive enough to see what could come of my revisiting old history. Take care of yourself and have a good life, Jim.

Everett Farnham had no such hesitation when we discussed flying the Stearman. We had met at an air show in Van Nuys, and he had a grin from ear to ear when the subject of a flight in the Stearman came up. He was even willing to break a golf date, which is like a religion to some retired folks.

Everett is a very meticulous man. I don't know him well enough to say that with total authority, but from what I have seen he is very careful about details of his appearance and possessions, and it was this character-istic that made our flight together in the Stearman ultimately so humorous.

His survival of fifty-four missions in P-38s no doubt had a lot to do with his attention to detail, because, after all, that is what flying is—a collection of details that must be done correctly or you don't come back to the barn. His recollections of those days were articulate, his memory accurate and detailed, and the stories absorbing.

But it was his appearance that fascinated me.

His slacks were pressed with razor-sharp creases and didn't have a wrinkle in them. The sport shirt was very preppy with a button-down col-lar and was equally fresh. His white hair was perfectly combed, without a hair out of place, and the shoes were perfect. A nifty yellow jacket rounded off the ensemble. My standard flying uniform of jeans, sweat-shirt, leather jacket, and the need of a shave paled by comparison. Even his black BMW didn't have a speck of dust on it. It was neat as a pin inside and the personalized license plate said "LTNG PLT." Every detail had been taken care of. I'll bet his P-38 never had a spot of grease on its twin Allison engines.

The day came and we were about to go fly the Stearman. It had been fifty-nine years since he had flown one and fifty-five since he had flown anything. He was to be my guest, and it was debatable which of us was most pleased to be doing this. Unfortunately, the flight was shaping up to be less than perfect.

The day before, the seal in the front compass of the Stearman had let go. I was at an air show; it was very hot and perhaps this had something to do with it—I don't know—sometimes, simple demonic possession afflicts airplanes. Not content to leak just a few drops and give me some warning, this instrument had all at once emptied its entire volume of compass fluid down the front of the newly painted instrument panel, then onto the fabric floor of the aircraft, where it ran down and made a pool around the tail wheel. I seem to be star-crossed when it comes to compasses. The compass card, which floats and is dampened in this liquid base, leaned drunkenly to one side, useless. Although there is a compass in the rear cockpit, it is not good for the soul to have to stare at any broken mechanical thing on an airplane, and this he would have to do. It's a bit disquieting for any passenger, and I was embarrassed.

Also making me very unhappy was the fact that some incredibly careless person had cracked the paint and left a gouge on the side of the fuselage while leaning on it with a camera. I was not feeling good about the airplane.

I warned Everett of these inadequacies before the flight—God forbid that you should look bad in front of a World War II pilot—but he waved them aside and we were off to the airport.

I did my usual preflight, going overboard to look professional, but when I got to the front cockpit I was stopped cold. There was no front seat cushion! It was three hundred miles away in a hangar. I had forgotten to put it in the airplane for this particular trip. The Stearman seat is designed to accept a parachute or a very thick cushion, and I had neither. I tried the local flight school but without luck. I was stumped, and it looked like we were not going flying this day.

Then I had an idea. I had three flight bags with me, and one of them had been earmarked for dirty laundry. It was quite full. Up it went into the front seat, where I tried it and found that although a bit lumpy, it would do. But my embarrassment in front of this gentleman was deep. I was about to take a World War II P-38 pilot up on a pile of laundry. Visions of Laurel and Hardy movies with parachutes full of dirty clothes filled my head. This was bad.

But Everett couldn't have cared less and quickly swung up into the cockpit and planted himself on top of my old sweatshirts and socks. Felix and Oscar were going flying.

Everett's flying that day was as impeccable as just about everything else about him. He nailed his altitude, and his turns didn't lose or gain a foot. We pulled some $g$'s, flew down among the weeds, and finished with a nice 360-degree overhead military approach.

I think that Everett would have been happy sitting on an orange crate.

## Air Cadet Everett Farnham
## Thunderbird Field, Arizona, 1942

### ". . . a split "S" down into the pattern."

We got approximately sixty hours' flying time in primary. When we finished all of the basic requirements, we practiced aerobatics constantly. You couldn't do anything to get in trouble with the Stearman if you used your head. We practiced spins in it all the time. We did snap rolls and slow rolls and loops and Immelmanns and everything else you could do.

The instructors were old barnstorming pilots. These guys really knew how to fly that type of airplane, and they were great instructors. When I was just about finished with my sixty hours—I remember that it was on one of those beautiful mornings about the end of September—we went out to do a little dual time.

My instructor said, "I was out among 'em last night and I don't feel very good this morning. I've got a terrible hangover, so I'll tell you what we'll do. You take it off, take it up a couple of thousand feet, and then we'll unwire the mixture control so that we can get a little altitude on this thing." So we flew that Stearman up to about 11,500 feet trying to get rid of his hangover! It was cool up there and he said, "I feel a lot better now."

After we flew around for a little while he asked, "Okay, now what's the fastest way to get it down to the ground?"

And I said, "Well, I guess just push it over into a power dive."

"Nope, we're going to spin it down. I'm going to put it in a spin and you count them." So he pulled it up into a spin at 11,500 feet, and I counted nineteen turns until he pulled out at the altitude at which we normally started doing spins, about four thousand feet.

And he said, "Okay, now you spin it on down," and I put another three or four turns on it. Well, that was a real experience for me.

But you got to know the airplane, its limitations, and what it could do. They taught you to fly it by the seat of your pants and by your instincts. You listened to the sound of the wind through the wires, and you used the wires to practice your precision maneuvers. You turned it over to where the cabane strut wires were laying on the horizon and made it stay there. [This will give the pilot an automatic sixty-degree angle of bank and provide an outside visual reference with which to hold it.] And you practiced and practiced precision work. You were not afraid of the airplane, because they had showed you right away what it would do.

I remember toward the end of my flying time at Thunderbird Field—our landing pattern was at five hundred feet—we would fly the reciprocal of the forty-five-degree pattern entry at about a thousand feet above pattern altitude, turn the Stearman over, and do a split-S down into the pattern!

I just can't envision people doing things like that now. We were at fifteen hundred feet starting a split-S and ending five hundred feet above the ground coming in on the forty-five-degree entry. Then we'd just make the normal pattern and land the plane. We really thought that we were something—that we were hot stuff. And we didn't think that there was a dangerous thing about it, because it was such a steady, safe-feeling airplane and we had such good instructors who we really trusted.

You know that they painted over the airspeed indicators. Oh, yeah. We never knew what our airspeed was. We only flew it with the tachometer and the sound of the engine and the way the wind sounded going through the wires. And it was totally safe. That's the way they taught you to fly, literally by the seat of your pants, and after you did that awhile, you felt totally secure in that airplane.

# Lt. Everett Farnham
# Italy, 1943

## . . . fifty missions and flimsies.

We are looking at Everett Farnham's mission flimsies. A flimsy is a small printed sheet of paper on which mission notes were jotted down. Call signs, times, distances, magnetic courses to rendezvous, and targets were all provided at the pilot briefing and filled in on these sheets of paper, which were indeed flimsy because of the poor quality wartime paper. They were kept in the flight suit during the mission and then usually disposed of.

Everett has kept almost all of his, fifty-odd, and made personal notes on the back of each to describe the mission outcome. A typical flimsy reads: "Escort 96 B-25s to bomb marshalling yards at Sofia, Bulgaria. First allied bombing of Sofia. First dogfight. Had shots at two 109s." Another reads: "Escort 36 B-24s to bomb marshalling yards at Bolzano, Italy. We were attacked by about 35 109s and 190s. Houtz and Judd each got a 109." And another: "Provide general cover for two Wings hitting the 109 factory at Wiener Neustadt. Twenty bomb groups hit the factory."

He says,

> Twenty bomb groups. That's a lot of bombers. They were probably B-17s and B-24s, and of the two we would much rather escort the B-17s than the B-24s, because the B-17s flew really good formations. The B-24 was not as good an airplane as far as being able to do some of the things that it was meant to do, like flying close formation and staying together. It didn't fly as easily as the B-17. The B-17 was a much better plane. They flew good formation. As for the B-24s, we used to say that their idea of flying formation was to be flying in the same direction on the same day!
>
> But they did a hell of a job. They were tough airplanes.

Another flimsy reads: "Escort B24s from Salzburg, Austria, home. They bombed Me-109 factory at Regensberg, Germany. Lt. Louis C. Champion went into the Adriatic off of Pescara, Italy, returning early from a mission. Bad weather, fog and haze. February 25,1944."

> Never recovered. He was from the Champion Spark Plug family. Nice fella. He just disappeared on the way back from a mission. Sometimes those things happened. He might have gotten disoriented. Maybe something happened to the airplane that he couldn't control. I think the weather was marginal that day and he probably got into an overcast

situation, lost his horizon and just flew into the water, because nobody saw him go down and we never ever heard from him again. The clue here is that he returned early from the mission so that he would have returned by himself and that's why nobody knew what happened to him.

Another: "Escort 36 B-24s to bomb M4 at Udine, Italy, Christmas Day, 1943. Lt. H. C. Pitts and Lt. R. Downing didn't return. Midair collision of two P-38s. One parachute. Lt. George Mitchell didn't return from mission to Sofia on December 20. Three P-38s shot down in flames. One parachute."

That was the day that we got into a big dogfight in the Venice area. You could easily run into another airplane, because you get so busy trying to shoot someone down. Maybe the two planes were going after the same aircraft and they didn't see each other. Neither of those fellows ever showed up anywhere.

And another: "Helped Lt. Dolezal. Flying 'BJ' [aircraft ID]. May 17, 1944, Cremona, at the mouth of the Po."

The whole group, which is forty-eight airplanes at sixteen per squadron, was detailed to strafe a couple of airfields in northern Italy, where the Germans had quite a few aircraft. We went up at low altitude out over the Adriatic, where you can avoid the radar.

The group commander was leading this mission and in the briefing said, "When we get to the coast I want everybody to be wingtip-to-wingtip, the whole forty-eight of us at full throttle with five degrees of flaps to keep the nose down."

So we went across these airdromes with forty-eight planes, wingtip-to-wingtip, and just shot at everything in sight. Airplanes, trucks, tanks, anything that looked like something the enemy would use we shot at. And then after we'd finished that, which doesn't take very long at three hundred miles per hour, we were free to take on targets of opportunity.

And that was the day that Lieutenant Dolezal, who was leading a four-ship flight, and I together found a Ju-88 flying in the area. He must have been the most surprised German in all of Italy when he saw forty-eight of these P-38s coming. We broke off, attacked, and we both shot him down. He went down in flames and bellied the thing in.

We got back to the base, were debriefed, and reported the shoot-down of the Ju-88.

"Well, which one of you did it?"

"We don't know. We both shot at him at the same time and we knocked him down."

"Well, we've got to decide who gets credit for him." So we drew cards and I drew a low card and he got the credit for the victory. And there went my claim to fame.

Finally, another of Everett's flimsies reads: "Escort two groups to bomb town of Banjalouca. Strafed airdrome and roads in vicinity. My wingman, Lieutenant Welsh, collided with me but we made it home OK. Lt. Gary Thomas shot down while strafing Banjalouca. Believed killed."

"Shot down by ground fire," he adds.

When I first got to Italy they said, "Okay, if you stay here, do your job, fly fifty missions and if you're still with us, then you are eligible to go home." A few people volunteered to stay and fly more missions, but mostly they sent everybody home. And you are very happy to get it over with and go home to do whatever else that they wanted you to do.

I'll never forget the day that we went in to the briefing for my fifti-eth mission. Our group commander in the briefing said, "Now you all know that we have been losing a lot of pilots lately through attrition. We've lost a few that were shot down and we've lost a few that have finished their missions and gone home. We're not getting enough re-placements in, so I'm going to ask anybody from now on who finishes fifty missions to stay around and fly a few more." My God, he did that on the briefing for my fiftieth mission. This was supposed to be my grad-uation day!

So I flew four additional missions. But on the fifty-second mission we were doing some strafing over Banjalouca, Yugoslavia. We were going down a river and shooting up some boats. My wingman and I were flying in the usual normal formation, and I started a turn to my right toward him. He didn't pick it up soon enough and our wingtips hit. We were about thirty feet off of the ground, and we hit so hard that the wheel jumped out of my hands. Well, that's a little bit exciting, about thirty feet off of the ground going at three hundred miles per hour.

I grabbed the wheel and thought, *What was that?* Then I realized that we had touched wings. His wingtip had hit my right aileron, so it made it a little bit hard to control, but it wasn't a big deal. We went home and landed and he had minor damage to his plane, but all the way home I thought, *This was my fifty-second mission. This shouldn't happen.* After you'd finished fifty you'd think that you'd get a break, but it doesn't seem to work that way.

## "The Germans"

I'm sure that they were far superior in experience than most of us. Here we were, just young kids who had learned to fly because a war that we didn't want had started. We jumped in, learned to fly and went over there with 300 to 350 hours of flight time. The German pilots, they were fighting to save their own country. Some of them did this from 1937 on. These guys had flown hundreds of missions by the time I even got overseas. So you can see their experience level was vastly higher than ours. Some of the German pilots had dozens or even hundreds of planes shot down, because they had been doing it for so long. They had much more experience than we did, but the plain fact is—we whipped their butts.

We just overcame everything that they did and all of their experience just in sheer numbers. And we wanted to win that war, because we were on the good side and they were on the bad side.

## "The Italians"

Our base was in Lecce. It's down in the heel of Italy at the very southern end. When I joined the 82nd Fighter Group, they had just moved in about a week before. Lecce had been an Italian air base and they had a number of Macchi and Fiat aircraft. We took over the operation of the base and it gave us a three-thousand-foot cement runway from which to operate. There were some very big trees at the end of the strip, which is pretty exciting when taking off with a full load of fuel and drop tanks, and you have to clear the trees at the end of the runway. But that's the way the Italians did things. They didn't worry about details.

We actually had two or three missions during the first part of my stay at Lecce that were coordinated with the Reggia Aeronautica [Italian air force]. They had only capitulated to the Allies about three weeks before, and all of a sudden they were on our side. We would go over to Yugoslavia on a dive-bombing mission, and they would fly top cover for us in their Italian fighter planes. They had been on the German side only until a few weeks before, and it must have been a little difficult for them to change their attitude, to all of a sudden be flying on the other side. But they liked to fly. When they were doing top cover for us on our dive-bombing or strafing missions, if you watched them carefully you'd see half of them up there doing slow rolls or just flying around and enjoying themselves. They were probably so happy to be out of the war that they didn't care. They were free spirits.

Everybody, after they had been there for a while, was assigned an airplane but that didn't mean that you always flew it. And sometimes, bad things would happen to your airplane when somebody else was flying it. Another pilot flew my airplane when we were still down in Lecce, in southern Italy. He took off on a mission with full drop tanks on and had what was called an "early return." He had to come back. His radio was out. He started out over the Adriatic and realized that he didn't have any communication, so he came back in to land. This was a three-thousand-foot cement runway and there was only one runway, so you had to hope that the wind was blowing down it one way or another. Well, that day it wasn't. It was a crosswind and it was fairly strong and gusty. He brought it on in and didn't do a real good job of landing. He dropped it in from a few feet and landed on one gear and collapsed the gear. He skidded down the runway, and the drop tank underneath, which was full of one-hundred-octane fuel, was skidding along and creating sparks. So before the airplane stopped, it had started burning. It ended up burning up right there on the runway.

The pilot didn't even think to pop the canopy; he just rolled down the window on the left side—didn't get out of his parachute, still had the parachute strapped on him—and he crawled out of that window, jumped off of the wing, and ran away from the airplane. He got out of it while it was burning. A one-hundred-octane fire really burns furiously, is very hot, and is a big incentive to get the hell away from it.

The day after that we wondered how in the hell he did that. How did he get out of that airplane with his parachute on and through the window, which is not very big? The side window is about like this. [His hands describe a very small opening.] We went out to try it and nobody could do it. We tried to crawl out that window with a parachute on and it was impossible. But I'll tell you that when an airplane is on fire, you can do amazing things. He did! He was motivated.

# CHAPTER 26

ROBERT POWELL JR., P-47s and P-51s in England

*". . . they would fire to show us the edge of the field as soon as they spotted us."*

Pine Bluff to Mineral Wells, Texas, September 11, 2000

It is a beautiful morning and quite clear after last night's little thunderstorm. It's early and I know that I'll be able to get a lot of good flying in before the cumulo-bumpus crew gets loose in the sky. I get a ride to the airport and roll the airplane out of the city hangar, somewhat to the puzzlement of the folks in the airport office, who can't quite figure how I got it in there. They ask but I shrug. *I ain't talkin', see.* Charles, the lineman, soon comes over and we chat a bit. I had noticed him the night before as he directed me into my tie-down space. He executed the hand parking signals with military precision, and his bearing was that of a military person.

"Yes, sir. Twenty years in the Air Force as a jet engine mechanic." I looked around the little rural field and saw there was nothing bigger than a Piper.

"Tried Chicago afterwards with an airline, but couldn't wait to get out of there. Came down here for a visit seven years ago. Heard the house across the street was for sale. Bought it and been here ever since." Now Charles pumps gas for the county, doesn't worry about turbojets, and is as happy as a clam.

I glanced up at the sky. I am dragging my feet here and enjoying the conversation, but there was scud beginning to move in from the south, dirtying up the clean blue sky of the morning. A lot of curious little clouds at about one thousand feet were moving along quite briskly. I picked up the pace of my preflight.

Thinking that we might have been at the same bases, I volunteer, "I was in for four years and got out of the Air Force in '61, Charles."

"I was nine years old in '61," he tells me.

*Damn. Thank you, Charles. I needed that.*

Another look at the sky tells me I'd better go—now! There has been no time to check weather, so I figure that I'll check it in the air. I've been following it for weeks, so I'm only a day behind the trends.

I shove the throttle forward and roll down Pine Bluff's runway one-seven. I lift it off and almost immediately have to dodge the scud layer. These are way lower than I thought. They are tiny little things, about a hundred feet across, in an even scattered-to-broken pattern, and there are a bunch of them coming in. It's gone from clear to an almost five-hundred-foot ceiling in less than an hour. I dodge left, right, find a hole, and yank. The airplane stands on its tail, punches through a clear spot, and I'm on top. I dump the nose to let it catch up with itself while it wallows at the apogee of its climb, engine bellowing while deciding whether to fall or fly. It grudgingly starts flying. I can see that the cloud deck stretches to the horizon in the direction that I want to go. What a way to start a morning. It's way too early for complicated problem solving—I haven't even had my coffee—but I decide to be optimistic, pick up my heading, and climb.

The good news is that it is smooth. I level off above the deck and enjoy the ride. The heat and humidity of Pine Bluff are behind me and the air smells fresh and cool. There are holes in the undercast and I can pick out highways, so things should be okay.

Soon though, I find it necessary to climb. The cloud layer is getting thicker, climbing higher, and the holes are getting smaller. I toy with the idea of going underneath before this layer goes solid, but the bases of the clouds look very close to the ground. I continue on my course, not quite as confident.

It's time to call Flight Watch. These are weather folks that can be reached from anywhere in the country while in flight. A simple call, tell them where you are, what weather you want, and they are happy to oblige.

"Flight Watch, Stearman five-five-seven-two-one, thirty miles out on the Pine Bluff two-four-zero radial at forty-five hundred feet, request."

Fort Worth Flight Watch replies and I'm in business. It doesn't look good. I keep hearing, "VFR flight not recommended." They give me the weather at a number of different places and that should tell me if I can go on. There is just one problem. I can't find the weather reporting points, the cities, that they are talking about. Aviation charts are about two feet by five feet. My route today takes me across three chart faces. Not being that familiar with Arkansas or Texas, I don't have a clue where, for example, Texarkana is. I try to unfold the charts to find the various areas of clear weather, but I'm unaware that I have neglected to lower my seat. Lowering the seat would reduce the ninety-mile-an-hour wind blast just enough to be helpful. As a result, each time I try to unfold the chart, it nearly blows out of my hands, and its fluttering makes it all but impossible to read. I lean forward, holding the chart down by my feet, and try to read it, but that, of course, requires letting go of the airplane. The one thing I really don't want to do is stall out and spin into a cloud deck. That could ruin my day.

I wrestle with my three charts in the slipstream, trying to find clear areas. I notice that my cloud deck has now gone solid under me and I'm up to sixty-five hundred feet and still climbing to avoid it. For me that forces the issue. As long as there are holes, I'm comfortable going on. Holes provide a way to go down, get under the deck, confirm my position, and land if necessary. If there are no holes, for me there is no safe way to go down. I have winds now, and I don't want my life to depend on a hastily plotted dead-reckoning course. Nor am I looking forward to a vintage needle, ball, and airspeed descent through six thousand feet of clouds into the unknown at the other end.

Tuning Little Rock Approach, I hear a fragment of drama going on.

A VFR pilot is trapped on top and lost. Approach is giving him vectors, but he is one scared puppy at the prospect of a descent through the overcast. It can be heard in his voice. The drama fades in my radio. I hope he makes it.

Prudence and wisdom, the virtues that had failed me before takeoff, now prevail. I still don't have a clear picture of the weather, so I do a 180 and head back to Pine Bluff, an area that the weather folks say is still open. I have been flying for an hour, so it is another hour back. I've burned a lot of gas and gone nowhere except a notch or two up the experience scale. I want to sit down with the radar, my charts, and have a session with a briefer, something that I should have done before I got in the airplane.

## Lt. Don Correa, P-38s
## Italy

*". . . five hundred miles per hour going straight down."*

I got out to the plane one morning and my crew chief said, "I'm sorry, but I put a new artificial horizon in and I can't get it uncaged." They won't work if they're caged.

He said, "I hope that you don't have to fly any instruments." You hate to fly a partial panel—needle, ball, and airspeed.

We took off and it was a strafing mission to Munich. We lost a couple of guys, but we got out of there and were over the Alps, just over an overcast around twenty thousand feet or so, when the fellow behind me said that he had an engine problem and would I come back and cover him.

So I started to turn . . . and the bottom engine quit. I was drawing fuel from the wingtip tanks, which were internal tanks, and there was no gauge on them. When a red light came on in the panel, you had twelve more minutes of fuel. So I had been timing it and I was into about six minutes on that tank. Obviously what had happened was that the gas had failed to flow to the bottom engine . . . and I went into the soup.

Fortunately they had made us fly a lot of instrument time, and every month we had to put an hour in the Link trainer. So the first thing I did was to go on needle, ball, and airspeed. I knew what had happened, so

I pulled back both throttles, since the airspeed was winding up, and switched tanks.

On to needle, ball, and airspeed. I got the needle centered and the ball centered, and I saw that the airspeed had continued to build up, so I started hauling back on the yoke. The airspeed just kept building. What I didn't know was that I was on my back!

I hit five hundred miles per hour going straight down between two Alps.

If I had been over a little one way or the other, I wouldn't have made it back.

## Lt. Robert Powell Jr., P-47s and P-51s in England

### ". . . we lost some planes and pilots in the North Sea . . ."

Weather flying out of England was our worst enemy by far. First, our fighters were only equipped with the following flight instruments: a magnetic compass, a gyro compass, an artificial horizon (not the sophisticated ones of today), airspeed indicator, altimeter, rate of climb indicator, and a needle and ball.

Navigation for missions was preplanned by our operations section based on where and when we were to rendezvous with the bombers—all on dead reckoning. We wrote (in ink) our general heading for a course back home from wherever we were going to be at the turning point of the missions. As we got closer to home, we could call in on our radio and get a "fix" as to our position and receive a reciprocal heading back to base, but it did not take wind drift into account.

In some of the bad weather, low on fuel, and bucking head winds usually on the return, we lost some planes and pilots in the North Sea, not so much from violent weather, but heavy fog and haze, which obscured many landmarks.

Of minimums, there were none. You could get vectored to other fields where the ceiling might be a little better, but there were no systems such as GCA, ILS, VOR, or markers to guide you. On one occasion returning from a mission leading three other planes (we had become separated after a fight), we crossed over Bodney (a grass field) at about three hundred feet and couldn't see it. They called us from radar control and told us we had just passed over the field. We could see to fly tight formation, but the ground haze obliterated the field.

To get us in they vectored us back around the field and gave us a heading (reciprocal) to bring us into the field landing diagonally across it. We stacked up in echelon about twenty-five feet apart in formation at about three hundred feet, put down partial flaps (twenty degrees), and lowered our wheels.

They had told us that they would have men stationed at the edge of the field with Very pistols, and they would fire to show us the edge of the field as soon as they spotted us. Still unable to see the ground, we hung on power as we approached and suddenly saw the colored Very pistol shots go up in front of us.

I called out on the radio to the other guys that we were "landing now" and we came in hot, almost line abreast, and landed safely. The term "minimums" wasn't in our vocabulary.

That's the day I learned the true meaning of that old Indian saying: "Never criticize the chief until you have walked in his moccasins."

While still in P-47s, and one of my first few missions, we went to briefing one day when it was snowing and the visibility was zilch. At briefing our C.O. said the mission would probably be scrubbed, but we briefed for it anyway, because only the local weather was bad. It was okay over the Continent. During briefing I heard and echoed the remark of most of the other pilots who said, "I don't have the balls to take off in this stuff." I was sure that I didn't.

Anyway no call to scrub the mission had come when the start-engine time came, so we cranked up and taxied out into takeoff position—forty-eight airplanes, in lines of four in the corner of the field. It was doing something rarely seen in England—snowing like crazy. We could hardly see the other planes. We sat there waiting for the takeoff signal, absolutely sure that it would not come.

That day I was flying wingman to our squadron C.O., Lt. Col. Everett Stewart, and sitting with my wingtip just fifteen to twenty feet off of his and a few feet back. I kept telling myself I couldn't do this, and I am sure there were many others saying the same thing to themselves at that moment.

Then, the signal came, not a green light from the tower, because we could not see the tower, but it came on the C.O.'s watch—takeoff time. Suddenly his head moved forward signaling that his throttle was moving forward, too. And mine, and the throttles of the other two planes taking off in our flight, moved forward, too. All forty-eight planes and two "spares" climbed out of the field and into the overcast, breaking out at about twelve hundred feet or so. Some may call that courage, but looking back on that moment of intense fear—and that's what it was—I think that it was pride, not courage, that moved those throttles forward to fly that mission. There was not a man in the squadron who could have faced himself in the mirror if he had chickened out.

By the time we returned from the mission a couple hours later the weather was much better—not great—but the ceiling and visibility were high enough that we could make a normal approach and landing. That was just another example of flying that winter.

# Lt. Channing Sargent, USNR
## South Pacific

## "Jesus Shoes"

The Navy had a real interesting instrument procedure that they advocated. If we came back to the ship and it was totally socked in and you couldn't get down through the overcast low enough to make a normal approach, this is what they wanted us to do.

They would shoot a five-inch gun flare straight over the ship and then tell you the direction the ship was heading. You were to go ahead of the ship, at a specified altitude, for so many minutes, and then bail out. They hoped to be able to pick you up as you came down through the overcast.

This was not appealing at all and some folks got their feet wet, but we never had to use the "Jesus Shoes" procedure. Others tried it but it didn't seem to work.

One giant breakfast later, it is now one in the afternoon and it's time to leave again. So far I've gone nowhere and I have two hours' flying time on the clock. I take off again, this time after exhaustive conversations with the weather people, and find conditions much improved. There is an inversion layer. My friends, the clouds of this morning, have broken up and now have their bases at sixty-five hundred feet. Below that it is cold and bumpy. At sixty-five to eighty-five hundred it is warm and smooth. I can lower my seat, kick the rudder pedals forward out of the way, hang my arm out, and enjoy the cloud shapes as I pass. I get busy with the camera and between struts, clouds, and flying wires, soon have enough wall art for the next millennium.

All too soon the party is over and I must come down from my aerie and put more gas into this airplane. Paris, Texas, is on the nose, and if the town is as pretty as the airport, it must be beautiful. The airport has three runways to take care of any crosswind contingency, and acres of freshly mown grass. If you don't like landing on the runways, choose the grass. The terminal looks like it was just built, and the folks are friendly. I wish I could stay, but I have a date with Breckenridge, Texas.

By the time I get back in the sky, there is no smooth air left. It's four in the afternoon and I'm getting bounced around badly on these Texas plains. I have more sense than to fly in this turbulence, but this morning's fiasco has wasted the day and I press on. The Stearman, although a heavy airplane at three thousand pounds, has a lot of wing area. Wing area, in square feet, divided by the weight of the airplane gives the wing loading. An aircraft with a high wing loading shrugs off most turbulence. One with a low wing loading, which the Stearman has, really gets knocked around. The Stearman has about the same wing loading as a Piper Cub, about nine pounds per square foot. A Beechcraft Bonanza, which is roughly the same size as the Stearman, has a wing loading of thirty-six pounds per square foot, giving it a much smoother ride. A 767 has 250 pounds per square foot. It's a Cadillac in most turbulence.

I pull the belts tight but I'm really getting hammered. Holding a heading and altitude is a joke as I herd the airplane across the sky. Instead of 265 degrees, I point it "over there." I only vaguely bother with holding my altitude. This isn't particularly dangerous, just fatiguing as I'm batted from one side of the cockpit to the other. The airplane looks frail but is immensely strong. I met an ex-marine once who instructed in these airplanes during the war. Since he was twenty-one at the time, a marine and therefore couldn't possibly be killed, he decided to see just how strong the Stearman really was. He set out to pull the wings off. He and a buddy put their aircraft into vertical dives at ten thousand feet and firewalled them. At two thousand feet they both pulled full aft stick, hard! The airplanes pulled many $g$'s on the pullout and mushed a bit as they curved back to level flight, but they were fine. A Beechcraft or a Cessna would have become a lawn dart as the wings peeled off. Many have.

## Capt. Robert Boyett, USAAF
## Europe, 1944

### "You're not getting shot at! That's just rough air."

We had an Oklahoma Indian one time who was coming back from a mission, and although he had been shot up pretty bad on a previous mission, we didn't think he was flak-happy. We got into some real turbulence and he was bouncing around pretty good, and we noticed that he opened his cockpit and stood up.

The flight leader told him to sit down, and the guy said, "No, I'm going to bail out. I can't take all this getting shot at."

"You're not getting shot at! That's just rough air."

Well, they talked him back in and he'd sit down, but in a bit they looked over and the airplane was trimmed, but he was gone and the airplane just flew on.

This would happen from time to time, people would get flak-happy. They would show no outward effect, but you could slam a table and they'd jump through the walls. But then they would go on and live a normal life. They didn't treat for all the illnesses of the world like they do now.

I give the Dallas airspace a very wide berth, and as I get close to Breckenridge, now a very tired pilot, I start hearing about a line of thunderstorms anchored in that city that are swinging toward me. This I don't need. I am still about thirty miles out when I spot the town of Mineral Wells and its runway off of my left wingtip. Between fatigue and the possibility of more weather problems there is no contest, and I head south. This night was made to be spent in Mineral Wells! After landing, I discover a bonus. During my taxi in to the ramp I spot three old empty hangars. With thunderstorms coming I can't believe my luck.

The lineman leads me to one of the hangars, but as I am taxiing up he begins acting very odd. He is applauding and waving wildly from inside the hangar. I'm mystified. I shut down and find the reason for the clapping. Pigeons. Hundreds of them in the rafters. We run them all out, but he isn't confident that they will stay out, since the hangars have no doors. My choice seems to be one of having the airplane rained on or shit on. I choose shit. It doesn't include hail and wind damage. The pigeons hopefully will make other arrangements.

Still another bonus, Mineral Wells has an airport courtesy car. Once fairly common, airport courtesy cars have pretty much disappeared with the invention of the lawyer and liability, but by God, Mineral Wells has two cars plus maps to all the good places to eat and sleep. I am in hog heaven. Soon I am in Pulido's Restaurant washing down chalupas and enchiladas with a Dos XX beer and carrying on a harmless flirtation with the waitress. The rains come soon, but I am sleeping the sleep of the untroubled. The pigeons are no doubt having a tougher time.

# CHAPTER 27

*". . . the bones of a Messerschmitt Bf-109."*

Mineral Wells to Le Chateau Messerschmitt, Texas, September 12, 2000

This morning I'm a man with a mission. The Stearman needs an oil change before I can fly anywhere. It's the third one on this flight. I don't have an oil filter on the engine, so I go roughly twenty-five hours between changes. Changing the oil is easy, but checking the filter screens for metal is a royal pain. The screens are hard to get at, the job is messy, and I inevitably wind up with nasty cuts all over my hands from the safety wire that's used to secure the various parts. You are, of course, always praying that you will find no metal in the screens, because that means the end of flying and beginning of big spending. It also means that the screens might have saved your butt.

Ed Wier runs the local maintenance facility, and I am camped on his ramp at 8:00 A.M., before he has even had his coffee. He invites me to join him in that activity, and in the ensuing conversation I find a kindred spirit. He is a lover of fine old airplanes and shows me his collection of antique parts, props, airframes, and manuals, including a complete Continental engine manual for the Stearman, which I lust after. In his hangar, sandwiched between a couple of sleek turboprops that he charters out, is an old Piper J3 Cub in need of a recover that is on his "gonna" list. Airplane guys, like car guys, all have "gonna" lists.

We work together on the oil change, which goes quickly.

"You owe me forty bucks for the oil and nothing for the labor. The conversation was worth it," he drawls. That's a first. No one had ever set a monetary value on my eloquence in the past.

I reach for my credit card to pay for the oil change, and he waves it aside. "Don't take plastic. Tried it and it didn't work. I take cash or you can mail me a check."

Mail him a check! Immediately start on a job. Let a customer help on his own plane. Courtesy cars. No charge for labor. Try all of that at your Chevy dealer. If you're ever near Mineral Wells, Texas, with an airplane, stop in and visit life as it should be. Perhaps life as it was in the forties and fifties and perhaps as it might still be in rural America. His name is Ed Wier and he is a good man.

I'm reluctant to leave this Oz, but I know all too well the penalty of a late start, so I fire up, rumble down runway one-seven, and point the nose toward Abilene. It is still fairly early and I stay down low for a while, experimenting with my navigation over this seemingly featureless landscape. But on closer inspection it is not really featureless. There is a road here and a road there, an unusual intersection, a ranch, a tower, a creek, and it is all there on the chart for the reading. Using the combination of landmarks and the compass, navigation is quite easy most of the time. Lay the course out on the chart and fly the heading. Landmark coming up and you are north of it instead of over it, correct a bit to the south. The wind is varying constantly. The later it gets, the harder it blows. The higher you climb, the harder it blows. Usually. See those clouds with the flat bottoms? Climb up there and the wind will be doing something entirely different above and below them. It will also be colder. Or warmer.

Of course, start dodging thunderstorms, dealing with mechanical problems, or getting distracted in major any way and it's easy to get "surrounded by lostness." Or get inattentive or careless . . .

I know a pilot who casually followed the interstate out of Laramie, Wyoming, heading for Cheyenne, the next city down the road. The next city he came to said Fort Collins on its runway! He was in Colorado, because he had followed the wrong highway. I know him well!

I know of another pilot, who, during the war became lost while out in a training mission in the States in his C-47. The crew didn't have a clue as to where they were, give or take a couple of states. The pilot got lucky and spotted a military field, but they still couldn't identify it on the chart, so they came up with a plan. They would land and when the "Follow Me" truck came out, it would no doubt have the base ID painted on it. They would then find their position and taxi back, take off, and set a course for home.

They landed, but no "Follow Me" truck came to meet them. They then taxied to the ramp, confident that the field name and elevation would be painted on the tower, as was the military custom. It was not. Undaunted, our resourceful aviators shut down their C-47 and simply went to a telephone to make an outside call. The base operator answered with, "Bryan Field. What number would you like?" They had their position and were on their way. Probably the first instance of telephonic navigation.

Not used to the old whiskey compass (so called because they were once filled with alcohol) after years of flying with convenient gyrocompasses and electronic navigation, we have an uneasy peace in the cockpit of the Stearman. Turn right and the compass initially shows a turn to the left. Turn left and it shows a turn to the right. Sometimes. Depending on what the heading is. Accelerate or decelerate and it will show a turn when none is occurring. Of course it is practically impossible to accelerate in a Stearman.

There are many mnemonics, such as ANDS—Accelerate/North, Decelerate/South—that pilots use to remember all of these normal but bizarre characteristics, but the fact remains that old whiskey compasses remain for me counterintuitive. I find that I have to constantly keep a visual picture of winds and headings before altering course. But that is not all bad. I should be doing that anyway.

Compasses are also subject to magnetic anomalies. For example, while scanning the chart I come across this interesting disclaimer: MAGNETIC DISTURBANCE OF AS MUCH AS 15 DEGREES EXISTS AT 7000 FT. ELEVATION BETWEEN RISON AND BUNN. Which way is it disturbed, plus or minus? That's a thirty-degree swing. And the town of Rison is only 263 feet above sea level. That makes the disturbance well over one mile straight up. Spooky. Add to that magnetic variation, compass deviation, and changing winds, and you have an instrument that makes you ache for a GPS. You've got to love a compass though, because with some notable exceptions (those would be mine), they rarely break.

But today navigation is easy and we are soon over Abilene. As I clatter by overhead, directly below lie the parallel runways of Dyess Air Force Base. The ramp is lined with the sleek shapes of B-1 jet bombers, their bellies filled with high-tech laser-guided bombs and standoff weapons of various types, waiting for "the call." But fifty years ago this base was known as Tye Army Air Field and a different kind of airplane, the P-47 Thunderbolt fighter, lined the ramps. And once they got to Europe, the P-47s would be asked to take care of these new jet flying machines every once in a while.

## Capt. Robert Boyett
## P-47s over Nuremberg

### ". . . he just disintegrated."

We did see a few German jets. I had one come down through the clouds one day as I was flying a flak-busting position with the group. I had the last element and we were the fifteenth or sixteenth plane in the flight. We flew the flak-busting position when we went in as ground support We looked for antiaircraft guns and went for them.

It was a low overcast at about five thousand feet down close to Nuremberg. We were tired; it had been a long mission, and everybody was kind of relaxing with an open canopy and lighted cigarettes.

Well, I was riding along there about half asleep, and I thought that it was a reflection off of a cloud. I kept watching it and it kept getting bigger and bigger, and all of a sudden it let down off of my right wing, and it was an Me-262 jet.

I looked at that pilot, he looked at me, and I fired my guns and yelled at the leader that we had a 262 in our midst. Then I pushed my turbo, throttle, and prop pitch all the way forward and rolled in on his tail. By the time I got all of that done, I didn't get half a dozen shots off at him. He put his foot in that carburetor and was gone.

We had several mix-ups with 262s. We met a couple of 262s head-on in flight one time. They looked like Stukas when we first saw them. They had that kind of broken gull wing and they were coming straight down on us. We alerted the whole flight, and they were coming so fast that we moved aside and they went right through us.

One of them had to be a hero though and made a head-on pass at sixteen P-47s, each with eight .50-caliber machine guns. He just disintegrated!

We couldn't touch them otherwise and they couldn't touch us either, because they couldn't turn with us. They were beautiful airplanes, and thank goodness Hitler didn't get those things into production two or three years earlier, because our heavy bombers just wouldn't have existed.

## ". . . a Texas chateau."

I'm well past Abilene now, and just over the nose on these endless Texas plains I can see my destination. Rising abruptly out of the sagebrush and almost defying all visual logic sits an elegant French chateau with a Romanesque tower. It is flanked by tennis courts, a long runway, and a complex of hangars. Nothing else exists for miles in any direction except the horizon and oil wells. Of course. Why not? It's not unreasonable. This is Texas.

I slide into the pattern, neatly using one of these wells on the base leg as a turn pylon. This is a private residence and I am here by invitation. I am promised some rare eye candy.

I touch down, taxi to the biggest hangar, which is very big indeed, shut down, and wander inside. I introduce myself to the two gentlemen engaged in reviving some old flying machine, and since the *padrone* is expecting me but is not presently in attendance, they tell me I am free to wander and have a look around. Fools.

The first direction I look is up. I'm looking at the bottom of the wing of a Consolidated PBY-5A Catalina flying boat, all 110 feet of it. And there is not one, but two of these old patrol bombers in this hangar. Catalinas were designed in the thirties and served the Navy throughout the war in dozens of roles all over the world. This is the premier American flying boat, the DC-3 of flying boats and, in fact, shares engines with that venerable old bird. There were ten thousand built, about ten remain. I'm looking at one-fifth of the existing fleet. I have not seen a PBY in almost forty years, not since I saw a line of surplus PBYs at the Santa Ana airport in 1963. I examine these closely, happy to see that they both retain their original observation blisters on the sides of the fuselage. These were usually the first things removed when this aircraft was civilianized. The "P" in PBY stood for "patrol" and it was from one of these patrolling aircraft that part of the Japanese fleet was first spotted during the Battle of Midway. These planes are in perfect shape, freshly painted and ready to go. One has a whimsical colorful paint scheme featuring a flying turtle on its side, and its interior has been fitted out for very comfortable travel.

Emerging from the hull of the Catalina, I check out the rest of the hangar residents. It is an aviary of flying boats and amphibians. To the right is an HU-16 Albatross, in front of that a Grumman Goose, and next to that a Grumman Widgeon. It appears that the entire Grumman lineup of amphibians from World War II is here. And nestled in the back of the hangar sits a Piaggio Gull, an elegant little Italian amphibian of remarkable performance. Tucked into every nook and cranny of the hangar are additional esoteric aircraft such as a Super Cub, an Air Tractor, and the most unlikely of all, a McCulloch Gyroplane. The rest of this amazing place is given over to a shop big enough to handle the maintenance of these aircraft. If I have skipped any or added any it is only because when there are more airplanes in a hangar than I have fingers, I am overwhelmed.

I walk outside and circle the building, passing additional dismantled Italian Piaggios and the hulls of a couple of more Grumman Widgeons, one of which has spent some time on its back.

But this is nothing. At one corner of the building sits the squat recognizable shape of a Sherman tank with both its cannon and its .50-caliber machine gun trained on the airstrip. In the weeds behind it, as if it were guarding its kill, rest the bones of a Messerschmitt Bf-109, the most widely used German fighter of World War II and probably one of the rarest in the world today. It's just lying there with the grass growing through it! On my value scale this is like finding a Rembrandt painting being used as a drawer liner. I look at it carefully. This is the real thing. It looks like an F-model fuselage with the motor mount, engine, cowlings, and wings missing. It is a beautiful aircraft, flush-riveted and reeking of the craftsmanship that the Germans of those times unfortunately were so good at. It looks all at once lethal, evil, and elegant, even lying there helpless under the hot Texas sun. This is one of the Holy Grails of aircraft lore. To possess or fly or even just see one of these pieces of history is a dream almost no one achieves, because there are so few of them. And here one sits, rusting out back like a '53 Nash. The last one of these I had seen was in a museum. I was stunned.

"Wait until you see what's in the other hangars," John, one of the craftsmen working on the Catalina, advised me with a grin, but I couldn't imagine what I could find to top what I had just seen. I cross the runway, passing by a Rolls-Royce Merlin engine, still in its crate, lying in the weeds, and let myself into another pair of large hangars.

Stacks of Messerschmitt wings lean against the hangar walls. Rows of Bf-109 fuselages sit on the floor.* A tandem two-place Bf-109G-12 sits on its splayed landing gear looking like it's ready to go. (It was!) And pushed into the back of the hangar almost as an afterthought sits a fully assembled Bf-109, limping on a collapsed landing gear strut and guarded on each side by its natural enemies, the North American P-51D Mustang and what appears to be a Mark V Spitfire. And towering over this whole assemblage of lethal fighter power, like some country bumpkin that stumbled into a country club, sits a Grumman TBF Avenger. All of these appear flyable in varying degrees, or very nearly so after bolting a few odd pieces together, and they were in a state of preservation that I love—well used.

Everything has a layer of dirt on it. Paint is thin, and there is oil on the engine cowlings. The cockpit glass is a bit scratched. It looks like time has stood still for these aircraft. It looks as if Chuck Yeager, Douglas Bader, and Adolph Galland had just parked them and walked away fifty-five years ago. It beats any museum with the pristine paint jobs, the yellow ropes, and the little pedestal with the bio cards on each aircraft. It is a spectacular sight.

I'm sure that there were more aircraft in that hangar. I have a dim awareness of a C-45, for example, but by now I have sensory overload. I again examine the Messerschmitts closely. Their leading edge slats weigh just ounces and jump right out when tugged at. The slats are one of the reasons that these airplanes could maneuver so well.

---

*Bf-109 and Me-109 are common usage terms for the same airplane.

But I'm not missing the big picture. Most of these "German" airplanes are really Spanish HA-1112 Buchons (the name of a deep-breasted pigeon found in the Seville area), essentially Spanish Messerschmitts, with Rolls-Royce Merlin 500 engines. During and after the war, Francisco Franco's air force acquired as much German equipment, bombers, fighters, and transports as possible and flew them well into the fifties and sixties. And why not? Their former owners had no further need for them, and this equipment had helped to defeat the Republicans in their civil war. They also picked up some of their aircraft out of the Spanish Sahara, where they were flown and abandoned by German pilots escaping from North Africa.

Until they acquired jets in the fifties, the Messerschmitt was the Spanish frontline fighter. Unable to get German Daimler Benz engines for their aircraft, they reengined the Messerschmitts, first with French Hispano Suiza engines, and then with the Rolls Royce Merlins, the engine of the Spitfire and the Mustang. They even built their own airframes and in later years when the unemployed Luftwaffe pilots flew these aircraft, they reported that they flew as well as the original item.

Closely examining the German-built hulk in the weeds, one could see where German craftsmanship ended and Spanish began. In the middle of the firewall of the F model out in the weeds is a cutout for the nose-mounted cannon. The Spanish version could not use the nose cannon because of the engine change, so they put a patch over this hole and a few smaller ones. The patches are serviceable but crudely fabricated. The steel screws that hold them in drip rust, and the patch itself is badly cut and has a corrosive patina over it. But I understand that the Spanish 109s served well and in fact became fighter trainers as they became obsolescent.

When operated by the Germans, Bf-109s were lost at a prodigious rate due to ground loops. But there was a war on. The Spanish, emulating the Germans in equipment but not in speed of training, used German Bucher-Jungmann biplanes as primary trainers and cautiously moved their pilots into the Messerschmitts at a slower pace. They had little trouble. And of course Franco, being no fool, soon started using American aircraft such as AT-6s and SabreJets. It took him quite awhile though to stop using the old Nazi helmets. Newsreels of him and his troops in that period are chilling.

I find another building to explore. A storage building. No aircraft here. Instead, in the dim light and dry environment stretch rows of Rolls-

Royce Merlin engines, and a few odd Daimler-Benz 601 series V12s, the engine of choice for the Bf-109. All in neat lines. Along the walls are wings, tails, canopies, landing gears, and assorted parts for Mustangs, Spitfires, and Messerschmitts. And it's not a small building.

I have no idea how many airplanes or parts of airplanes I have seen, how they got here, or what will happen to them. When the owner of these airplanes, Connie Edwards, appears, he turns out to be a genial, hospitable Texan, who tells me that the airplanes collected him, not the other way around. He is very casual about them and occasionally trades them for things he wants or needs. Did you know that a P-51 Mustang roughly equates to a large skip loader?

Connie has flown all of them, and we are soon into a discussion of the relative qualities of each. Fifty years of flying, including a stint in the Nicaraguan air force in the 1969 Soccer Wars, and a seat in A-26s for the CIA in the Bay of Pigs invasion gives him a certain cachet on these matters.

He is curiously adamant over the qualities of the Messerschmitt versus the Mustang or the Spitfire. Not many people have flown all three of these aircraft, and certainly not many have a lot of hours in each. He does. I'm surprised at his views though.

There are any number of pilot combat reports detailing the advantages of each aircraft that can lead to a shoot-down, but the big variable is always the pilot and the circumstances. A new kid or an old hand? No way of telling. Connie swears by the Messerschmitt. He has flown it in dogfights against Mustangs and Spitfires and modestly claims to have waxed their butts every time. Just play of course.

The Spitfire? Overrated. The Mustang? Average, with weak wings. The Bf-109? A fine aircraft. It's hard to separate the moral ideals that each aircraft represents from their engineering, so I don't want to believe him. There are very few of each type left, and unless I can talk him into swapping a Messerschmitt for a Stearman I'll never know firsthand. But it's fun to hangar-fly with this man who has seen so much.

He looks at my Stearman. Referring to my flight across the country in this airplane, he says, "It's a beauty, but you must have the sorest ass in the world." I don't know if he is right about the Messerschmitts, but he is correct about the Stearman.

# CHAPTER 28

*"Which ones were better?"*

Le Chateau Messerschmitt to Las Cruces, New Mexico, September 13, 2000

Of all the mornings to oversleep I have chosen the one where I am a houseguest, and the host, who normally gets up quite early, is too polite to awaken me. So, unavoidably violating the Carter Teeter rule of early takeoffs because of my slothful indolence, I leave the ground around ten, knowing that I'll soon have to pay the price in turbulence.

I have time for a quick 180 from my takeoff and a low pass down the runway of Le Chateau but with nothing wilder than a wing wave, and then set my course for Carlsbad, New Mexico, which is a bit north of west and out of my way, but necessary as a fuel stop. I'm still astonished by what I saw back at Le Chateau, particularly the quantities of German aircraft casually filling those hangars. Our hangar-flying session regarding which of these legendary aircraft surrounding us was the better flying and fighting machine was intriguing. German, Italian, American, and British pilots rarely got to fly the aircraft of their adversaries, so their opinions of their respective aircraft were based not unnaturally on what they saw going on around them in their particular theater of operations. Talking to a man who could literally walk out to his backyard, strap on an example of the best technology each country had to offer and go fly it anytime was breathtaking. "You take the Spitfire, I'll take the one-oh-nine. We'll meet at twenty thousand feet over Abilene. Loser buys lunch!"

I've always tried to ask each pilot how they felt about the equipment they were provided with during that war. Not surprisingly, each are confident that they had the best (although one has to wonder what a 160-mph B-17 was doing in the same sky with a 600-mph Me-262—and how the pilot felt about that).

When posing that question to one of the pilots I flew with, I got a very comprehensive and thoughtful answer. As a twenty-year-old Air Corps pilot in the Mediterranean, Arthur Fiedler, with eight confirmed victories, was able to offer considerable insight into this question.

## Col. Arthur Fiedler, USAF (Ret.)

*"It's not just the airplane alone."*

First, you must remember that an aircraft is a machine, and without man to operate it, it is just something beautiful, just as a computer is nothing without the software and man or some other input device to tell it what to do. Of course in both cases, with man's input it is transformed into something entirely different. Second, what I say is based on my experiences and on what other pilots in my fighter group said, but all pilots do not agree on the answers to this type of inquiry. We have an expression that when you look out the right side of the bird you may see something entirely different than from the left side. And what happened to me might be entirely different from what happened to another pilot in the same situation. The explanation for that is that the training, ability, and experience of the pilots involved are major factors in the outcome of any air-to-air combat.

Let me limit the discussion to only German planes, with minimal reference to Italian ones. Regarding their basic performance, there are many books that list the top speed, rate of climb, endurance, armament, and range. But you must realize that all the aircraft went through nu-

250

merous modifications from the early days of the war right to the end of it. The modifications provided improved characteristics such as a higher ceiling, greater speed, enhanced maneuverability, and increased firepower. The Me-109E at the beginning of World War II was a far different bird than the models being used at the end of the war. In addition, there were many submodifications such as the Me-109G-7 or the G-10, and so forth. The same was true of the FW-190A and the FW-190D. They were like two entirely different airplanes, exactly as the P-51A was nothing like the P-51D.

Generally speaking, I would say the German aircraft at the beginning of the war were superior to the majority of Allied aircraft. The Spitfire could pretty well hold its own against the Messerschmitt and could outturn it, but was available only in limited numbers. The German fighters had fuel injection rather than carburetors, which were used on English fighters. This allowed the Germans to disengage from combat by pushing the stick forward and diving straight down. When the English plane tried to follow, his engine would momentarily quit—and Jerry was gone. When the FW-190 was introduced into combat, it was superior to even the latest Spitfire IX. But of course the English made many improvements in later versions, which once again leveled the playing field.

In the first German/American combat in North Africa, our P-40 was outclassed in every category except turning ability. Thus if the Germans wanted to fight, we fought. Their tactics usually involved trying to get above us, dive, fire on us, and zoom back up. We would immediately respond by turning into them. We did have pilots in the group who claimed they outsped a German Me-109 that was chasing them, but this appears to be the exception rather than the rule. Despite all this, our P-40s racked up a seven-to-one advantage in German planes shot down. At times they would get into a turning contest with us, and then we had them. The P-39 was also in limited use (not by my group) and was an unmitigated disaster. It was often referred to as being good target practice for the Germans. The Italian planes were very maneuverable but were lightly armed compared to ours, and there was some question about the ability or desire of the Italians to actually fight. But a determined Macchi 202 or 205 on your tail was not something to be taken lightly.

In November of 1943, we transitioned into P-47s. This was a completely different bird from the P-40 and ushered in new missions and tactics.

Whereas we seldom were over twenty thousand feet in the P-40, with the P-47 we were often above thirty thousand feet. Most of our missions were now long-range escort missions of B-24s and B-17s. "Long-range" is relative though, because a 450-mile mission was stretching it. The P-47 really gulped fuel.

It was not recommended that we engage German fighters below fifteen thousand feet; however, above fifteen thousand we certainly held our own and more against the German fighters. We could turn and climb with them and outspeed and outdive them.

The tactics used were dependent upon the specific conditions of combat. The P-47 with eight .50-caliber machine guns had formidable firepower. At all times we would try to intercept enemy fighters before they could hit the bombers. At the lower altitudes, there were instances in which a P-47 would be seen turning with an Me-109 or a FW-190 on the deck and not come back, but other times our pilots would come back saying they had outmaneuvered the enemy bird on the deck. This undoubtedly had to do with pilot training and experience.

In May of 1944, we transitioned into P-51s—originally the B and C models and about two months later the D models. This was the most fantastic airplane I was ever in. You did not fly a P-51; you became part of the airplane. We did everything better than the Germans; we turned better, climbed better, dived better, and were faster than they were. In addition, our phenomenal range was what allowed daylight long-range bombing to continue. When the '51s arrived, the bomber losses dropped dramatically as we escorted them to whatever target was assigned. Initially the Germans tried to mix it up with the '51s, with disastrous results. They rapidly realized they had problems, and their normal response as soon as they saw us was to head for the deck and scatter in all directions. But there was no way they could get away from us if our pilot was competent. Once he tacked onto the tail of a German fighter, it was usually a foregone conclusion as to what would happen unless he was a lousy shot. There are numerous incidents when we were badly outnumbered, attacked anyway, only to have them try to get away instead of fighting.

During the later stages of the war, when the Germans introduced jets, once again the tactics changed—but right back to what they were when we used P-40s against them. We could easily outturn the jets, and so if we saw them they usually did no damage. If they attacked from below and behind and we did not see them, they could make a pass with their higher speed and climb away from us. On our part, we would fly in the vicinity of their bases over southern Germany, and if we saw them trying to take off, we would dive on them. By the time we hit the deck, our speed would be approaching five hundred miles per hour, which was much higher than theirs on takeoff. Thus we would overtake them and blow them away.

I have not even touched on the most important part—that of man, the pilot. I will not address the Japanese situation, as their philosophy, environment, and logic was far different from the Western world and led to their cruel, barbarous, savage, inhuman, and uncivilized conduct by our standards in all phases of the war. Accordingly tactics in the Far East reflected this and remained far different from that experienced in the Western European theaters of combat.

For Americans, a tour of combat was finite. That is it might be 200, 250, or 300 hours of combat. It also might be 35, 50, or 70 missions. For the Germans this did not exist. As I have discussed with my German counterparts, when they began flying combat, it ended only with their death, being seriously wounded, or the end of the war. Many Germans flew well over a thousand missions and many of their top aces were shot down numerous times. I met one who was shot down fourteen times. They were often in the hospital for extended periods trying to recover—to go back into combat.

In North Africa, several of our pilots witnessed Germans shoot a pilot in his parachute. I have overheard some of our pilots who indicated they replied in kind when it appeared the German would land within his territory. I think the situation changed when we moved from North Africa to Italy. All our pilots bailing out now were over enemy territory, and I never heard of one being shot at by an enemy pilot. Ground troops and antiaircraft guns often did fire at them as they were coming down. Logic demanded that we should try to kill any German pilot bailing out, but I know of no one who did so. Their attrition rate would have been much greater if we had, but the thought of shooting someone helpless in a parachute seemed to go against the grain of most Americans.

Early on the Germans had the advantage of combat experience from their support of Franco in Spain. They also benefited in this respect from their invasion of Poland. Combat experience is extremely critical. It is important to know how to look, where to look, what to do, when to do it, how to aim, when to fire, and just as important, what not to do. Just as an example, if you come in behind and below, open fire at close range, and the opponent's aircraft explodes, it seems to stop in midair and drop straight down. You need to be ready to take evasive action and hope to avoid his debris, which could down you too.

But that is another whole subject. When the Germans began the blitzkrieg against the western European nations, they had better aircraft, tactics, and more experience than their opponents. And although I cannot attest to this, I presume since Hitler had been preparing for combat for some time, their training may have been more complete also.

No nation had an advantage in the areas of patriotism or outstanding pilots. In fighter planes, there were two kinds of pilots: fighter pilots, who were often aces, and pilots flying a fighter plane. There were excellent pilots who were lousy fighter pilots—and average and mediocre ones too. There was a tremendous difference, which I am sure is attributable to motivation and capability. I know some who got into the Air Force because they did not want to be in the infantry. I personally know pilots who flew the same missions I did, were in the same battles I was, but never fired a shot at an enemy bird in the sky. I am sure they never dreamed of being a fighter pilot as I had all during my childhood. But since they were usually older than I was, I imagine their maturity told them not to get into tight spots if they could help it, while my philosophy was "damn the torpedoes, full speed ahead." But then what could one expect from a twenty-year-old fighter pilot?

Recognize that it's not just the airplane alone, but also the combination of the pilot and plane. An outstanding or experienced pilot often could and did win over a mediocre pilot in a better plane. But if two good pilots encountered each other, it was usually the one in the better aircraft who prevailed.

I have 370 hours in the P-47 and instructed in them prior to going overseas. The ones I flew in the States were much different than the ones overseas. In combat we had all eight guns loaded, we had water injection (never heard of it stateside), and we could draw seventy inches Hg. [inches of Mercury]. War emergency power was supposed to be fifty-six inches with 100/115-octane fuel. The seventy inches we could pull drove the factory reps crazy. We could not use emergency power in the States with 91-octane fuel. We could with the 100/115-octane that we used in combat. We had drop tanks overseas but not in the U.S. So you see—very different airplanes.

The difference in the '47 and '51? The '47 was much better for strafing. The '47 flew like two different birds at low and high altitude. At high altitude it was quite tender, and a sudden movement of the controls would give a high-speed stall unless you caught it. Down on the deck, one could rack it around as much as you wanted. The '51 flew much the same both on the deck and at thirty thousand feet. I believe both birds were better than the other birds we encountered (Me-109s and Focke-Wulf 190s) above fifteen thousand feet except for the jets. The '47 was of course much more rugged than the '51, but it also gulped fuel. We planned on 100 to 120 gph [gallons per hour] in the '47 on a mission. With the '51 we planned on 60 gph on the way out and 50 gph on the way back. Of course these are not maximum endurance figures but what we planned on for mission use.

## Capt. Joseph C. Pimentel, Thunderbolt pilot
## Germany, 1945

### *". . . went through there like a lawn mower."*

The Spitfire. What a beautiful airplane. If I had to go to air-to-air instead of air-to-ground, I would have loved nothing better than trying the Spit against the Luftwaffe. It was such a sweet flying machine. That elliptical wing plan aerodynamically is such an ideal form. The airplane has its own structural disadvantages, such as the narrow spacing of the landing gear (the RAF boys nicknamed it "the strawberry machine"; when it ground looped on landing, the pilot ended up wrapped around the engine like a coating of strawberries). But as far as a flying machine is concerned you couldn't ask for more. Just beautiful. Absolutely sweet, a pilot's delight. I had a checkout flight in a Hurricane and it was nice too, but once I had flown that Spitfire it spoiled me for the rest.

On the other hand, for air-to-ground combat I wouldn't swap the P-47 for anything else. That old Jug could take such punishment and still get you home. When you are doing that air-to-ground mission *everybody* shoots at you, including your own friends. There is something about an air attack, especially out of a fighter airplane, that makes everybody mad. They shoot first and ask questions later.

Here is a pretty good illustration of why anybody trying to do an air-to-ground job, on a combat basis, would like the Jug.

I'm pretty sure that you know about the bridge at Remagen, over which American forces first crossed the Rhine River. This was a big goal. The Allied armies wanted a foothold on the German side of that river, so that the war could then be fought on German soil. Remagen, however, wasn't in the Third Army area. We, at the time, were supporting Patton's Third Army drive and he wanted to get across the Rhine on his own. That was the kind of person he was and more power to him. He had selected a point of attack that he favored to try to establish a new crossing of the Rhine River.

Patton was a tough fighter. He was unrelentingly demanding and confident of his intended successes. One of the things that he was meticulous about was demanding constant radio voice communications between his armored spearhead columns and the air support. Patton had found out long since that when his armor was supported with adequate communication, air-to-ground, we could cut a path for him ahead of his armored spearheads. If we got there first and, via communications, could avoid hitting friendly troops on the ground, minimum casualties would result to both ground and air forces. So he evolved a system of radio communication call signs, markings, smoke signals, and so on, so there would be a minimum likelihood of friendly fire interfering with his attack.

Suffice to say, in supporting the particular assault I am describing now against the far side of the Rhine River, my cohorts and I in our P-47s had long since developed an air-to-ground strafing system, which we crudely labeled "circuits and bumps." We'd neutralize the enemy ground fire by maintaining a steady presence of air-to-ground machine gun strafing on whatever width of tactical front was dictated by the local terrain and the enemies' positioning. Such decisions were jointly brought about through constant radioed exchanges, mainly directed by Patton and his staff.

Circuits and bumps. That meant that we were in a constant parade in a kind of circular or elliptical pattern on both the left and the right flanks so that we didn't interfere with one another. The aim was to try to maintain as constant an air-to-ground strafing fire as possible so that the German gunners had to do their best to dodge what we were delivering rather than shooting back or directing their gunfire at the river-crossing assault.

So we were doing our circuits and bumps. In this particular attack I wasn't flying with a wingman. We had broken up our pairings in order to expand the width of our assault. I was by myself then, but by design. Then on one of my strafing attacks I suddenly realized that the splashes in the Rhine River ahead of me, and some of the tracers, were not coming from my airplane or my guns.

I jammed the stick forward, dumped the Jug, and headed for the surface of the river. The P-47 had a war emergency setting on the throttle quadrant where you'd get water injection. It lasts about five minutes and it really gives you a balls-out get-go.

I got down onto the surface of the river. The Rhine River at that particular place had lots of curves to it, with steep banks on both sides. There were two Germans attacking me, yellow-nosed Focke-Wulf 190s, and one got right behind, while the other stayed about level with the cliffs on both sides to keep me from pulling up and escaping that way. The 190 at six o'clock was able to shoot if I'd sit still long enough, but with the war emergency, I was putting up a rooster tail with the P-47, and that screwed up his aiming. Jinking down the Rhine River I was desperately looking for a way out that wouldn't commit me to suicide from the other guy who was sitting up there waiting for me.

With just plain Portugee luck, we came to a place where the river turned almost ninety degrees, hard right, and I hogged that Jug around as hard as I could, pulling about six g's. I got around the corner and momentarily clear out of sight of both of them when I noticed that the left side cliff bank was covered with tall conifers. So I just drove that dear old Jug right into them—oh, maybe ten to fifteen feet below the treetops—and went through there like a lawn mower. Neither one of them saw me. I just disappeared into the woods and got away.

That's the kind of thing that you could do with that airplane and that's why I liked the Jug. I don't think that I would have been able to survive that day if I had been in a Spitfire or a Mustang. I don't think that things would have ended quite so nicely.

And what about the Navy fighters? Where did they fit in the mix?

## Lt. Channing Sargent, USNR
## Barbers Point, Hawaii

*"They'd make a pass and run, get on your rear, laugh at you, and away they'd go."*

The F6F Hellcat was a fine air machine; rugged as all get-out. It would take all kinds of junk. I've seen them come back so shot up it was absolutely ridiculous; there was no reason in the world why they should keep flying. Didn't seem to bother them. They'd pull out the clock—that was the only salvageable item in it—and push the rest over the side. The mechanics liked them; they were easy to work on and easy to service. Good engine, systems in it were simple.

We used to tangle a lot with Air Force planes, dogfight for fun, particularly when we were at Barbers Point. There were Air Force fields scattered all over the place, and we'd go up the valley and if we spotted Air Force types, why, we'd jump them and pretty soon you've got a real gaggle going on.

There would be a bunch of P-47s and some Black Widows and P-51sand here we've got F6Fs and F4Fs, and there would be a mess of airplanes all over the place. The P-51s would wax us; we couldn't do anything. They'd sit up on a perch, and when the time was right they'd come down like a bullet and jump your rear end. If you tried to turn with them they'd take off. If you could get them to turn, we could take them, but they were smart enough that they wouldn't try. They'd just make a pass and run, get on your rear end, laugh at you, and away they'd go.

The P-47s would turn with us and we could wax them, and they were just about the same as the F6F as far as performance at low altitude. Now, at high altitude they could have probably taken us apart.

The Black Widows strangely enough gave us an awful tussle when we were in a dogfight with them, but we could usually take them too. But it was a mess. There would be airplanes from the deck up to ten thousand feet trying to get on everybody's tail. No air control. You're on your own, just having fun.

There was one F8F [Bearcat] that got out there about this time. It was an experimental model and it could handle P-51s. It was speedy; it was a goer and light as all get-out. It had no armament on it at all, because it was experimental, so it was really a going cat. But that was the only thing that could handle the '51s, and there was only one of them on the island.

Fifteen miles out of Carlsbad I call and ask for wind and traffic information but get no response. I try again at ten miles. Nothing. My last call is at four miles and still there is silence. That's odd. The last time I came through here, five weeks ago, near the start of this journey, I got a prompt, helpful response from the Unicom. It is no big thing though. I do a wind check, circle, and land on runway three-two. The airplane is in a foul mood today and gives me a sorry lurching landing, just like the last time I landed here. The karma's bad at Carlsbad. Couldn't be me.

I find the source of the lack of response from the Unicom. The fuel service girl is deep into a conversation about her love life and is ignoring the radio.

I refuel and set sail for El Paso and across one of the more desolate parts of the southwest. The first forty miles are a very pretty high desert, but then the elevation abruptly drops a couple of thousand feet at the Guadalupe Mountains and the terrain becomes parched and relatively featureless for navigation. You fly forty miles and hope that you can see the ranch house or the rock outcropping depicted on the chart. Oh, can't find it, don't worry, there is another ranch in another twenty miles. I arrive at a peak, Wind Mountain, that looms in isolation out of the desert floor. I've been using it as an aiming point, because it lies along my course line. Hopefully I've picked correctly among the peaks. Finally my ranch comes up, as advertised, and yes, I am on course. The ranch is a cluster of buildings, a dirt road, and a hundred miles of nothing in any direction. Who can live here, and what do they do when they need a quart of milk? Where do the children go to school, and who do they play with? This is a strange part of the country.

El Paso is now on the horizon, and I carefully negotiate the crazy quilt of restricted airspace surrounding it. I hit the Rio Grande and head north along the river to Las Cruces. My work for the day is almost done, and all that remains is to land this bird and belly up to the great food at the little restaurant in the terminal.

My last landing here was a relatively graceless affair, but that was five weeks and six thousand miles ago. I see that we are using the same runway today, so I slide into the downwind leg, focused on really greasing this one on. There is little wind today at Las Cruces, so I know I can't miss. I glide over the runway numbers, flair the machine—and balloon. I let it settle back down, flair again—and balloon again. By now my airspeed is getting on the low side, so I add a little power, lower the airplane back down, and balloon a third time. I'm starting to consider a go-around, but I try one more time. Four is the charm. This time the wheels nicely kiss the pavement and my little self-torture session is over. If I live to be a hundred, I'll never be consistent in this airplane. I taxi over to the terminal, tie down, off-load, and lay into a Southwest chicken sandwich.

# CHAPTER 29

LT. HIRAM J. PECKHAM, USAAF/Martin test pilot, 1943
*"The A-30 was probably one of the meanest airplanes on
the ground that I'd ever flown."*

Las Cruces to Marana Field, Arizona, September 15, 2000

Although this airport is a long way out of town, I've managed to get an early ride and I'm on the ramp at 7:15. It is a beautiful morning, and I'm looking forward to this leg and the landing at Ryan Field, where good food, friends, and accommodations await me. It's early enough and the leg is short enough to give me some time at that airport I enjoyed so much at the beginning of this flight. As usual, with a forty-two-hundred-foot field elevation, the Stearman isn't eager to fly and gives me a long ground run before reluctantly lifting into flight. As we flash by the overrun (things flash when they are close to you) at the far end, we're not more than fifty feet high. I stay low this morning, five to six hundred feet does it, since I'm stopping at Lordsburg for fuel and it's not much more than one hundred miles from Las Cruces, all downhill. I check the chart carefully for towers and, finding none, sit back to enjoy the ride.

The course to Lordsburg is a straight line, but the highway comes and goes. Fifty miles out I pass farther north of Deming than I should and have to correct for a southerly wind. That is odd at this hour of the morning, as it was quite calm at Las Cruces. Soon Lordsburg comes up, but I find that I'm north of it also. Suspicions are confirmed when my radio conversation with the airport manager reveals a crosswind on their single east-west runway. I go through my usual angst as to whether this should be a three-pointer or a wheel landing and decide to wheel land it. I grease it on straight, but things get a little interesting for a few seconds during rollout and I'm happy when the tail wheel finally hits the ground.

As I'm fueling I notice that the wind is snatching at the control surfaces, beating them up and down, and I have to put the gust lock on. This is not good. So far I've been spared really high winds, but it looks like it's going to blow today. It's already taken me longer than it should to get to Lordsburg, so the winds are significant. The airport manager is in the middle of an excellent story about an airline pilot who passed over Lordsburg in a Cessna 152 and ran out of gas down the road, when I notice the windsock is out straight and sideways to the runway. I excuse myself, fire up, and with a takeoff run requiring lots of right rudder to keep things straight, haul the Stearman off of the ground.

The course to Tucson leaves the highway and passes over some good-sized mountains and a national wilderness area. I must give this area at least a two-thousand-foot altitude buffer. The mountains are about eighty-five hundred feet, so the plan is to go around them to the south, and not over them. In spite of my best intentions and the world's biggest crab angle, the wind from the south blows me directly over the Dos Cabezas Mountains Wilderness Area, barely clearing the mountains. There are downdrafts that defeat all attempts to climb. This wind by now really has my attention. I angle my way across a dry lakebed and, true to form, remain constantly blown north of my desired course, even though I keep increasing my wind correction angle.

Getting close to Tucson, I pick up the Ryan Field airport winds, which are gusting to thirty-five knots and will present me with a forty-five-degree crosswind. It's said that a crosswind landing requires two things: pilot judgment and pilot skill. The judgment part is "knowin' when to hold 'em and knowin' when to fold 'em." I know enough to fold 'em and start looking for a runway that is more reasonably aligned with the wind.

After the normal battle with the blowing charts, I find a possibility in Marana Regional, a small strip to the north of Tucson. Marana was a fighter training base during the war, so the attraction is there and off I go. Altering course to the north, the Stearman covers the distance in record time with its newfound tailwind. I monitor Marana's frequency and, not surprisingly with this wind, can hear no other aircraft in the air. Entering the pattern I happily find that the wind is straight down the runway—blowing hard. Turning base, even with a big crab angle, I can feel myself being blown sideways across the ground. My approach to the runway is almost a crawl. I could eat my lunch during final approach.

This should be an easy landing. All I have to do is motor on down and kiss the ground at a pace not much faster than a walk. It will be like operating an elevator. "Main floor—fuel, charts, and tie-downs." I creep up on the numbers and flair, but just as I touch and suck the stick back into my gut to pin the tail down for steering, the Stearman gracefully arcs back in the sky. Wrong move. The problem is, with the wind so strong, almost at takeoff speed, the normally fully deflected (up) elevators simply lift the airplane back up about ten feet into the air and we're flying again. I should be alarmed, but I'm not. In fact I'm almost amused. I feel like an observer discovering a new and interesting natural aeronautical phenomenon. I relax the back pressure, the airplane settles back to earth, but I reflexively bring the stick back into my lap once again, this time, predictably, with the same result. Old habits die hard. I do this one more time before I comprehend completely what the airplane is trying to tell me and lower it cautiously to the ground, this time letting the elevators trail. It must have been very entertaining from the ramp to see the Stearman standing quite still except for great leaping bounds straight up and down. Who said that this airplane is touchy? It's not. It simply goes where it's pointed. Even up. The trick is knowing where to point it. I taxi in, my dignity only slightly ruffled.

## Lt. Channing Sargent, USNR

### "Oh, that was a great landing!"

Some of the training situations were kind of interesting, I thought. I particularly remember night qualification when I was at Memphis, Tennessee, flying Stearmans. I don't think that the instructors were too crazy about taking people out at night—so here it is, no runway lights, just flare pots laid out on this big mat. Memphis had two huge dumbbell mats, and the instructor was going to check me out on making night landings and then he would turn me loose to solo.

And of course he's talking me through this thing, telling me how wonderful I'm doing, and I'm trying to move the stick and it won't move, trying to move the rudder pedals and they won't move. I let go of the stick and it keeps on moving, and he's telling me how great I'm doing, and I just watch this activity, and the plane lands and he says, "Oh, that was a great landing! Okay, you've got it, I'm getting out."

And away I went and that was it. That was my night checkout. Absolutely, absolutely, he was doing the flying. He wasn't going to take any chances.

A real interesting thing happened when I was going through field carrier landing practice up at Glenview. We went through hours of landings before we went out to the carrier to qualify, primarily so that we could answer the landing signal officer's signals and paddles automatically. You didn't even think; it just happened.

So we are getting ready to go out to the carrier in the TBF Avenger and one of our group was on downwind. Of course you're rarely over three hundred feet, if you ever get even that high during a field carrier landing. Well, he ran a tank dry with the gear and the flaps down. He quickly switched tanks, but of course he was so low that the engine didn't catch and down he came.

The ground was soft. It had been raining a lot, and by rights he should have gone head over heels and just really ripped this airplane up, but he caught a barbed wire fence with his tail wheel and it just brought him to a stop. The airplane just dropped and didn't move.

Didn't do a bit of damage to that airplane. By rights it should have torn it to smithereens. I don't know how they ever got it out of there. It had sunk in way over the hubs, because the ground was so soft.

The guy used up his luck there, I think, because later on we were out at Barber's Point and he had switched to LSO [Landing Signals Officer] training. There was a field on the opposite side of the island of Oahu, a small field that we used a lot for field carrier landing practice. He took an F6F Hellcat up and he was to bring a TBF Avenger back. At that time we wore these quick attachable seat-pack chutes that had a fitted harness that you wore. The chute pack itself was on the seat, and you snapped onto the risers when you got into the airplane.

He apparently was in a hurry when he got out of the F6F and into this TBF, and as he was flying across the island back to Barber's Point it caught fire. He bailed out and he didn't have his risers attached to the chute, so he went right into the ground and made a large hole. It used him up pretty well, so I think he had all of his luck there at Glenview on that landing.

The field carrier landing practice was actually worse than the carrier landings as far as I was concerned. You didn't have the speed of the ship, and you always felt like you were going too slow. After you got through with the field carrier landing practice and went out to the ship, it seemed like a piece of cake.

Some people have asked me, "What was your airspeed when you were on final?" I have no idea. I didn't care. On field carrier landing you watched the LSO very closely, particularly if you were working night carrier.

The poor LSO was always trying to slow you down. He was beating his leg to death with the fast signal. But when you went out to the ship, even at night, once you got in the groove, picked up the center lights, and picked up the LSO, it was all downhill. But you didn't watch your airspeed. You felt it. You had total reliance on the LSO. You had total faith in him, and it worked.

The first carrier landing that I made was on one of the Great Lakes, and it was the worst landing I ever made. I dove for the deck and hit main wheels first, bounced, caught a wire on my way up, and it snatched me back down on the deck. That was the worst one I ever made. I got my rear end chewed but good. I got hauled up to the bridge and the air boss raked me over. Made an impression.

# Lt. George Campbell, B-17 pilot
# Italy

## ". . . the B-17 reared straight up."

I was tower officer one day, and a crew had taken a plane up to test fly it. When they came back they asked permission to do a formation landing. Well, a formation landing for us was a pass down the runway and a peel off. If the first one did it properly, he closed his throttle, made his circle, and never touched the throttle until he set down.

This B-17 made his circle and was starting his flair about fifty feet off of the ground when all of a sudden the B-17 reared straight up about 150 feet, stalled, fell over on a wing, and went straight in.

I can still see the nose, crunching in like an accordion and then a big ball of fire. By the time the plane hit, the crash crew was rolling. Didn't do any good. They were all killed.

In the investigation, they came and talked to me and I said, "I wasn't in it but I can tell you what happened. They hadn't set up the autopilot. Somebody standing in the center, between the two pilots, brushed the autopilot switch on, all the servos took over and did what they were told to do, and the crew couldn't recover fast enough to get the nose back down. You really had to push the controls. You could overpower the autopilot, but you had to be right with it, and these guys were already pulling back, starting to flare."

## Lt. Hiram J. Peckham, USAAF/Martin test pilot, 1943

### "The A-30 was probably one of the meanest airplanes on the ground that I'd ever flown."

I completed advanced training at Aloe [Texas] in AT-6s. When I graduated from Aloe Field, I was the only one in my class sent to Dayton, Ohio, to Wright Field—Material Command.

I didn't know what the dickens Material Command was, so I asked a number of the other fellows. They didn't know but supposed that it would be transport work, hauling things. I asked a couple of the instructors, and they didn't have any idea of what it was either.

When I reported in to Wright Field, I found I was to be a test pilot. So I was put into test pilot school along with a few other fellows who had just been transferred in there. I was there two or three weeks and flew odds and ends, just little jobs that came up.

Then a program was begun in which test pilots were transferred into different aircraft factories to let them become acquainted with the engineering personnel, company flight test procedures, and to really get to know the aircraft and equipment. We'd spend a few months in one factory, and a few months in another, and so on. It was a good program.

I went to the Eastern Procurement District Office in New York and from there was assigned to the Glenn L. Martin Company in Baltimore. Bill Hodding came to the district office about the same time I did. He was a twin-engine pilot; I was a single-engine pilot. Our orders got mixed up and he was sent to Republic at Farmingdale (single-engine), Long Island, and I to the Martin company in Baltimore (multi-engine). I didn't know the difference and we didn't question orders anyway.

I got to Glenn Martin in the latter part of February or the first part of March, and the weather was awful. I had graduated February 16, 1943, from Aloe Field.

I had sat on the right-hand side on two or three short flights on the B-26 when the weather broke a little bit. One morning, Colonel Saehleno called over and told Seiberling, the chief of flight test, to have the three new pilots—Kircher, Edmonds, and myself—check out in A-30s. Kircher and Edmonds were twin-engine pilots, I wasn't. I guess people just assumed that I was a twin-engine pilot.

The A-30 had been built for the British. It was a lot like the A-20, and it had a conventional landing gear, Wright 2600 engines, and only one cockpit; do it all yourself, just like a fighter.

I went out and did a cockpit check and familiarized myself with the airplane, then found that I didn't know how to taxi a twin-engine airplane. The radio equipment was such that I could call the tower but couldn't receive. It really wasn't a good situation.

After I finally got the plane out on the runway, I called the tower and asked them to let me make two or three taxi runs to figure out how to keep a twin-engine aircraft going straight. I got a green light and ran the plane up and down the runway two or three times.

I finally decided that I'd try a takeoff. I didn't have any trouble getting the plane off of the ground, and it flew nice in the air. It was quite fast and maneuverable. Then I decided to shoot the first landing and came in way too high. Good Lord, it just wasn't settling out like a B-26 did.

One of the company test pilots, Poplosky, was sitting at the end of the runway in an A-30. Well, the A-30s could talk to each other; the tower was the only place that we had a problem. I was coming in on the approach, and of course I was sweating it when Poplosky pushed his mike button and said, "Hey, Peck, did you file a cross-country?"

I couldn't get it on the field the first time. I wanted to be careful and stay on the runway, as there were buildings and haystacks all over the place. So I made another approach. The A-30 was probably one of the meanest airplanes on the ground that I'd ever flown. The props were right even with your head, so the noise was something terrible.

Your head felt like it was puffing up and down. The planes had big, low-pressure, no-tread balloon tires. The gear had real soft oleo struts and practically no brakes. You could tap the brakes about three times before they just faded. If you tightened the friction on the throttles to hold them in place, you couldn't move them. If you loosened them up enough to move them, the vibration from the airplane would move them.

This second approach gave me a pretty good bounce. With that plane, if you tried to correct the bounce, the next one would be about twenty times higher. It was a crazy airplane on concrete. It should have been flown only on a dirt or grass strip like it was in England.

So I didn't get down the second time. I got all screwed up on the runway and ran off, but missed all the camouflaged equipment. I got the power on and got back in the air again.

On my third attempt I finally got the plane on the ground and stayed on the runway too. I got it stopped and turned around and taxied back.

Well, I climbed out of the plane in front of the administration building, and here were all the company test pilots, an ornery bunch of guys, all out there exchanging money. They'd been betting on the whole episode.

I walked inside the building and Colonel Saehleno, who had just come over to the field, was in the lobby of flight test. "Peck," he said, "it looks like you were having a little trouble with that airplane."

"Yes, sir, but I think I've got it figured out."

"Didn't you fly AT-11s in advanced training?" The AT-11 is a hot little twin-engine Curtiss.

"No, sir."

"What'd you fly?"

"AT-6s."

"Where'd you get your twin-engine training?"

I said, "I just did, Colonel, right out there."

He said, "Oh, my God!"

# CHAPTER 30

LT. CLARENCE A. (Bill) MOORE, in Japanese waters, 1945

*". . . the last Japanese airplane shot down in World War II."*

M arana Field to Buckeye, Arizona, September 16, 2000

Today is the last leg and the last day of this journey. I'm like a horse that can smell the barn, and I'm in a hurry. The psychology of this flight is curious. Going east I took my sweet time and savored every flight and every stop. It took five weeks to get to the Atlantic and the trip was pure pleasure. No place to be, no due dates to meet, not much of a plan, just a rolling stone and a trusty biplane. How lucky can one get? Coming back with a sore ass and half deaf, I've taken the express route and crossed the country in a little over a week. The romance of flight is taking a backseat to the prospect of a home-cooked meal and my own bed.

Reveille is at 4:15 this morning, and I'm at the airport at 5:30 loading the aircraft and preflighting by the lights of the rental car. At 6:15 Marana is treated to the sound of the old inertial starter winding up. It is dead calm, so I use the east-west runway for my departure. Conditions today look very much the same as they did yesterday, so I hope to be long gone before the wind comes up again. I'm headed for Buckeye, Arizona, this morning for a final fuel stop before crossing the desert, and it's only a hundred miles away, so I stay fairly low again this morning.

Pima County Airport is only ten miles northwest of Marana, so I make sure to give it enough vertical clearance. It's right on my course line, but I'm so wrapped in the reverie of the morning I don't see the 747 until it slides into view under my wing. The Stearman is great that way. The view of where you are going is practically nonexistent. The view of where you have been is excellent. Fortunately this 747 is parked on the ground at Pima County Airport along with dozens of DC-9s, DC-10s, 737s, and 727s. Apparently, aircraft salvage is one of the businesses at this airport. It's startling to see this on the desert floor in the half dark of the morning. The airplanes are out of context. They don't belong on the floor of a desert. Viewed at LAX or O'Hare they wouldn't be given a second glance, but I know that something sad is happening here. Most of these airplanes are dead, their useful life used up or time expired. They will be stripped of parts and their aluminum bones will be left to bleach out in the Arizona sun. They will become organ donors for other aircraft.

I pass over a 707 with its engines missing. Four little pylon stubs mark the amputations. There is a DC-10 with an empty socket in the tail where one of its engines once sat. I can remember when both of these aircraft were brand-new and were being introduced into airline service. They represented the ultimate cleverness of man. They were the future. Cars were growing tailfins, television was getting color, and airliners suddenly had jet engines. They were the exciting machines that carried us to new jobs, vacations, weddings, and reunions. They had names like the *City of Denver* or the *Flagship Los Angeles*. They had silver-haired pilots who you could trust with your life and beautiful stewardesses who couldn't do enough for you.

Now these airplanes are junk. Used up. The owners' names have been painted out in a crude effort to disclaim these sad relics, but it conceals nothing. TWA and United airplanes simply look like TWA and United airplanes with their names painted out. Good-bye, old friends.

Fortunately for my mood, Pima County Airport with its dead airplanes passes quickly and Buckeye, another ex-military field, is just over the nose. So is a C-47, the first airplane I've seen even remotely close to the Stearman in almost eight thousand miles. It must be coming out of Avondale, which is off to my right. I land at Buckeye, refuel, and I'm back in the air in fifteen minutes, heading for Thermal, California. The flight is coming to an end, and my turn-arounds are no longer leisurely affairs.

## Capt. William M. Thompson, USAAF

### ". . . the Germans have surrendered."

We continued to fly support and resupply missions from A-58 at Coulemmiers, France. On May 9, 1945, I flew a mission landing at Rheims, France. As I was taxiing to operations I noticed an airplane with British General Montgomery's flag on it and another, which appeared to be that of General Eisenhower, and several others carrying VIPs.

I asked the operations officer, "What's going on?"

The major replied, "Well, I understand the Germans have surrendered and they are over there in that small red school building signing the treaty."

This was about 10:00 A.M. I could hardly wait to get to home base and report to my squadron commander, Les Ferguson, what I had heard. As we had nothing official, we could not really announce it to the troops, so we had to just sit and wait. Sure enough about 10:00 P.M. the BBC confirmed that what I had heard that morning was true.

It was hard for us to believe. However, we had lots of missions to fly going into Germany and hauling POWs out to different embarkation points to process them to their home countries, England, France, and the U.S.A.

We picked up some French soldiers who had been held in Germany ever since the overrun of France by the Germans in 1940. Prior to loading on our aircraft at the German strip, many of the French soldiers had a woman hanging onto them, tearfully saying their good-byes. Then when we landed the French soldiers at Le Bourget in Paris to a grand welcoming home by the city with much fanfare, I noted many of the same soldiers who had tearfully said good-bye to a lady two hours previously in Germany were now being greeted by some other nice young ladies with tears in their eyes. What do they say? All is fair in love and war.

## Capt. Fred Selle, USAAF
## Ie Shima, August 1945
### *". . . a big double flash down below."*

We were on this little island called Ie Shima off Okinawa, and we didn't even know that the atom bomb had been dropped on Hiroshima, that's how secret it was. On my next to last mission I was leading a flight of Thunderbolts, this particular morning to be at thirty thousand feet and sweep the skies above Nagasaki. I had made the sweep around the Nagasaki area and was off to the south of it when there was a big double flash down below. We didn't even know that there was such a thing as an atom bomb. This plume started coming up, and I was about twenty miles away when it mushroomed out.

I was looking at it like that from about thirty thousand feet, so I actually witnessed the second atom bomb.

We were on radio silence, and about the time this column of smoke got to our level, some guy broke radio silence and said, "Jesus Christ, somebody sure got a big one today."

When the Japanese surrendered, their envoys had to fly down to the Philippines to see [General Douglas] MacArthur, and on the way they had to land on our fighter strip on Ie Shima. There were two white G4M-1 *Betty* bombers with green crosses on them. The Japanese airmen emerged in their spit-and-polish leather flight suits along with others in their tuxes and top hats, carrying bouquets of flowers.

## Lt. Richard J. Burnett, USAAF
## Japan, 1945
### *". . . lost at least a million men."*

I flew over Nagasaki a couple of days after the bomb was dropped, and it was as flat as a table. You could see where the sides of the hills around it were scorched from the effects of the blast.

When the Japanese sued for peace, they had to uncover the camouflaged coastal defense weapons and airfields. I think it was patently obvious, after seeing what they had down there to defend themselves with, that President Truman's decision to drop the atomic bomb was justified, because we would have lost at least a million men trying to storm the beaches of Japan.

# Lt. Clarence A. (Bill) Moore, in Japanese waters, 1945

## ". . . the events that occurred during the day of August 15th."

We were operating off the USS *Belleau Wood*, CVL24. On the morning of August 15, 1945, we were scrambling to make a strike on Tokyo. Our efforts that day were to go to the electric works in Tokyo and destroy the final source of power for the Tokyo area.

We were up around twenty thousand feet and climbing, getting into position to make our bombing run, but we were also flying cover for bombers that were in the flight.

We were in sight of our target—it was still early in the morning—when we heard, "All planes, all planes. Now hear this. This is the admiral. An armistice has been declared. All planes return to their bases."

Needless to say there was chaos in the air. We all had five-hundred-pound bombs under our wings. We had rockets and we had a full load of ammunition for the six .50-caliber machine guns. When the armistice announcement came over the air, I believe every pilot dropped all of his bombs and jettisoned all of his rockets. It looked like the Fourth of July. It's an amazing thing that someone didn't actually get killed in that particular episode.

We were so thrilled and excited that we lost formation integrity, and there was no order or anything of the sort returning to the ship. We had to get there on our own, because our flights were all broken up.

We all finally did get down. Our particular flight was down on the deck, and we had relaxed for just a few minutes when all of a sudden we heard over the speaker that Flight Ten of the Second Wing Division was to go aloft and fly cover for the fleet. We'd been down only about half an hour when we were ordered to resume flight, which we did. We climbed to around ten thousand feet.

But it was kind of a monotonous day. We figured everybody was having a grand time on board the ship and here we were, having to fly cover for what we thought was no particular reason. After all, the armistice had been declared.

Not long after we'd reached our cruising altitude, we received word from the combat information center that there was a bogey approaching at twelve thousand feet and headed right toward the fleet. We were ordered to scramble, and find and destroy it. We all did everything that we could to gain altitude so that we could come in from above, and we were able to do just that.

It just so happened that I had the liveliest plane in the bunch, so I was able to get to the target first. It turned out to be a Japanese Judy, which intended to make a kamikaze attack on our fleet. And of course the target, I'm sure, was the carrier.

I was able to get into position above the Judy and drop down behind and surprise him. I hit the plane with a full burst of six guns, three on each side. He burst into flames and exploded.

It wasn't until earlier this year that I learned that the Judy I shot down was the last Japanese airplane shot down in World War II.

## Capt. Robert Boyett, USAAF
## Longview, Texas

### *". . . wonderful memories."*

I wouldn't take a thing for the experience. People don't understand it and they won't believe it when you tell them, but people during World War II were the happiest and had the best time of any people at any time. Although there was so much sorrow, everybody had one goal. There were no "isms." We were not mad at each other. We had one goal in life and that was to win the war.

I never saw the good humor of the American soldier or the American pilot fail. They always had something to joke about, always something to laugh about, even when things were at their worst. They could always see the humor in a situation. Sometimes I'm afraid we're losing the sense of humor that we had in those days. We can't joke with one another, we can't laugh with one another, we can't laugh at each other, and it's a sad thing.

I can look back on those days with great memories, wonderful memories of the people we had, and the people I served with.

I hope that this information will be of some benefit to some people, sometime, somewhere.

# CHAPTER 31

*"The first thing Martin did was to drain all of the aviation gasoline out of this huge fleet and immediately make back a good portion of his $2.78 million."*

Buckeye to the San Fernando Valley, California, September 16, 2000

The desert between Buckeye and Thermal is serious terrain. Words like *parched, barren, scorched,* and *dangerous* all come to mind as I blink away the combined heat of the engine and the 115-degree desert. The wind has removed anything not anchored securely in the soil. Every so often a small mountain range erupts through the desert floor like a set of decayed teeth needing to be capped. They're rock all the way to the top. Not a tree or a bush in sight. Much of this is designated as a national wildlife refuge, and some people find it beautiful, but I would rather be flying over Iowa or someplace where things actually grow. Aeronautically it is a patchwork of restricted areas, military operational areas, and other places that I would rather not be. The only good thing seems to be that there are no antennas. Out here, they are put on mountaintops.

The Continental engine doesn't miss a beat. I think it knows the consequences of faltering.

The bleakness, however, ends abruptly at the Colorado River. On both sides of the river, extending two to three miles from its banks, it is lush with a patchwork of intense agriculture supported by the river water. The town of Blythe sits down there, with its former military airfield essentially abandoned, its taxiways, streets, and barracks foundations still evident in the sand. A single runway struggles for survival alongside a huge truckstop.

I swing into the pattern at nearby Thermal. Three California Highway Patrol Cessna 185s are doing touch and gos on the airstrip and finish just as I land. At the ramp we all get out of our aircraft at about the same time. I'm wearing my standard jeans and a sweatshirt and feel like a vagrant next to these guys. They are resplendent in immaculately pressed flight suits, with patches, gleaming gold helmets, and badges. They have utility belts with little black leather pouches, straps, radios, clubs, guns, holsters, and ammo belts. Everything is trimmed in brass and nickel and they all sport the same model of sunglasses, mustaches, and boots. They look terrific and professional, but it's 110 degrees in Thermal and they must be extremely uncomfortable in all of that gear. They look at me like I stole the airplane.

Thermal is another ex-military primary training base. The typical World War II hangars are a giveaway. Some type of curious tall plant, perhaps a reed of some sort, grows along the verge of the taxiways so that it is impossible to see the entire airport from any one place. An aircraft could crash in the middle of the Thermal airport and no one would know it. I do the world's fastest refueling job, burning my hands on just about anything metallic that I touch, and jump back in the plane, again burning myself on the leather seat cushion. I get out of there as quickly as I can.

Instantly I'm in contact with a harried controller at Palm Springs Approach, who fits me in with the Lears, Citations, and Gulfstreams that move in and out of that resort airport. I cruise over the top of it and into the Banning Pass, where I'm handed off to SoCal Approach. Now I know that I'm home. I hug the southern edge of the San Gabriel Mountains at sixty-five hundred feet, pretty much out of everybody's way and getting traffic advisories. There are airplanes zipping all over, but if I keep the wing stuffed into the pine trees, no one can get to the right or below me.

Chapter 31

These mountains are so incredibly steep that if there is a mechanical problem it is quite possible to simply glide to the valley floor from their peaks. Not that it would do much good since the San Gabriel Valley has houses from one end to the other.

Soon all of the interesting airports of the valley are ticked off in rapid succession: Banning Field, another primary base during the war; Hemet, where I hopped rides three years ago at the cadet reunion and listened to them debate whether they should have any more reunions since they were all dying off. For that reunion there were two of us there giving rides. They had another one two years later, and it was mobbed with cadets and with over fifty aircraft giving rides.

March Field is below me, where B-17s once lived and I was once stationed; and there's Chino Airport, where both Julian Kahn and I learned to fly this beast armed with the same Army training films but a half century apart.

After serving as a primary training base for four years, in 1945 Chino became an elephant burial ground. It was where aircraft came to die. Kingman, 270 miles to the east and one of the first stops on this flight six long weeks ago, was another.

B-17s and 24s with names such as *Fearless Fosdick* and *5 Grand* that had struggled to stay alive in the skies over Germany came back to Chino and Kingman to be parked in endless rows and be destroyed by their creators. P-38s, P-39s, and P-47s took up station on them, parked at the same fields, now flying silent escort on the great doomed bomber fleets and destined to share their fate. Acres of glittering aluminum covered the San Gabriel Valley pasturelands and the Arizona desert, barely leaving room on the runways as the government debated what to do with its huge surplus Air Force. Attempts were made to sell the aircraft. A four-hundred-mile-per-hour P-47 fighter could be had for $3,500. A $250,000 B-17 bomber, in case you didn't like your neighbor, went for $10,000, "fly it away," and there were plenty of pilots around who knew how to do just that. But they didn't sell. People wanted cars and washing machines and aluminum awnings. So with no more enemies to slay, the government put them up for bid as scrap. That's "scrap" as in melted ingots rather than dismantled airplane parts. It was found to be far more cost effective to melt the aircraft down rather than to part them out. The winning bid at Kingman was $2.78 million for 5,437 aircraft—all parked at one airport.

Martin Wunderlich, a Jefferson City, Missouri, contractor, was now the proud owner of the world's second largest air force. The first thing Martin did was to drain all of the aviation gasoline out of this huge fleet and immediately make back a good portion of his $2.78 million. The aircraft of Chino went to the Sharp and Fellows Contracting Company. They paid $404,593 for 1,390 aircraft. That's $291.00 per plane. Tires and engines were removed for parts, then the destruction of the airframes began. A giant blade, not unlike a guillotine, was devised. It was hung from a crane and could be dropped on an aircraft from a considerable height. When it hit it would neatly slice the airplane into as many pieces as desired. A smelter was set up to receive the pieces and turn them into ingots. Nearly new airplanes were flown from bases all over the world to Kingman, Chino, and a handful of other depots in this country—and ripped apart.

To this day it's possible to wander the desert floor in Kingman and uncover forgotten pieces of a B-17 or a B-24. The actual site of the smelter at Kingman constantly yielded parts until it became an object of the Environmental Protection Agency's Superfund Cleanup and was capped.

Today one B-17 is worth about three million dollars. Just slightly more than was paid for all of the 5,437 aircraft that were scrapped in 1946 at Kingman.

## Col. D. J. Beggerly, USAF, Ret. 1945

### "... buy ten to keep two flying."

At the close of the war I was assigned as a property disposal officer, closing bases and disposing of property, airplanes, and equipment. We would go to places like Midland and Marfa, training bases, and some of the other bases that were being closed down or phased out, and dispose of all the aircraft and equipment. We had another team that did ground equipment and tools. Another group closed out the quarters and got rid of all the furnishings. I did the rolling equipment and airplanes.

What we would do was to sort them into lots of aircraft, jeeps, or weapons carriers and sell them in these lots. We sold B-17 or B-24 type aircraft in lots of twelve to eighteen. Sometimes the highest bid was less than $50,000. If it was a flyable B-17, it would go anywhere from $1,500 to $10,000. We would strip off the armament, bombsights, and military classified material.

A lot of people who would bid on these lots would come in as soon as their bid was accepted and they were notified. They would bring tanker trucks in, empty the gasoline and oil out of the aircraft, and they would recoup their bid by the resale of the gasoline and oil. It was sad to see the airframes smelted down.

A lot of them they flew out. The flyable small aircraft like C-45s, Stearmans, PT-19s, and the AT-6s, were immediately picked up. We sold droves of AT-6s. The Stearmans were sold for crop dusting. They'd buy ten to keep two flying and use them for parts. A lot of people wouldn't take the whole airplane. They'd just take the engine and leave the rest of the airplane and we'd have to dispose of it.

# Capt. Everett Farnham
# Firth, Germany, 1945

## *". . . you almost felt like crying."*

At Firth, the air base where we were stationed after the war, there were a lot of wrecked German planes out at the far end of the field. And sadly enough, there were a lot of wrecked P-38s out there, which had been destroyed by the Americans. When the war ended, there were thousands of airplanes all over Europe, and it wasn't worth spending the money to supply the fuel to fly them back home. They didn't cost that much and the Army didn't need them, so they had to get rid of them somehow. What they did at Nuremberg was to take them out to the far end of the base and remove what they felt was of value and whatever instruments they could use on other aircraft. They put sticks of dynamite on each of the booms and blew them up. They weren't totally destroyed, but they would never fly again. There was no way that you could put them back together. They'd knock the wings off and break the booms in half and just leave them there. You almost felt like crying to see them sitting there, but what could be done with them?

## Lt. Carl D. Cuthright, USAAF B-26 pilot
## August 1945

## ". . . kind of sad."

I want to tell you about the conditions in the ETO after the war ended. The preparations to get ready for Japan were already on the minds of people. We were scheduled for A-26 bombers if we were sent on to Japan. The B-26 had become obsolete, I'm sorry to say, by the end of the European war.

When the war ended, we were still based in Belgium, but we moved to Schleissheim, north of Munich, and took over a German air base. We were told we were going to start to fly L-4s in place of B-26s, because the B-26 was to be phased out.

Our A-26 situation never materialized. The war in the Pacific ended before any major changes took place, but we did get the L-4s and got some flying time. The Army had to figure out what to do with the obsolete B-26s. They started blowing them up next to the runways and burying them there, but it was such a long, drawn-out process that they stopped doing that.

One of the sad things I remember is taking off in a B-26 and flying it about sixty miles north and west of Schleissheim to a potato field, coming in as low as I could to get over a barbed wire fence and dropping it in on a dirt strip. It was a rough ride once we hit the ground. We pulled to a stop with B-26s and other planes lined up all over the place. The object was just to wheel them out of the way.

As a matter of fact, we had to get out of the way in a hurry, because other planes were coming behind us. All we did was taxi down another dirt area between rows and rows of planes, which were all destined for junk. We pulled the lifeboat rings before we got out of the area, and those were popping all over the place. And we took the radio equipment off just for our own fun and the smoke bombs—those kinds of things.

The plane that came in right after me didn't make it to a stop in time and nosed over. That stopped the flights into that junk pile. But there were rows and rows of B-26s in perfect condition. They were just going to be scrapped by the Germans.

Today, when we think about the one B-26 left flying in the world, it's kind of sad.

I call up Whiteman tower and give them my position and intentions. I do a low pass down the runway and wave to my family, who has come out to meet me. My landing stinks (will I ever master this thing?) and I skip refueling and head straight for the hangar. I guess I'm tired. The kids and grandkids have a "welcome home" banner and champagne. It's good to be home.

I switch the mags off and on again to make sure that they are grounded, and then pull the mixture to lean. There is a slight rise in the rpm, and the engine clatters to a stop. That's what it is supposed to do and the carburetor must still be in adjustment. It has done well. This airplane has traveled almost eight thousand miles in six weeks and never missed a beat. Not bad for tractor technology. There are some holes in the fabric from rocks being kicked up off the runway, but they can be patched. The biggest maintenance item was the prop decal that came off of the wooden prop. But the manufacturer agrees to make good on it. The prop was only eight years old!

Maybe in another forty years the owner of this airplane will say, "Hey, just for grins let's take the summer and fly this old Stearman to every field that it was ever stationed at during that war one hundred years ago."

To which I would say, "Do it. It will make it, but watch out for that damn tower in Burnet, Texas."

# ABOUT THE AUTHOR

James M. Doyle has been flying for thirty-five years and roaming the country in airplanes for almost that long. A former flight instructor, he holds a commercial license with multiengine and instrument ratings. Jim was in the U.S. Air Force for four years and the U.S. Naval Reserve for six years as an air intelligence officer. He has owned the Stearman for ten years and far more sensible airplanes for eighteen.

He holds a master's degree from UCLA, and his day job for thirty years has been advertising.

Jim lives with his wife, Mary Ann, in Columbia, California, where he flies the Stearman off of Columbia's grass strip, as God, Boeing, and Lloyd Stearman intended.